Discovering Biblical Treasures

UNDERSTANDING: PROVERBS

A commentary using Ancient Bible Study Methods

Michael Harvey Koplitz

This edition 2020 copyright © by Michael H. Koplitz
All rights reserved. No part of this publication may be reproduced or transmitted in any form or by any means without the permission of the publisher.

All Scripture quotations, unless otherwise noted, are taken from the New American Standard Bible®, Copyright © 1960, 1962, 1963, 1968, 1971, 1972, 1973, 1975, 1977, 1995 by the Lockman Foundation. Used by permission (www.Lockman.org)

The NASB uses italic to indicate words that have been added for clarification. Citations are shown with large capital letters.

Published by Michael H. Koplitz

ACKNOWLEDGMENTS

This work could not have been accomplished without Dr. Anne Davis, who taught me the Ancient Bible (Hebraic) study methods, and my two study partners, Rev. Dr. Robert Cook and Pastor Sandra Koplitz. We know that the journey has just started and will last a lifetime. The discovery of the depths of God's Word is waiting for us to find.

Table of Contents

INTRODUCTION

After 2000 years of Christian theology and thought, the original meaning to the Scriptures, especially the Christian Scriptures, has come to us today with a vast number of filters. These filters include the theological interpretations that have developed over the years about the meaning of the Scriptures. Unfortunately, Christianity divorced itself from its mother religion, Judaism, by the end of the first century C.E. By doing so, combined with the dwindling number of Jews in the church, the Hebraic understanding of the Scriptures was mostly lost and eventually considered invalid by the church Bishops. Ignatius of Antioch (died in 107 C.E.) in his Epistle to the Magnesians wrote, "To profess Jesus Christ while continuing to follow Jewish customs is an absurdity. The Christian faith does not look to Judaism, but Judaism looks to Christianity."[1]

In addition to the filters, there is much cultural information not contained in the narratives of the Scriptures because the people of the Bible knew their own culture. A modern example is this. If you were to write in your diary you went to church on Sunday; there would be a lot of information you would not include. Anyone reading your diary entry would know certain things intuitively. Some of these things would be (1) You drove your car; (2) The car had gasoline in it; (3) You had a driver's license; (4) You had paid for car insurance, to list a few items. The same applies when the narratives of the Scriptures are read. When a narrative says that Yeshua's disciples went into a field and picked grain, the narrator does not have to explain how grain was picked and how it was prepared for consumption.

---

[1] Friedman, David. *They Loved the Torah: What Yeshua's First Followers Really Thought about the Law*. Baltimore, MD: Lederer Books, 2001.

Another example would be the marriage story. The original listeners of the Scriptures did not need an explanation of what happened at a Jewish wedding. Read the account of Yeshua at the wedding at Cana, and you will find there is much cultural information left out about the ceremony and celebration because the people knew it of the day.

So, to obtain a complete understanding of the Scriptures, especially the words of Yeshua, we need to learn how to think as a person did in Yeshua's days. This can be done by combining the culture and customs of the people with a linguistic approach of the Scriptures. The people "listened" intently for the linguistic clues that led to a depth of meaning because they did not have books or copies of the Scriptures to read. The Scriptures were passed down through the generations by a mouth to ear method.

Much has been written about the customs and manners of the ancient world; therefore, current research is sufficient. What makes this dissertation unique is that it is the combination of culture and to offer a Hebraic understanding of Scripture from Yeshua's day as the Jewish listener heard it.

Dr. Robert Price makes an argument in his article <u>New Testament Narrative as Old Testament Midrash</u> that the New Testament is a retelling of the Old Testament, thus creating aggadah.[2] "The New Testament gospels and the Acts of the Apostles can be shown to be Christian aggadah upon Jewish scripture, and these narratives can be

---

[2] Aggadah is "the non legal or narrative material, as parables, maxims, or anecdotes, in the Talmud and other rabbinical literature, serving either to illustrate the meaning or purpose of the law, custom, or Biblical passage being discussed or to introduce a different, unrelated topic." Source: "The Definition of Aggadah." *Dictionary.com*. N.p., n.d. Web. 1 Aug. 2016.

neither fully understood nor fully appreciated without tracing them to their underlying sources, the object of the present article."[3]

What is the Greek system of learning? J. Parsons expresses an overview of this system of learning in his article <u>Theology and the Greek Mindset</u>. "The modern university, for example, was modeled after the ideals of Plato's Academy in which (it was hoped) the entire universe would be explained within its halls."[4] Today's Seminaries and Bible Colleges are part of the modern university system and therefore, are using the learning methodology that Plato and his contemporaries used to view the universe. This system of learning and understanding is a part of our current education system. Therefore, when teachers, who are considered experts in their field of study, instruct students, it is often frowned upon for the student to challenge the teacher or to create a debate when the student might not agree with the teacher's interpretation. Besides, the Greek method of learning calls the study of Scripture hermeneutics. Hermeneutics is "the science of interpretation, especially of the Scriptures."[5] This Greek approach is very different from the Hebraic method proposed by this study.

The learning methods of Socrates and his contemporaries make sense when studying, for example, "The Iliad" by Homer or other Greek philosophic documents, but these methods do not necessarily bring to life all of the flavors of ancient Middle Eastern documents. This Greek approach is the method of Bible study that has been employed by Christianity for over 1900 years.

---

[3] Price, Robert M. "New Testament Narrative as Old Testament Midrash." In *The Christ-myth Theory and Its Problems*, 1. Cranford, NJ: American Atheist Press, 2011. Accessed August 01, 2016. http://www.robertmprice.mindvendor.com/art_midrash1.htm.

[4] Parsons, John. "Theology and the Greek Mindset - a Brief Look." Theology and the Greek Mindset - a Brief Look. Accessed August 01, 2016. http://www.hebrew4christians.com/Articles/Hellenism/hellenism.html.

[5] "Hermeneutics." Dictionary.com. Accessed April 14, 2016. http://dictionary.reference.com/browse/hermeneutics.

Near Eastern teachers used parables and proverbs as their main teaching tool. The proverbs leave a lasting vivid picture in the minds of their students. Many of the proverbs are attributed to King Solomon. When he became King he asked the LORD for Wisdom. The LORD granted him Wisdom and wealth.

THE MAIN DIFFERENCES BETWEEN THE GREEK METHOD AND THE HEBRAIC METHOD OF TEACHING

Once a student becomes aware of these two teaching styles, the student will be able to determine if the class attended or if a book read, whether the teaching method is either a Greek or Hebraic method. In the Greek manner, the instructor is always right because of advanced knowledge. In the college situation, it is because the professor has his/her Ph.D. in some area of study, so one assumes that he or she knows everything about the topic. For example, Rodney Dangerfield played the role of a middle-aged man going to college. His English midterm was to write about Kurt Vonnegut Jr. Since he did not understand any of Vonnegut's books, he hired Vonnegut himself to write the midterm. When he received the paper from the English Professor told Dangerfield that whoever wrote the paper knew nothing about Vonnegut. The professor's words are an example of the Greek method of teaching. Did the Ph.D. English professor think that she knew more about Vonnegut's writings than Vonnegut did? [6]

In the Greek teaching method, the professor or the instructor claims to be the authority. If one attends a Bible study class and the class leader says, "I will teach you the only way to understand this biblical book," you may want to consider the implications. This method is standard since most Seminaries and Bible colleges teach a Greek mode of learning, which is the same method the church has been utilizing for centuries.

Hebraic teaching methods are different. The teacher wants the students to challenge what they hear. It is through questioning that a student can learn. Also, the teacher wants his/her students to excel to a point where the student becomes the teacher.

---

[6] *Back to School*. Performed by Rodney Dangerfield. Hollywood: CA: Paper Clip Productions, 1986. DVD.

If two rabbis come together to discuss a passage of Scripture, the result will be at least ten different opinions. All points of view are acceptable if each is supported by biblical evidence. It is permissible and encouraged that students develop many ideas. There is a depth to God's Word, and God wants us to find all His messages contained in the Scripture.

Seeking out the meaning of the Scriptures beyond the literal meaning is essential to understand God's Word fully.[7] The Greek method of learning the Scriptures has prevailed over the centuries. One problem is that only the literal interpretation of Scripture was often viewed as valid, as prompted by Martin Luther's "sola literalis," meaning that just the literal translation of Scripture was accurate. The Fundamentalist movements of today base their beliefs on the literal interpretation of the Scripture. Therefore, they do not believe that God placed more profound, hidden, or secret meanings in the Word.

The students of the Scriptures who learn through Hebraic training and understanding have drawn a different conclusion. The Hebrew language itself leads to different possible interpretations because of the construction of the language. The Hebraic method of Bible study opens avenues of thought about God's revelations in the Scripture never considered. Not all questions about the Scripture studied will have an immediate answer. If so, it becomes the responsibility of the learners to uncover the meaning. Also, remember that many opinions about the meaning of Scripture are also acceptable.

---

[7] Davis, Anne Kimball. *The Synoptic Gospels.* MP3. Albuquerque: NM: BibleInteract, 2012.

METHODOLOGY

The methodology employed is to use First Century Scripture study methods integrated with the customs and culture of Yeshua's day to examine the Hebrew and Christian Scriptures, thus gathering a more in-depth understanding by learning the Scriptures in the way the people of Yeshua's day did.

I have titled the methodology of analyzing a passage of Scripture in a Hebraic manner the "Process of Discovery." The author developed this methodology, which brings together various areas of linguistic and cultural understanding. There are several sections to the process, and not all the parts apply to every passage of Scripture. The overall result of developing this process is to give the reader a framework for studying the word in more depth.

The "Process of Discovery" starts with a Scripture passage. An examination of the linguistic structure of the passage is next. The linguistic structure includes parallelism, chiastic structures, and repetition. Formatting the passage in its linguistic form allows the reader to be able to visualize what the first century CE listener was hearing. Their corresponding sections label the chiasms, for example, A, B, C, B', A.' Not all passages of the Scriptures have a poetic form.

The next step is to "question the narrative." The questioning the narrative process assuming the reader knows nothing about the passage. Therefore, the questions go from the simple to the complex. The next task is to identify any linguistic patterns. Linguistic patterns include, but are not limited to, irony, simile, metaphor, symbolism, idioms, hyperbole, figurative language, personification, and allegory.

A review of any translation inconsistencies discovered between the English NAU version and either the Hebrew or Greek versions is done. There are times when a Hebrew or Greek word is translated in more than one way. Inconsistencies also can be created by the translation committee, which may have decided to use traditional language instead of the actual translation. The decision of the translation committee is in the Preface or Introduction to the Bible. Perhaps some of the inconsistencies were intentionally added to convey some deeper meaning. An examination for every discrepancy is done.

The passage is analyzed for any echoes of the Hebrew Scriptures in the Christian Scriptures. Using a passage from the Hebrew Scriptures in the Christian Scriptures, an echo occurs.[8] Also, echoes are found when Torah (Genesis through Deuteronomy) passages are used in other Hebrew Bible books. Cross-references in the Scripture are references from one verse to another verse which can assist the reader in understanding the verse.

The names of persons mentioned in the passage are listed. Many of the Hebrew names have meaning and may be associated with places or actions. Jewish parents used to name their children based on what they felt God had in store for their child. An example of this is Abraham, whose original name was Abram and was changed to mean eternal father (God changed Abram's name to Abraham, indicating a function he was to perform). When the Hebrew Bible gives names, many of the occurrences mean

---

[8] Mitzvot are the 613 commandments found in the Torah that please God. There are positive and negative commandments. The list was first development by Maimonides. The full list can be found at: ttp://www.jewfaq.org/613.htm.

something unique. The same importance can occur for the names of places. The time it takes to travel between locations can supply insight into the event.

Keyphrases are identified in verses when they are essential to an understanding of that passage. There are no rules for selecting the keywords. Searching for other occurrences of the keywords in Scripture in a concordance is necessary to understand the word's usage; this must be done in either Hebrew or Greek, not in English. A classic Hebraic approach is to find the usage of a word in the Scripture by finding other verses that contain the word. The usage of a word, in its original language, is discovered by searching the Scripture in the language of the word. Verses that contain the word are identified, and a pattern for the usage of the word discovered. Each verse is examined to see what the usage of the word is which, may reveal a model for the word's usage. For Hebrew words, the first usage of the word in the Scripture, primarily if used in the Torah, is essential. For the Greek words, the Christian Scriptures are used to determine the word usage in the Scripture. Sometimes finding the equivalent Greek word in the Septuagint then analyzing its usage in Hebrew can be very helpful.

The Rules of Hillel are used when applicable. Hillel was a Torah scholar who lived shortly before Yeshua's day. Hillel developed several rules for Torah students to interpret the Scriptures which refer to halachic Midrash. In several cases, these rules are helpful in the analysis of the Scripture.

The cultural implications from the period of the writing are done after the linguistic analysis is completed. The culture is crucial because it is not explicitly referenced in the biblical narratives, as indicated earlier.

From the linguistic analysis and the cultural understanding, it is possible to obtain a deeper meaning of the Scripture beyond the literal meaning of the plain text. That is what the listeners of Yeshua's time were doing. They put the linguistics and culture together without even having to contemplate it. They did it.

The analysis will lead to a set of findings explaining what the passage meant in Yeshua's day. Most of the time, the Hebraic analysis leads to the desire for more in-depth analysis to fully understand what Yeshua was talking about or what was happening to Him. Whatever the result, a new, more in-depth understanding of the Scripture is obtained.

The components of the Process of Discovery are:

Language

  Process of Discovery

    Linguistics Section

      Linguistic Structure

      Discussion

      Questioning the Passage

      Verse Comparison of citations or proof text

      Translation Inconsistencies

      Biblical Personalities

      Biblical Locations

      Phrase Study

      Scripture cross-references

      Linguistic Echoes

Only the application sections are included in this document.

Chapter One

Language

New American Standard 1995	Hebrew
[1] The proverbs of Solomon the son of David, king of Israel: [2] To know Wisdom and instruction, To discern the sayings of understanding, [3] To receive instruction in wise behavior, Righteousness, justice and equity; [4] To give prudence to the naive, To the youth knowledge and discretion, [5] A wise man will hear and increase in learning, And a man of understanding will acquire wise counsel, [6] To understand a proverb and a figure, The words of the wise and their riddles. [7] The fear of the LORD is the beginning of knowledge; Fools despise Wisdom and instruction. [8] Hear, my son, your father's instruction And do not forsake your mother's teaching; [9] Indeed, they are a graceful wreath to your head And ornaments about your neck. [10] My son, if sinners entice you, Do not consent. [11] If they say, "Come with us, Let us lie in wait for blood, Let us ambush the innocent without cause; [12] Let us swallow them alive like Sheol, Even whole, as those who go down to the pit; [13] We will find all *kinds* of precious wealth, We will fill our houses with spoil;	מִשְׁלֵי שְׁלֹמֹה בֶן־דָּוִד מֶלֶךְ יִשְׂרָאֵל: [2] לָדַעַת חָכְמָה וּמוּסָר לְהָבִין אִמְרֵי בִינָה: [3] לָקַחַת מוּסַר הַשְׂכֵּל צֶדֶק וּמִשְׁפָּט וּמֵישָׁרִים: [4] לָתֵת לִפְתָאיִם עָרְמָה לְנַעַר דַּעַת וּמְזִמָּה: [5] יִשְׁמַע חָכָם וְיוֹסֶף לֶקַח וְנָבוֹן תַּחְבֻּלוֹת יִקְנֶה: [6] לְהָבִין מָשָׁל וּמְלִיצָה דִּבְרֵי חֲכָמִים וְחִידֹתָם: [7] יִרְאַת יְהוָה רֵאשִׁית דָּעַת חָכְמָה וּמוּסָר אֱוִילִים בָּזוּ׃ פ [8] שְׁמַע בְּנִי מוּסַר אָבִיךָ וְאַל־תִּטֹּשׁ תּוֹרַת אִמֶּךָ: [9] כִּי לִוְיַת חֵן הֵם לְרֹאשֶׁךָ וַעֲנָקִים לְגַרְגְּרֹתֶיךָ: [10] בְּנִי אִם־יְפַתּוּךָ חַטָּאִים אַל־תֹּבֵא: [11] אִם־יֹאמְרוּ לְכָה אִתָּנוּ נֶאֶרְבָה לְדָם נִצְפְּנָה לְנָקִי חִנָּם: [12] נִבְלָעֵם כִּשְׁאוֹל חַיִּים וּתְמִימִים כְּיוֹרְדֵי בוֹר: [13] כָּל־הוֹן יָקָר נִמְצָא נְמַלֵּא בָתֵּינוּ שָׁלָל: [14] גּוֹרָלְךָ תַּפִּיל בְּתוֹכֵנוּ כִּיס אֶחָד יִהְיֶה לְכֻלָּנוּ: [15] בְּנִי אַל־תֵּלֵךְ בְּדֶרֶךְ אִתָּם מְנַע רַגְלְךָ מִנְּתִיבָתָם:

¹⁴ Throw in your lot with us, We shall all have one purse,"

¹⁵ My son, do not walk in the way with them. Keep your feet from their path,

¹⁶ For their feet run to evil And they hasten to shed blood.

¹⁷ Indeed, it is useless to spread the *baited* net In the sight of any bird;

¹⁸ But they lie in wait for their own blood; They ambush their own lives.

¹⁹ So are the ways of everyone who gains by violence; It takes away the life of its possessors.

²⁰ Wisdom shouts in the street, She lifts her voice in the square;

²¹ At the head of the noisy *streets* she cries out; At the entrance of the gates in the city she utters her sayings:

²² "How long, O naive ones, will you love being simple-minded? And scoffers delight themselves in scoffing And fools hate knowledge?

²³ "Turn to my reproof, Behold, I will pour out my spirit on you; I will make my words known to you.

²⁴ "Because I called and you refused, I stretched out my hand and no one paid attention;

²⁵ And you neglected all my counsel And did not want my reproof;

²⁶ I will also laugh at your calamity; I will mock when your dread comes,

²⁷ When your dread comes like a storm And your calamity comes like a whirlwind, When distress and anguish come upon you.

²⁸ "Then they will call on me, but I will not answer; They will seek me diligently but they will not find me,

כִּי רַגְלֵיהֶם לָרַע יָרוּצוּ וִימַהֲרוּ לִשְׁפָּךְ־דָּם: ¹⁶

כִּי־חִנָּם מְזֹרָה הָרָשֶׁת בְּעֵינֵי כָל־בַּעַל כָּנָף: ¹⁷

וְהֵם לְדָמָם יֶאֱרֹבוּ יִצְפְּנוּ לְנַפְשֹׁתָם: ¹⁸

כֵּן אָרְחוֹת כָּל־בֹּצֵעַ בָּצַע אֶת־נֶפֶשׁ בְּעָלָיו יִקָּח: פ ¹⁹

חָכְמוֹת בַּחוּץ תָּרֹנָּה בָּרְחֹבוֹת תִּתֵּן קוֹלָהּ: ²⁰

בְּרֹאשׁ הֹמִיּוֹת תִּקְרָא בְּפִתְחֵי שְׁעָרִים בָּעִיר אֲמָרֶיהָ תֹאמֵר: ²¹

עַד־מָתַי ׀ פְּתָיִם תְּאֵהֲבוּ פֶתִי וְלֵצִים לָצוֹן חָמְדוּ לָהֶם וּכְסִילִים יִשְׂנְאוּ־דָעַת: ²²

תָּשׁוּבוּ לְתוֹכַחְתִּי הִנֵּה אַבִּיעָה לָכֶם רוּחִי אוֹדִיעָה דְבָרַי אֶתְכֶם: ²³

יַעַן קָרָאתִי וַתְּמָאֵנוּ נָטִיתִי יָדִי וְאֵין מַקְשִׁיב: ²⁴

וַתִּפְרְעוּ כָל־עֲצָתִי וְתוֹכַחְתִּי לֹא אֲבִיתֶם: ²⁵

גַּם־אֲנִי בְּאֵידְכֶם אֶשְׂחָק אֶלְעַג בְּבֹא פַחְדְּכֶם: ²⁶

בְּבֹא (כְשַׁאֲוָה) [כְשׁוֹאָה] פַּחְדְּכֶם וְאֵידְכֶם כְּסוּפָה יֶאֱתֶה בְּבֹא עֲלֵיכֶם צָרָה וְצוּקָה: ²⁷

אָז יִקְרָאֻנְנִי וְלֹא אֶעֱנֶה יְשַׁחֲרֻנְנִי וְלֹא יִמְצָאֻנְנִי: ²⁸

תַּחַת כִּי־שָׂנְאוּ דָעַת וְיִרְאַת יְהֹוָה לֹא בָחָרוּ: ²⁹

לֹא־אָבוּ לַעֲצָתִי נָאֲצוּ כָּל־תּוֹכַחְתִּי: ³⁰

וְיֹאכְלוּ מִפְּרִי דַרְכָּם וּמִמֹּעֲצֹתֵיהֶם יִשְׂבָּעוּ: ³¹

כִּי מְשׁוּבַת פְּתָיִם תַּהַרְגֵם וְשַׁלְוַת כְּסִילִים תְּאַבְּדֵם: ³²

<table>
<tr>
<td>

29 Because they hated knowledge And did not choose the fear of the LORD.

30 "They would not accept my counsel, They spurned all my reproof.

31 "So they shall eat of the fruit of their own way And be satiated with their own devices.

32 "For the waywardness of the naive will kill them, And the complacency of fools will destroy them.

33 "But he who listens to me shall live securely And will be at ease from the dread of evil."

</td>
<td>

וְשֹׁמֵעַ לִי יִשְׁכָּן־בֶּטַח וְשַׁאֲנַן מִפַּחַד 33 רָעָה: פ

</td>
</tr>
</table>

Process of Discovery

Linguistics Section

Linguistic Structure

A [1] The proverbs of Solomon the son of David, king of Israel:

> **B** [2] To know Wisdom and instruction, To discern the sayings of understanding, [3] To receive instruction in wise behavior, Righteousness, justice and equity; [4] To give prudence to the naive, To the youth knowledge and discretion,

A' [5] A wise man will hear and increase in learning, And a man of understanding will acquire wise counsel,

> **B'** [6] To understand a proverb and a figure, The words of the wise and their riddles. [7] The fear of the LORD is the beginning of knowledge; Fools despise Wisdom and instruction.

A [8] Hear, my son, your father's instruction And do not forsake your mother's teaching; [9] Indeed, they are a graceful wreath to your head And ornaments about your neck.

> **B** [10] My son, if sinners entice you, Do not consent. [11] If they say, "Come with us, Let us lie in wait for blood, Let us ambush the innocent without cause; [12] Let us swallow them alive like Sheol, Even whole, as those who go down to the pit; [13] We will find all *kinds* of precious wealth; We will fill our houses with spoil; [14] Throw in your lot with us, We shall all have one purse,"

> > **C** [15] My son, do not walk in the way with them. Keep your feet from their path, [16] For their feet run to evil And they hasten to shed blood. [17] Indeed, it is useless to spread the *baited* net In the sight of any bird; [18] But they lie in wait for their own blood; They ambush their own lives. [19] So are the ways of everyone who gains by violence; It takes away the life of its possessors.

A' [20] Wisdom shouts in the street, She lifts her voice in the square; [21] At the head of the noisy *streets* she cries out; At the entrance of the gates in the city she utters her sayings:

B' [22] "How long, O naive ones, will you love being simple-minded? And scoffers delight themselves in scoffing And fools hate knowledge? [23] "Turn to my reproof, Behold, I will pour out my spirit on you; I will make my words known to you. [24] "Because I called and you refused, I stretched out my hand and no one paid attention; [25] And you neglected all my counsel And did not want my reproof; [26] I will also laugh at your calamity; I will mock when your dread comes, [27] When your dread comes like a storm And your calamity comes like a whirlwind, When distress and anguish come upon you.

C' [28] "Then they will call on me, but I will not answer; They will seek me diligently but they will not find me, [29] Because they hated knowledge And did not choose the fear of the LORD. [30] "They would not accept my counsel, They spurned all my reproof. [31] "So they shall eat of the fruit of their own way And be satiated with their own devices. [32] "For the waywardness of the naive will kill them, And the complacency of fools will destroy them. [33] "But he who listens to me shall live securely And will be at ease from the dread of evil."

(For verses 8 to 33) A: Voice of Wisdom. B: Words of evil companions/words of Wisdom. C: The way.[9]

Discussion

This chapter consists of two chiasms. The first chiasm introduces the book as a work of King Solomon. The second chiasm concentrates on Wisdom.

Questioning the Passage

1. What is a proverb? (v. 6)

A proverb is a saying of Wisdom that is being conveyed by the use of metaphors.

---

[9] Hajime Murai, "Literary Structure (Chiasm, Chiasmus) of Book of Proverbs," Literary structure (chiasm, chiasmus) of each pericopes of Book of Proverbs, accessed May 30, 2020, http://www.bible.literarystructure.info/bible/20_Proverbs_pericope_e.html.

2. What does "a figure mean" in verse six?

   "Figure" can be translated as "satire." Satire is "the use of humor, irony, exaggeration, or ridicule to expose and criticize people's stupidity or vices, particularly in the context of contemporary politics and other topical issues."[10]

3. What does it mean to fear the LORD? (v. 7)

   The Sage Malbim[i] said that fear of the LORD means that one believes in the LORD and the unquestioning acceptance and fulfillment of His dictates.[11]

4. What is the meaning of verse eight?

   A child (or can be viewed as a student) must be ready to accept learnings in three ways. The first way is physical hearing with the ears. The second is understanding with the heart and obeying. The third way is by accepting the yoke of the mitzvot and mussar.[12] The first mussar that must be accepted is that of his/her parents. In Solomon's day, parents tried to install Wisdom and knowledge in their children. Today this is not always the case. Also, many single parents are trying to offer both motherly and fatherly advice.

---

[10] Google Search. Google. Accessed June 1, 2020.
https://www.google.com/search?sxsrf=ALeKk00INN_6n4EuhzGigiZP9onMg16p3Q%3A1591025699153&source=hp
&ei=IyDVXpi8BsyHytMP3Ymp8Ac&q=satire%2Bdefinit&oq=satire%2Bdefinit&gs_lcp=CgZwc3ktYWIQAzIHCAAQRhD
5ATICCAAyAggAMgIIADICCAAyAggAMgIIADICCAAyAggAMgIIADoHCCMQ6gIQJzoECCMQJzoFCAAQkQI6BQgAEIMBO
gQIABAKOgkIABAKEEYQ-
QFQzQ9YkypghERoAnAAeAKAAfUOiAGzLpIBDjExLjUuMS4wLjEuOC0ymAEAoAEBqgEHZ3dzLXdperABCg&sclient=psy
-ab&ved=0ahUKEwjY2f7M-ODpAhXMg3IEHd1ECn4Q4dUDCAk&uact=5.
[11] Eliezer Ginsburg, *Mishlei = Proverbs: a New Translation with a Commentary Anthologized from Talmudic, Midrashic and Rabbinic Sources* (New York: Mesorah Publications Ltd, 1998).
[12] Mussar (also spelled Musar), a Jewish spiritual practice that gives concrete instructions on how to live a meaningful and ethical life, arose as a response to this concern. Source: IBID.

5. What do the wreath and ornaments mean in verse nine?

    The Vilna Gaon[ii] explained that these are symbols. In the Sages' days, it was customary to make jewelry for one's wife according to her qualities. A head ornament was made for a woman with superior intelligence. A necklace was made for a woman who performed good deeds.[13]

6. What is the warning of verses eleven to fourteen?

    These verses warn about the ways of sinners seeking out compatriots for their crimes of murder and robbery.

7. What does the baited net in verse seventeen mean?

    When attempting to catch birds, a net was laid out on the ground with legumes and wheat spread. The birds think that the grains are free and approach the net. Then the trap is set, and the birds are caught. It is incorrect thinking to believe that working with criminals will result in riches. Eventually, the criminals get caught and punished.[14]

8. What Wisdom is in the streets? (v. 20)

    The Hebrew word for Wisdom is plural in this verse. It tells us that the Wisdom of the LORD and everything that one needs to be a good person can be found in the Torah. The Torah is the essence of the LORD's Wisdom. One can see the LORD's work in all of nature.

---

[13] IBID.

[14] IBID.

9. What is the reference to the city gates in verse twenty-one?

   The elders and judges of the people held their administrative offices at the city gates. If a person had a dispute or a question about how to live by the LORD's law, they would go to the city gate. The Wisdom of the LORD rested with the elders and judges.

Phrase Study

1. מָשָׁל. (V. 1) "Proverb, parable, allegory, byword, taunt, discourse. Of great interest is the wide number of translations for this word in most English translations of the Old Testament. The substantive appears thirty-nine times (eight times in Ezek).

   To translate מָשָׁל simply as "proverb" misses the wide sweep of the word, suggested by the many suggested translations. We are accustomed to think of a proverb as a short, pithy, epigrammatic saying which assumes the status of gnomic truth. In the Old Testament, however, the word מָשָׁל may be synonymous with an extended parable (and hence the frequent LXX translation παραβολή) (Ezek 17:2 and vv. 2–24; 20:49 [H 21:5] and vv. 45–49 [H 21:1–5]; 24:3 and vv. 3–14). It may refer to an extended didactic discourse (Prov 1:8–19 for example). A person (Saul, 1 Sam 10:12; Job, 17:6) or a group of persons (Israel, Ps 44:14 [H 15]), may function as a מָשָׁל.

   In this last connection notice the verse in 1 Sam 10:12, "So the saying, 'Is Saul also among the prophets?' became a proverb." What is involved here is the creation of a public example, in this case the example of one, a royal figure, whose public antics were questionable. The "proverb" would then be applicable to anyone charged with unorthodox behavior.

In a similar vein, note passages which translate מָשָׁל as "byword": Ps 44:14 [H 15~}; 69:11 [H 12]; Jer 24:9; Ezek 14:8; Deut 28:37; 1 Kgs 9:7; 2 Chr 7:20; Job 17:6. In each of these verses some kind of doom has, or will, come upon Israel or an individual. The result? God has made Israel a מָשָׁל among the nations. Job has become a מָשָׁל to his counselors and acquaintances. What can this mean? Much more is involved than simply scorn or derision. The point is that God has made Israel/Job a public example, an object lesson to their respective contemporaries. "Look, observe, and see your own life under my judgment," the Lord says.

Analogous to these are the three times prophets are told to lift a מָשָׁל, Isaiah against the king of Babylon (Isa 14:4f.); Micah against his own people (Mic 2:4) and similarly Habakkuk (Hab 2:6). One might also add the passages in the Balaam narratives, "And Balaam took up his מָשָׁל (KJV discourse)" (Num 23:7, 18; 24:3, 15, 20, 21, 23). In each of these instances there is an object lesson painted. The haughty are humbled. Those to be cursed are blessed and vice versa. The first are last."[15]

2. מְלִיצָה *(mᵉlîṣā) satire, mocking poem* (Hab 2:6), *figure, enigma* (Prov 1:6).

"Fools scorn and mock at sin (14:9) and judgment (19:28). The scorner (Qal participial form) himself may be described as proud and haughty (21:24),

---

[15] R. Laird Harris, Gleason L. Archer, and Bruce K. Waltke, *Theological Wordbook of the Old Testament* (Chicago: Moody Press, 2004).

incorrigible (9:7), resistant to all reproof (9:8; 15:12), and hating any rebuke (13:1). Wisdom and knowledge easily elude him (Prov 14:6).

So despicable is the scorner that he may be labelled as odious to all men (24:9). Therefore he must be avoided (Ps 1:1) by all who would live godly lives. Further, he should be punished by hitting so that the easily pursuaded naive fool may benefit from the lesson (Prov 19:25; 21:11). One good way to remove contention from a group is to eject the scorner, and then "strife and reproach will cease" (22:10). A prepared judgment awaits all such scorners (19:29), for their trademark of life has been "to delight" in their scorning (1:22). They shall be brought to nothing and consumed (Isa 29:20).

That the particular type of wickedness of the scorner is pride is suggested by Prov 3:34. Here the scorner is contrasted with the humble. In this verse the LXX renders "scorner" by "proud" which is followed in the NT Jas 4:6 and 1 Pet. 5:5. Cf. Prov 21:24. Dahood points out a parallel of this word with "evil" in the Karatepe I inscription *(Psalms, I, in AB, p. 2)*.

Among the various mockers and scorners are wine (Prov 20:1), the proud (Ps 119:51), the king of Samaria's henchmen (Hos 7:5), and Job's friends (Job 16:20).

As a Hiphil participle, the word means an interpreter, such as Joseph used to fool his brothers (Gen 42:23). The interpreters in Isa 43:27 are the teachers of Israel, God's priests and prophets who have sinned by refusing to give out God's word as he first gave it. In 2 Chr 32:31, the word represents ambassadors or representatives of Babylon.

The most interesting text is Job 33:23. Elihu speaks of God graciously teaching men through the discipline of suffering the more perfect path of the Lord. Then God sends an angel, i.e. a messenger otherwise known as an interpreter, ambassador, or even a mediator to show man what is right."[16]

Culture Section

Questioning the passage

1. What does "therefore shall they eat of the fruit of their own way" mean? (v. 31) This phrase is a Semitic idiom, which means the results of their own devices will punish them. It is called the Law of Compensation. A person who sows wheat will reap wheat, while a person who sows tares shall reap tares.[17]

Thoughts

This chapter is a simple lesson written in symbolism. The LORD offers Wisdom to all His people. The reward for following the Wisdom of the LORD is far greater than ignoring it. Evil is not the way to live. It is better to be in the graces of the LORD. The reward is that the LORD's Wisdom will be with you.

---

[16] Harris, R. L., "Proverbs," in WBC, p. 560.

[17] Rocco A. Errico and George M. Lamsa, *Aramaic Light on Ezra through the Song of Solomon* (Smyma, GA: Noohra Foundation, 2010).

Chapter Two

Language

New American Standard 1995	Hebrew
[1] My son, if you will receive my words And treasure my commandments within you,	¹ בְּנִי אִם־תִּקַּח אֲמָרָי וּמִצְוֹתַי תִּצְפֹּן אִתָּךְ: ²
[2] Make your ear attentive to Wisdom, Incline your heart to understanding;	לְהַקְשִׁיב לַחָכְמָה אָזְנֶךָ תַּטֶּה לִבְּךָ לַתְּבוּנָה:
[3] For if you cry for discernment, Lift your voice for understanding;	³ כִּי אִם לַבִּינָה תִקְרָא לַתְּבוּנָה תִּתֵּן קוֹלֶךָ:
[4] If you seek her as silver And search for her as for hidden treasures;	⁴ אִם־תְּבַקְשֶׁנָּה כַכָּסֶף וְכַמַּטְמוֹנִים תַּחְפְּשֶׂנָּה:
[5] Then you will discern the fear of the LORD And discover the knowledge of God.	⁵ אָז תָּבִין יִרְאַת יְהוָה וְדַעַת אֱלֹהִים תִּמְצָא:
[6] For the LORD gives Wisdom; From His mouth *come* knowledge and understanding.	⁶ כִּי־יְהוָה יִתֵּן חָכְמָה מִפִּיו דַּעַת וּתְבוּנָה:
[7] He stores up sound Wisdom for the upright; *He is* a shield to those who walk in integrity,	⁷ (וְצָפַן) [יִצְפֹּן] לַיְשָׁרִים תּוּשִׁיָּה מָגֵן לְהֹלְכֵי תֹם:
[8] Guarding the paths of justice, And He preserves the way of His godly ones.	⁸ לִנְצֹר אָרְחוֹת מִשְׁפָּט וְדֶרֶךְ (חֲסִידוֹ) [חֲסִידָיו] יִשְׁמֹר:
[9] Then you will discern righteousness and justice And equity *and* every good course.	⁹ אָז תָּבִין צֶדֶק וּמִשְׁפָּט וּמֵישָׁרִים כָּל־מַעְגַּל־טוֹב:
[10] For Wisdom will enter your heart And knowledge will be pleasant to your soul;	¹⁰ כִּי־תָבוֹא חָכְמָה בְלִבֶּךָ וְדַעַת לְנַפְשְׁךָ יִנְעָם:
[11] Discretion will guard you, Understanding will watch over you,	¹¹ מְזִמָּה תִּשְׁמֹר עָלֶיךָ תְּבוּנָה תִנְצְרֶכָּה:
[12] To deliver you from the way of evil, From the man who speaks perverse things;	¹² לְהַצִּילְךָ מִדֶּרֶךְ רָע מֵאִישׁ מְדַבֵּר תַּהְפֻּכוֹת:
[13] From those who leave the paths of uprightness To walk in the ways of darkness;	¹³ הַעֹזְבִים אָרְחוֹת יֹשֶׁר לָלֶכֶת בְּדַרְכֵי־חֹשֶׁךְ:
	¹⁴ הַשְּׂמֵחִים לַעֲשׂוֹת רָע יָגִילוּ בְּתַהְפֻּכוֹת רָע:
	¹⁵ אֲשֶׁר אָרְחֹתֵיהֶם עִקְּשִׁים וּנְלוֹזִים בְּמַעְגְּלוֹתָם:
	¹⁶ לְהַצִּילְךָ מֵאִשָּׁה זָרָה מִנָּכְרִיָּה אֲמָרֶיהָ הֶחֱלִיקָה:
	¹⁷ הַעֹזֶבֶת אַלּוּף נְעוּרֶיהָ וְאֶת־בְּרִית אֱלֹהֶיהָ שָׁכֵחָה:
	¹⁸ כִּי שָׁחָה אֶל־מָוֶת בֵּיתָהּ וְאֶל־רְפָאִים מַעְגְּלֹתֶיהָ:
	¹⁹ כָּל־בָּאֶיהָ לֹא יְשׁוּבוּן וְלֹא־יַשִּׂיגוּ אָרְחוֹת חַיִּים:
	²⁰ לְמַעַן תֵּלֵךְ בְּדֶרֶךְ טוֹבִים וְאָרְחוֹת צַדִּיקִים תִּשְׁמֹר:

¹⁴ Who delight in doing evil And rejoice in the perversity of evil; ¹⁵ Whose paths are crooked, And who are devious in their ways; ¹⁶ To deliver you from the strange woman, From the adulteress who flatters with her words; ¹⁷ That leaves the companion of her youth And forgets the covenant of her God; ¹⁸ For her house sinks down to death And her tracks *lead* to the dead; ¹⁹ None who go to her return again, Nor do they reach the paths of life. ²⁰ So you will walk in the way of good men And keep to the paths of the righteous. ²¹ For the upright will live in the land And the blameless will remain in it; ²² But the wicked will be cut off from the land And the treacherous will be uprooted from it.	²¹ כִּי־יְשָׁרִים יִשְׁכְּנוּ אָרֶץ וּתְמִימִים יִוָּתְרוּ בָהּ׃ ²² וּרְשָׁעִים מֵאֶרֶץ יִכָּרֵתוּ וּבוֹגְדִים יִסְּחוּ מִמֶּנָּה׃ פ

Process of Discovery

Linguistics Section

Linguistic Structure

[Saying One] [1] My son, if you will receive my words And treasure my commandments within you, [2] Make your ear attentive to Wisdom, Incline your heart to understanding; [3] For if you cry for discernment, Lift your voice for understanding; [4] If you seek her as silver And search for her as for hidden treasures; [5] Then you will discern the fear of the LORD And discover the knowledge of God. [6] For the LORD gives Wisdom; From His mouth *come* knowledge and understanding. [7] He stores up sound Wisdom for the upright; *He is* a shield to those who walk in integrity, [8] Guarding the paths of justice, And He preserves the way of His godly ones.

[Saying Two] [9] Then you will discern righteousness and justice And equity *and* every good course. [10] For Wisdom will enter your heart And knowledge will be pleasant to your soul; [11] Discretion will guard you, Understanding will watch over you, [12] To deliver you from the way of evil, From the man who speaks perverse things; [13] From those who leave the paths of uprightness To walk in the ways of darkness; [14] Who delight in doing evil And rejoice in the perversity of evil; [15] Whose paths are crooked, And who are devious in their ways;

[Saying Three] [16] To deliver you from the strange woman, From the adulteress who flatters with her words; [17] That leaves the companion of her youth And forgets the covenant of her God; [18] For her house sinks down to death And her tracks *lead* to the dead; [19] None who go to her return again, Nor do they reach the paths of life.

[Saying Four] [20] So you will walk in the way of good men And keep to the paths of the righteous. [21] For the upright will live in the land And the blameless will remain in it; [22] But the wicked will be cut off from the land And the treacherous will be uprooted from it.

Discussion

This chapter consists of four saying about Wisdom and evil.

Questioning the Passage

1. What does it mean to make one's ear attentive to Wisdom? (v. 3)

   Wisdom in this verse is defined as what one learns from one's teacher because the teacher is being listened to. The sage Rabbi Yonah[iii] offered the following five steps that are necessary to acquire Wisdom:

   a. Listen carefully to your teachers' words

   b. Concentrating your heart to the exclusion of all else

   c. Pray to merit wisdom

   d. Love wisdom[18]

2. What does verse three mean?

   To obtain Wisdom, one must pray. King Solomon offered his prayers for Wisdom, and the LORD granted him Wisdom. Therefore, if one wants Wisdom today, one must pray for it.

3. What does verse four mean?

   To own silver, one has to trade for it or dig for it. Obtaining silver requires work of some kind. Therefore, to search for the hidden treasure, which is Wisdom, requires work. Obtaining Wisdom from the LORD requires work on the seeker's part.[19]

---

[18] Eliezer Ginsburg and Nosson Scherman, *Mishlei: Proverbs = Mishlei: a New Translation with a Commentary Anthologized from Talmudic, Midrashic and Rabbinic Sources* (Brooklyn, NY: Mesorah, 2003).

[19] IBID.

4. What does verse five mean?

    While working to obtain the Wisdom of the LORD, one will learn to have a strong reverence for the LORD. When this occurs, the seeker will have both Wisdom and knowledge. Wisdom and knowledge work together.

5. What are the paths of justice? (v. 8)

    Through the study and implementation of the Torah, a person will be protected from the path of evil and will not stumble from the righteous path.[20]

6. What does "for wisdom will enter your heart" mean? (v. 10)

    When one reaches the spiritual level of Wisdom, Evil inclination will no longer battle with him. Wisdom will be his heart, and he will no longer suffer from the inner strength and influence of outside forces.

7. What is the meaning of verse eleven?

    Wisdom will save an individual from mishap; (1) character traits, (2) deeds, (3) Torah study.

8. What paths are crooked? (v. 15)

    The ways of evil people are described as a crooked path. This comes from the understanding that if a person is not following the Torah's ways, then they are committing sins against the LORD.

---

[20] IBID.

9. Who is the strange woman in verse sixteen?

The Sage Vilna Gaon[iv] said that the strange woman is a metaphor referring to coveting and sin. The Sage Rashi[v] said that this is referring to the dangers of idolatry or heresy. The Sages believed that the Torah must be protected. When the people followed the Torah, they will be performing mitzvot that are pleasing to the LORD.[21]

Thoughts

The ways of Wisdom, which leads to righteousness, is discussed. Justice for all is a result of a leader who is full of Wisdom. Wisdom comes from the LORD and must be worked for through prayer as any other gift or talent that one may receive from the LORD. After Wisdom is obtained, there is a requirement to continue the study of the Torah in order to keep the Wisdom from the LORD. The LORD's Wisdom is worthy of anything. The study of the Torah will keep a person on the pathway of righteousness. It pleases the LORD when people study the Torah to obtain knowledge, and through the knowledge, one can obtain Wisdom.

---

[21] IBID.

Chapter Three

Language

New American Standard 1995	Hebrew
NAU **Proverbs 3:1** My son, do not forget my teaching, But let your heart keep my commandments; 2 For length of days and years of life And peace they will add to you. 3 Do not let kindness and truth leave you; Bind them around your neck, Write them on the tablet of your heart. 4 So you will find favor and good repute In the sight of God and man. 5 Trust in the LORD with all your heart And do not lean on your own understanding. 6 In all your ways acknowledge Him, And He will make your paths straight. 7 Do not be wise in your own eyes; Fear the LORD and turn away from evil. 8 It will be healing to your body And refreshment to your bones. 9 Honor the LORD from your wealth And from the first of all your produce; 10 So your barns will be filled with plenty And your vats will overflow with new wine. 11 My son, do not reject the discipline of the LORD Or loathe His reproof, 12 For whom the LORD loves He reproves, Even as a father *corrects* the son in whom he delights. 13 How blessed is the man who finds Wisdom And the man who gains understanding.	בְּנִי תּוֹרָתִי אַל־תִּשְׁכָּח וּמִצְוֹתַי יִצֹּר לִבֶּךָ: 2 כִּי אֹרֶךְ יָמִים וּשְׁנוֹת חַיִּים וְשָׁלוֹם יוֹסִיפוּ לָךְ: 3 חֶסֶד וֶאֱמֶת אַל־יַעַזְבֻךָ קָשְׁרֵם עַל־גַּרְגְּרוֹתֶיךָ כָּתְבֵם עַל־לוּחַ לִבֶּךָ: 4 וּמְצָא־חֵן וְשֵׂכֶל־טוֹב בְּעֵינֵי אֱלֹהִים וְאָדָם: פ 5 בְּטַח אֶל־יְהוָה בְּכָל־לִבֶּךָ וְאֶל־בִּינָתְךָ אַל־תִּשָּׁעֵן: 6 בְּכָל־דְּרָכֶיךָ דָעֵהוּ וְהוּא יְיַשֵּׁר אֹרְחֹתֶיךָ: 7 אַל־תְּהִי חָכָם בְּעֵינֶיךָ יְרָא אֶת־יְהוָה וְסוּר מֵרָע: 8 רִפְאוּת תְּהִי לְשָׁרֶּךָ וְשִׁקּוּי לְעַצְמוֹתֶיךָ: 9 כַּבֵּד אֶת־יְהוָה מֵהוֹנֶךָ וּמֵרֵאשִׁית כָּל־תְּבוּאָתֶךָ: 10 וְיִמָּלְאוּ אֲסָמֶיךָ שָׂבָע וְתִירוֹשׁ יְקָבֶיךָ יִפְרֹצוּ: פ 11 מוּסַר יְהוָה בְּנִי אַל־תִּמְאָס וְאַל־תָּקֹץ בְּתוֹכַחְתּוֹ: 12 כִּי אֶת אֲשֶׁר יֶאֱהַב יְהוָה יוֹכִיחַ וּכְאָב אֶת־בֵּן יִרְצֶה: 13 אַשְׁרֵי אָדָם מָצָא חָכְמָה וְאָדָם יָפִיק תְּבוּנָה: 14 כִּי טוֹב סַחְרָהּ מִסְּחַר־כָּסֶף וּמֵחָרוּץ תְּבוּאָתָהּ: 15 יְקָרָה הִיא (מִפְּנִיִּים) [מִפְּנִינִים] וְכָל־חֲפָצֶיךָ לֹא יִשְׁווּ־בָהּ: 16 אֹרֶךְ יָמִים בִּימִינָהּ בִּשְׂמֹאולָהּ עֹשֶׁר וְכָבוֹד: 17 דְּרָכֶיהָ דַרְכֵי־נֹעַם וְכָל־נְתִיבוֹתֶיהָ שָׁלוֹם: 18 עֵץ־חַיִּים הִיא לַמַּחֲזִיקִים בָּהּ וְתֹמְכֶיהָ מְאֻשָּׁר: פ 19 יְהוָה בְּחָכְמָה יָסַד־אָרֶץ כּוֹנֵן שָׁמַיִם בִּתְבוּנָה:

[14] For her profit is better than the profit of silver And her gain better than fine gold.

[15] She is more precious than jewels; And nothing you desire compares with her.

[16] Long life is in her right hand; In her left hand are riches and honor.

[17] Her ways are pleasant ways And all her paths are peace.

[18] She is a tree of life to those who take hold of her, And happy are all who hold her fast.

[19] The LORD by Wisdom founded the earth, By understanding He established the heavens.

[20] By His knowledge the deeps were broken up And the skies drip with dew.

[21] My son, let them not vanish from your sight; Keep sound Wisdom and discretion,

[22] So they will be life to your soul And adornment to your neck.

[23] Then you will walk in your way securely And your foot will not stumble.

[24] When you lie down, you will not be afraid; When you lie down, your sleep will be sweet.

[25] Do not be afraid of sudden fear Nor of the onslaught of the wicked when it comes;

[26] For the LORD will be your confidence And will keep your foot from being caught.

[27] Do not withhold good from those to whom it is due, When it is in your power to do *it*.

[28] Do not say to your neighbor, "Go, and come back, And tomorrow I will give *it*," When you have it with you.

בְּדַעְתּוֹ תְּהוֹמוֹת נִבְקָעוּ וּשְׁחָקִים יִרְעֲפוּ־ טָל: [20]

בְּנִי אַל־יָלֻזוּ מֵעֵינֶיךָ נְצֹר תֻּשִׁיָּה וּמְזִמָּה: [21]

וְיִהְיוּ חַיִּים לְנַפְשֶׁךָ וְחֵן לְגַרְגְּרֹתֶיךָ: [22]

אָז תֵּלֵךְ לָבֶטַח דַּרְכֶּךָ וְרַגְלְךָ לֹא תִגּוֹף: [23]

אִם־תִּשְׁכַּב לֹא־תִפְחָד וְשָׁכַבְתָּ וְעָרְבָה שְׁנָתֶךָ: [24]

אַל־תִּירָא מִפַּחַד פִּתְאֹם וּמִשֹּׁאַת רְשָׁעִים כִּי תָבֹא: [25]

כִּי־יְהוָה יִהְיֶה בְכִסְלֶךָ וְשָׁמַר רַגְלְךָ מִלָּכֶד: [26]

אַל־תִּמְנַע־טוֹב מִבְּעָלָיו בִּהְיוֹת לְאֵל (יָדֶיךָ) [יָדְךָ] לַעֲשׂוֹת: [27]

אַל־תֹּאמַר (לְרֵעֲיךָ) [לְרֵעֲךָ] לֵךְ וָשׁוּב וּמָחָר אֶתֵּן וְיֵשׁ אִתָּךְ: [28]

אַל־תַּחֲרֹשׁ עַל־רֵעֲךָ רָעָה וְהוּא־יוֹשֵׁב לָבֶטַח אִתָּךְ: [29]

אַל־(תָּרוֹב) [תָּרִיב] עִם־אָדָם חִנָּם אִם־לֹא גְמָלְךָ רָעָה: [30]

אַל־תְּקַנֵּא בְּאִישׁ חָמָס וְאַל־תִּבְחַר בְּכָל־ דְּרָכָיו: [31]

כִּי תוֹעֲבַת יְהוָה נָלוֹז וְאֶת־יְשָׁרִים סוֹדוֹ: [32]

מְאֵרַת יְהוָה בְּבֵית רָשָׁע וּנְוֵה צַדִּיקִים יְבָרֵךְ: [33]

אִם־לַלֵּצִים הוּא־יָלִיץ (וְלַעֲנִיִּים) [וְלַעֲנָוִים] יִתֶּן־חֵן: [34]

כָּבוֹד חֲכָמִים יִנְחָלוּ וּכְסִילִים מֵרִים קָלוֹן: פ [35]

²⁹ Do not devise harm against your neighbor, While he lives securely beside you.
³⁰ Do not contend with a man without cause, If he has done you no harm.
³¹ Do not envy a man of violence And do not choose any of his ways.
³² For the devious are an abomination to the LORD; But He is intimate with the upright.
³³ The curse of the LORD is on the house of the wicked, But He blesses the dwelling of the righteous.
³⁴ Though He scoffs at the scoffers, Yet He gives grace to the afflicted.
³⁵ The wise will inherit honor, But fools display dishonor.

Process of Discovery

Linguistics Section

Linguistic Structure

[Blessings of Wisdom][1] My son, do not forget my teaching, But let your heart keep my commandments;[2] For length of days and years of life And peace they will add to you.

[Blessings of Wisdom] [3] Do not let kindness and truth leave you; Bind them around your neck, Write them on the tablet of your heart. [4] So you will find favor and good repute In the sight of God and man.

[Blessings of Wisdom] [5] Trust in the LORD with all your heart And do not lean on your own understanding. [6] In all your ways acknowledge Him, And He will make your paths straight.

[Blessings of Wisdom] [7] Do not be wise in your own eyes; Fear the LORD and turn away from evil. [8] It will be healing to your body And refreshment to your bones.

[Blessings of Wisdom] [9] Honor the LORD from your wealth And from the first of all your produce; [10] So your barns will be filled with plenty And your vats will overflow with new wine.

A [11] My son, do not reject the discipline of the LORD Or loathe His reproof, [12] For whom the LORD loves He reproves, Even as a father *corrects* the son in whom he delights.

> **B** [13] How blessed is the man who finds Wisdom And the man who gains understanding. [14] For her profit is better than the profit of silver And her gain better than fine gold.

> > **C** [15] She is more precious than jewels; And nothing you desire compares with her. [16] Long life is in her right hand; In her left hand are riches and honor.

> **B'** [17] Her ways are pleasant ways And all her paths are peace. [18] She is a tree of life to those who take hold of her, And happy are all who hold her fast.

A' [19] The LORD by Wisdom founded the earth, By understanding He established the heavens. [20] By His knowledge the deeps were broken up And the skies drip with dew.

A [21] My son, let them not vanish from your sight; Keep sound Wisdom and discretion, [22] So they will be life to your soul And adornment to your neck. [23] Then you will walk in your way securely And your foot will not stumble. [24] When you lie down, you will not be afraid; When you lie down, your sleep will be sweet.

    B [25] Do not be afraid of sudden fear Nor of the onslaught of the wicked when it comes; [26] For the LORD will be your confidence And will keep your foot from being caught.

        C [27] Do not withhold good from those to whom it is due, When it is in your power to do *it*. [28] Do not say to your neighbor, "Go, and come back, And tomorrow I will give *it*," When you have it with you.

        C' [29] Do not devise harm against your neighbor, While he lives securely beside you. [30] Do not contend with a man without cause, If he has done you no harm.

    B' [31] Do not envy a man of violence And do not choose any of his ways. [32] For the devious are an abomination to the LORD; But He is intimate with the upright.

A' [33] The curse of the LORD is on the house of the wicked, But He blesses the dwelling of the righteous. [34] Though He scoffs at the scoffers, Yet He gives grace to the afflicted. [35] The wise will inherit honor, But fools display dishonor.

Discussion

Chapter three begins with five sayings about the blessings of Wisdom. The first chiasm is about the gifts of Wisdom. The second chiasm is about the exhortation of Wisdom.[22]

---

[22] Murai, Hajime. "Literary Structure (Chiasm, Chiasmus) of Book of Proverbs." Literary structure (chiasm, chiasmus) of each pericopes of Book of Proverbs. Accessed June 25, 2020. http://www.bible.literarystructure.info/bible/20_Proverbs_pericope_e.html.

Questioning the Passage

1. How does the study of the Torah increase one's life expectancy? (v. 2)

    The Sage Rashi said that the LORD's Torah study and performing the Mitzvot would extend life because the Torah defends the person against evil. The length of days and years are the rewards for the study of the Torah.[23]

2. What does "bind them around your neck" mean? (v. 3)

    The Sage Metzudos[vi] said that this means that one must continuously speak and think about the ways of the Torah.[24]

3. What does it mean to "not rely upon your own understanding" in verse five?

    The Sage Bahya Ben Joseph ibn Paquda[vii] said that there are ten progressive levels of human trust

    a. A newborn infant trusts his/her mother's breasts for life.

    b. The newborn grows, and the trust moves to his mother.

    c. When the child sees that his/her mother depends on his/her father for protection, he/she transfers his/her trust to his/her father (Bahya did live in a time that men ensured a wife's survival)

    d. When he/she grows up and earn a livelihood or marriage, a man transfers his trust to his strength and skill while a woman trusts in her husband.

    e. As the man grows, he recognizes his human deficiencies and realizes his need for his Creator.

    f. His trust for the LORD grows stronger as he matures.

    g. Eventually, he places his trust in the LORD for all affairs.

---

[23] Eliezer Ginsburg and Nosson Scherman, *Mishlei: Proverbs = Mishlei: a New Translation with a Commentary Anthologized from Talmudic, Midrashic and Rabbinic Sources* (Brooklyn, NY: Mesorah, 2003).
[24] IBID.

h. When a higher realization of divine mercy is attained, he accepts divine Will.

i. When his knowledge of the LORD becomes still stronger, he understands why he was created and realizes the World's enduring value to come.[25]

4. What does it mean to have a smooth path? (v. 6)

The LORD will make life's journey easier if the Torah is followed.

5. What does it mean to be wise in your own eyes? (v. 7)

Do not be wise in your own eyes. This statement means that one must not rely only upon what one sees and thinks. It is wise to count on life's direction from the LORD.

6. What does the beatitude in verse thirteen mean?

"Wisdom and Understanding are two separate matters. Wisdom is the source of knowledge; Understanding is knowing how to carefully and properly use Wisdom."[26] Wisdom without Understanding is dangerous.

7. What does verse sixteen mean?

This verse is referring to the study of the Torah. The "right side" refers to persons who study it in preparation for the World to Come. The "left side" refers to persons who study the Torah to attain wealth or honor.[27]

---

[25] IBID.

[26] Rocco A. Errico and George M. Lamsa, *Aramaic Light on Ezra through the Song of Solomon* (Smyma, GA: Noohra Foundation, 2010).

[27] Eliezer Ginsburg and Nosson Scherman, *Mishlei: Proverbs = Mishlei: a New Translation with a Commentary Anthologized from Talmudic, Midrashic and Rabbinic Sources* (Brooklyn, NY: Mesorah, 2003).

8. What does verse eighteen mean?

   The Torah is compared to a Tree of Life because the study of the Torah and practice of the Mitzvot will prolong one's life.

9. What does verse twenty-eight mean?

   The Sage Rashi said that if a poor person asks for alms or if someone needs a favor and you can comply immediately, you need to do it immediately.

Translation Inconsistencies

1. בְּנִי תּוֹרָתִי אַל־תִּשְׁכָּח

   This phrase is from verse one. It says, "My child, do not forget My Torah." The English NAU translates this phrase as "My child, do not forget my teaching." King Solomon is writing this phrase in the name of the LORD. He writes it as if the LORD is saying it. The children of the LORD must never forget the words of the Torah.

Culture Section

Questioning the passage

1. What does verse thirty-three mean?

   People in the ancient world believed that the LORD was patient with sinners and gave them time to turn from their evil ways. Evil ways were also called crooked ways. If they refused to change, they destroyed themselves.[28]

---

[28] Rocco A. Errico and George M. Lamsa, *Aramaic Light on Ezra through the Song of Solomon* (Smyma, GA: Noohra Foundation, 2010).

Straightening a crooked road is a metaphor for repenting for one's sins.

Thoughts

An emphasis of this chapter is on having trust in the LORD. One will develop a trust for the LORD by studying the Torah. The performance of the Mitzvot and the avoidance of sinful acts will allow a person to grow in the knowledge of the LORD, which then brings trust in the LORD.

46

Chapter Four

Language

New American Standard 1995	Hebrew
[1] Hear, O sons, the instruction of a father, And give attention that you may gain understanding, [2] For I give you sound teaching; Do not abandon my instruction. [3] When I was a son to my father, Tender and the only son in the sight of my mother, [4] Then he taught me and said to me, "Let your heart hold fast my words; Keep my commandments and live; [5] Acquire Wisdom! Acquire understanding! Do not forget nor turn away from the words of my mouth. [6] "Do not forsake her, and she will guard you; Love her, and she will watch over you. [7] "The beginning of Wisdom *is*: Acquire Wisdom; And with all your acquiring, get understanding. [8] "Prize her, and she will exalt you; She will honor you if you embrace her. [9] "She will place on your head a garland of grace; She will present you with a crown of beauty." [10] Hear, my son, and accept my sayings And the years of your life will be many. [11] I have directed you in the way of Wisdom; I have led you in upright paths. [12] When you walk, your steps will not be impeded; And if you run, you will not stumble.	שִׁמְעוּ בָנִים מוּסַר אָב וְהַקְשִׁיבוּ לָדַעַת בִּינָה: [2] כִּי לֶקַח טוֹב נָתַתִּי לָכֶם תּוֹרָתִי אַל־תַּעֲזֹבוּ: [3] כִּי־בֵן הָיִיתִי לְאָבִי רַךְ וְיָחִיד לִפְנֵי אִמִּי: [4] וַיֹּרֵנִי וַיֹּאמֶר לִי יִתְמָךְ־דְּבָרַי לִבֶּךָ שְׁמֹר מִצְוֹתַי וֶחְיֵה: [5] קְנֵה חָכְמָה קְנֵה בִינָה אַל־תִּשְׁכַּח וְאַל־תֵּט מֵאִמְרֵי־פִי: [6] אַל־תַּעַזְבֶהָ וְתִשְׁמְרֶךָּ אֱהָבֶהָ וְתִצְּרֶךָּ: [7] רֵאשִׁית חָכְמָה קְנֵה חָכְמָה וּבְכָל־קִנְיָנְךָ קְנֵה בִינָה: [8] סַלְסְלֶהָ וּתְרוֹמְמֶךָּ תְּכַבֵּדְךָ כִּי תְחַבְּקֶנָּה: [9] תִּתֵּן לְרֹאשְׁךָ לִוְיַת־חֵן עֲטֶרֶת תִּפְאֶרֶת תְּמַגְּנֶךָּ: [10] שְׁמַע בְּנִי וְקַח אֲמָרָי וְיִרְבּוּ לְךָ שְׁנוֹת חַיִּים: [11] בְּדֶרֶךְ חָכְמָה הֹרֵתִיךָ הִדְרַכְתִּיךָ בְּמַעְגְּלֵי־יֹשֶׁר: [12] בְּלֶכְתְּךָ לֹא־יֵצַר צַעֲדֶךָ וְאִם־תָּרוּץ לֹא תִכָּשֵׁל: [13] הַחֲזֵק בַּמּוּסָר אַל־תֶּרֶף נִצְּרֶהָ כִּי־הִיא חַיֶּיךָ: [14] בְּאֹרַח רְשָׁעִים אַל־תָּבֹא וְאַל־תְּאַשֵּׁר בְּדֶרֶךְ רָעִים: [15] פְּרָעֵהוּ אַל־תַּעֲבָר־בּוֹ שְׂטֵה מֵעָלָיו וַעֲבוֹר: [16] כִּי לֹא יִשְׁנוּ אִם־לֹא יָרֵעוּ וְנִגְזְלָה שְׁנָתָם אִם־לֹא (יִכְשׁוֹלוּ) [יַכְשִׁילוּ]: [17] כִּי לָחֲמוּ לֶחֶם רֶשַׁע וְיֵין חֲמָסִים יִשְׁתּוּ: [18] וְאֹרַח צַדִּיקִים כְּאוֹר נֹגַהּ הוֹלֵךְ וָאוֹר עַד־נְכוֹן הַיּוֹם: [19] דֶּרֶךְ רְשָׁעִים כָּאֲפֵלָה לֹא יָדְעוּ בַּמֶּה יִכָּשֵׁלוּ: פ [20] בְּנִי לִדְבָרַי הַקְשִׁיבָה לַאֲמָרַי הַט־אָזְנֶךָ:

¹³ Take hold of instruction; do not let go. Guard her, for she is your life.

¹⁴ Do not enter the path of the wicked And do not proceed in the way of evil men.

¹⁵ Avoid it, do not pass by it; Turn away from it and pass on.

¹⁶ For they cannot sleep unless they do evil; And they are robbed of sleep unless they make *someone* stumble.

¹⁷ For they eat the bread of wickedness And drink the wine of violence.

¹⁸ But the path of the righteous is like the light of dawn, That shines brighter and brighter until the full day.

¹⁹ The way of the wicked is like darkness; They do not know over what they stumble.

²⁰ My son, give attention to my words; Incline your ear to my sayings.

²¹ Do not let them depart from your sight; Keep them in the midst of your heart.

²² For they are life to those who find them And health to all their body.

²³ Watch over your heart with all diligence, For from it *flow* the springs of life.

²⁴ Put away from you a deceitful mouth And put devious speech far from you.

²⁵ Let your eyes look directly ahead And let your gaze be fixed straight in front of you.

²⁶ Watch the path of your feet And all your ways will be established.

²⁷ Do not turn to the right nor to the left; Turn your foot from evil.

²¹ אַל־יַלִּיזוּ מֵעֵינֶיךָ שָׁמְרֵם בְּתוֹךְ לְבָבֶךָ:

²² כִּי־חַיִּים הֵם לְמֹצְאֵיהֶם וּלְכָל־בְּשָׂרוֹ מַרְפֵּא:

²³ מִכָּל־מִשְׁמָר נְצֹר לִבֶּךָ כִּי־מִמֶּנּוּ תּוֹצְאוֹת חַיִּים:

²⁴ הָסֵר מִמְּךָ עִקְּשׁוּת פֶּה וּלְזוּת שְׂפָתַיִם הַרְחֵק מִמֶּךָּ:

²⁵ עֵינֶיךָ לְנֹכַח יַבִּיטוּ וְעַפְעַפֶּיךָ יַיְשִׁרוּ נֶגְדֶּךָ:

²⁶ פַּלֵּס מַעְגַּל רַגְלֶךָ וְכָל־דְּרָכֶיךָ יִכֹּנוּ:

²⁷ אַל־תֵּט־יָמִין וּשְׂמֹאול הָסֵר רַגְלְךָ מֵרָע:

Process of Discovery

Linguistics Section

Linguistic Structure

[Father's instruction] [1] Hear, *O* sons, the instruction of a father, And give attention that you may gain understanding, [2] For I give you sound teaching; Do not abandon my instruction. [3] When I was a son to my father, Tender and the only son in the sight of my mother, [4] Then he taught me and said to me, "Let your heart hold fast my words; Keep my commandments and live; [5] Acquire Wisdom! Acquire understanding! Do not forget nor turn away from the words of my mouth.

[Wisdom] [6] "Do not forsake her, and she will guard you; Love her, and she will watch over you. [7] "The beginning of Wisdom *is:* Acquire Wisdom; And with all your acquiring, get understanding. [8] "Prize her, and she will exalt you; She will honor you if you embrace her. [9] "She will place on your head a garland of grace; She will present you with a crown of beauty."

[Father's sayings] [10] Hear, my son, and accept my sayings And the years of your life will be many. [11] I have directed you in the way of Wisdom; I have led you in upright paths. [12] When you walk, your steps will not be impeded; And if you run, you will not stumble. [13] Take hold of instruction; do not let go. Guard her, for she is your life. [14] Do not enter the path of the wicked And do not proceed in the way of evil men. [15] Avoid it, do not pass by it; Turn away from it and pass on. [16] For they cannot sleep unless they do evil; And they are robbed of sleep unless they make *someone* stumble. [17] For they eat the bread of wickedness And drink the wine of violence.

[Righteousness] [18] But the path of the righteous is like the light of dawn, That shines brighter and brighter until the full day.

[The wicked] [19] The way of the wicked is like darkness; They do not know over what they stumble.

[Father's words] [20] My son, give attention to my words; Incline your ear to my sayings. [21] Do not let them depart from your sight; Keep them in the midst of your heart. [22] For they are life to those who find them And health to all their body. [23] Watch over your heart with all diligence, For from it *flow* the springs of life. [24] Put away from you a deceitful mouth And put devious speech far from you. [25] Let your eyes look directly ahead And let your gaze be fixed straight in front of you. [26] Watch the path of your feet And all your ways will be established. [27] Do not turn to the right nor to the left; Turn your foot from evil.

Discussion

This chapter is a collection of instructions from a father to his son.

Questioning the Passage

1. What is the instruction of the father? (v. 1)

   King Solomon was speaking in the LORD's name according to the sage Metzudos. Therefore, Solomon was referring to the Torah. The LORD gave Israel His Torah to teach them how to become the righteous people whom the LORD wanted them to become.[29]

2. How does one acquire Wisdom? (v. 5)

   The Sage, the Vilna Gaon, said that verse five is saying that if one cannot find a teacher who will teach Wisdom for free, then the student must find a willing person to teach it to them for a cost.[30]

3. Whom is verse six referring to? (v. 6)

   The author is referring to the Torah. The Torah is always identified as "she."

4. What is the crown of beauty in verse nine?

   Other persons esteem this crown because the one who learned Torah obtained Wisdom and demonstrated it. The study of the Torah leads to wisdom.

---

[29] Eliezer Ginsburg and Nosson Scherman, *Mishlei: Proverbs = Mishlei: a New Translation with a Commentary Anthologized from Talmudic, Midrashic and Rabbinic Sources* (Brooklyn, NY: Mesorah, 2003).
[30] IBID.;

5. What does verse twenty-one mean?

In all that one does, the words of the Torah must stand in front of the eyes. Never lose sight of the righteousness expressed in the Torah.[31]

6. What does verse twenty-two mean?

There are two aspects to the Torah, as there are two aspects to humans. The flesh and the spirit comprise a human. There is the written word of the Torah and the secret work of the Torah, which Moses orally gave to the people, which are the two aspects of Torah.[32]

7. What does verse twenty-three mean?

A person must watch over their heart to prevent improper thoughts from entering the soul.

Culture Section

Questioning the passage

1. What is the wine of violence? (v. 17)

"Wine" is used metaphorically in verse seventeen. It means "extortation, rage, and other evil things that dominate the lives of the wicked. Wine can cause a person to rejoice, but it also can be used in excess and can cause a person to sin before the LORD. Wine can destroy a person when abusively consumed.[33]

---

[31] IBID.

[32] IBID.

[33] Rocco A. Errico and George M. Lamsa, *Aramaic Light on Ezra through the Song of Solomon* (Smyma, GA: Noohra Foundation, 2010).

2. What does verse eighteen mean?

   A righteous person will bring light into their communities. The light is the love and grace of the LORD.

3. What does verse twenty-six mean?

   The path of evil refers to the broad and dangerous ways filled with temptations and lead to destruction. It is best to stay far away from this path.[34]

Thoughts

How does one achieve righteousness? This chapter says that following the ways of the Torah will move a person to righteousness. Everything that is needed to have a righteous life is contained in the Torah. At the same time, one has to be on guard because Evil inclination will try to trick a person into leaving the ways of the Torah and move toward evil. The Torah study is always necessary to keep the words of the LORD fresh in one's mind. The mind can then control the desires of the flesh and keep a person righteous.

---

[34] IBID.

Chapter Five

Language

New American Standard 1995	Hebrew
[1] My son, give attention to my wisdom, Incline your ear to my understanding;	בְּנִי לְחָכְמָתִי הַקְשִׁיבָה לִתְבוּנָתִי הַט־אָזְנֶךָ: [2]לִשְׁמֹר מְזִמּוֹת וְדַעַת שְׂפָתֶיךָ יִנְצֹרוּ:
[2] That you may observe discretion And your lips may reserve knowledge.	[3] כִּי נֹפֶת תִּטֹּפְנָה שִׂפְתֵי זָרָה וְחָלָק מִשֶּׁמֶן חִכָּהּ:
[3] For the lips of an adulteress drip honey And smoother than oil is her speech;	[4]וְאַחֲרִיתָהּ מָרָה כַלַּעֲנָה חַדָּה כְּחֶרֶב פִּיּוֹת:
[4] But in the end she is bitter as wormwood, Sharp as a two-edged sword.	[5] רַגְלֶיהָ יֹרְדוֹת מָוֶת שְׁאוֹל צְעָדֶיהָ יִתְמֹכוּ:
[5] Her feet go down to death, Her steps take hold of Sheol.	[6] אֹרַח חַיִּים פֶּן־תְּפַלֵּס נָעוּ מַעְגְּלֹתֶיהָ לֹא תֵדָע: פ
[6] She does not ponder the path of life; Her ways are unstable, she does not know *it.*	[7] וְעַתָּה בָנִים שִׁמְעוּ־לִי וְאַל־תָּסוּרוּ מֵאִמְרֵי־פִי:
[7] Now then, *my* sons, listen to me And do not depart from the words of my mouth.	[8] הַרְחֵק מֵעָלֶיהָ דַרְכֶּךָ וְאַל־תִּקְרַב אֶל־פֶּתַח בֵּיתָהּ:
[8] Keep your way far from her And do not go near the door of her house,	[9] פֶּן־תִּתֵּן לַאֲחֵרִים הוֹדֶךָ וּשְׁנֹתֶיךָ לְאַכְזָרִי:
[9] Or you will give your vigor to others And your years to the cruel one;	[10] פֶּן־יִשְׂבְּעוּ זָרִים כֹּחֶךָ וַעֲצָבֶיךָ בְּבֵית נָכְרִי:
[10] And strangers will be filled with your strength And your hard-earned goods *will go* to the house of an alien;	[11] וְנָהַמְתָּ בְאַחֲרִיתֶךָ בִּכְלוֹת בְּשָׂרְךָ וּשְׁאֵרֶךָ:
[11] And you groan at your final end, When your flesh and your body are consumed;	[12] וְאָמַרְתָּ אֵיךְ שָׂנֵאתִי מוּסָר וְתוֹכַחַת נָאַץ לִבִּי:
[12] And you say, "How I have hated instruction! And my heart spurned reproof!	[13] וְלֹא־שָׁמַעְתִּי בְּקוֹל מוֹרָי וְלִמְלַמְּדַי לֹא־הִטִּיתִי אָזְנִי:
[13] "I have not listened to the voice of my teachers, Nor inclined my ear to my instructors!	[14] כִּמְעַט הָיִיתִי בְכָל־רָע בְּתוֹךְ קָהָל וְעֵדָה:
[14] "I was almost in utter ruin In the midst of the assembly and congregation."	[15] שְׁתֵה־מַיִם מִבּוֹרֶךָ וְנֹזְלִים מִתּוֹךְ בְּאֵרֶךָ:
[15] Drink water from your own cistern And fresh water from your own well.	[16] יָפוּצוּ מַעְיְנֹתֶיךָ חוּצָה בָּרְחֹבוֹת פַּלְגֵי־מָיִם:
	[17] יִהְיוּ־לְךָ לְבַדֶּךָ וְאֵין לְזָרִים אִתָּךְ:
	[18] יְהִי־מְקוֹרְךָ בָרוּךְ וּשְׂמַח מֵאֵשֶׁת נְעוּרֶךָ:
	[19] אַיֶּלֶת אֲהָבִים וְיַעֲלַת־חֵן דַּדֶּיהָ יְרַוֻּךָ בְכָל־עֵת בְּאַהֲבָתָהּ תִּשְׁגֶּה תָמִיד:
	[20] וְלָמָּה תִשְׁגֶּה בְנִי בְזָרָה וּתְחַבֵּק חֵק נָכְרִיָּה:
	[21] כִּי נֹכַח עֵינֵי יְהוָה דַּרְכֵי־אִישׁ וְכָל־מַעְגְּלֹתָיו מְפַלֵּס:
	[22] עַווֹנוֹתָיו יִלְכְּדֻנוֹ אֶת־הָרָשָׁע וּבְחַבְלֵי חַטָּאתוֹ יִתָּמֵךְ:

<table>
<tr>
<td>

¹⁶ Should your springs be dispersed abroad, Streams of water in the streets?

¹⁷ Let them be yours alone And not for strangers with you.

¹⁸ Let your fountain be blessed, And rejoice in the wife of your youth.

¹⁹ *As* a loving hind and a graceful doe, Let her breasts satisfy you at all times; Be exhilarated always with her love.

²⁰ For why should you, my son, be exhilarated with an adulteress And embrace the bosom of a foreigner?

²¹ For the ways of a man are before the eyes of the LORD, And He watches all his paths.

²² His own iniquities will capture the wicked, And he will be held with the cords of his sin.

²³ He will die for lack of instruction, And in the greatness of his folly he will go astray.

</td>
<td>

²³ הוּא יָמוּת בְּאֵין מוּסָר וּבְרֹב אִוַּלְתּוֹ יִשְׁגֶּה׃

פ

</td>
</tr>
</table>

Process of Discovery

Linguistics Section

Linguistic Structure

A [1] My son, give attention to my wisdom, Incline your ear to my understanding;

> **B** [2] That you may observe discretion And your lips may reserve knowledge.

> **B'** [3] For the lips of an adulteress drip honey And smoother than oil is her speech; [4] But in the end she is bitter as wormwood, Sharp as a two-edged sword.

A' [5] Her feet go down to death, Her steps take hold of Sheol. [6] She does not ponder the path of life; Her ways are unstable, she does not know *it*.

A [7] Now then, *my* sons, listen to me And do not depart from the words of my mouth. [8] Keep your way far from her And do not go near the door of her house, [9] Or you will give your vigor to others And your years to the cruel one; [10] And strangers will be filled with your strength And your hard-earned goods *will go* to the house of an alien;

> **B** [11] And you groan at your final end, When your flesh and your body are consumed; [12] And you say, "How I have hated instruction! And my heart spurned reproof! [13] "I have not listened to the voice of my teachers, Nor inclined my ear to my instructors! [14] "I was almost in utter ruin In the midst of the assembly and congregation."

A' [15] Drink water from your own cistern And fresh water from your own well. [16] Should your springs be dispersed abroad, Streams of water in the streets? [17] Let them be yours alone And not for strangers with you. [18] Let your fountain be blessed, And rejoice in the wife of your youth. [19] *As* a loving hind and a graceful doe, Let her breasts satisfy you at all times; Be exhilarated always with her love.

> **B'** [20] For why should you, my son, be exhilarated with an adulteress And embrace the bosom of a foreigner? [21] For the ways of a man are before the eyes of the LORD, And He watches all his paths. [22] His own iniquities will capture the wicked, And he will be held with the cords of his sin. [23] He will die for lack of instruction, And in the greatness of his folly he will go astray.

Discussion

This chapter consists of two chiasms. The chapter is about King Solomon advising about avoiding adultery.

Questioning the Passage

1. What does it mean to have lips like dripping honey? (v. 3)
   This phrase means that the woman is enticing and beautiful. She may be considered irresistible. The warning that follows is that a man can be trapped into doing evil for such a woman.

2. What does it mean that the woman can be as bitter as wormwood? (v. 4)
   A woman who appears to be sweet as honey, but evil is compared to a two-edged sword, one edge smooth while the other is sharp. The wormwood is a bitter-tasting item that symbolizes the evil of a woman who is an adulteress.[35]

3. What does it mean that feet go down to death? (v. 5)
   The Sage Alshich[viii] said that this means that Evil inclination is looking to take the man through the woman. An adulterous woman must be avoided because Evil inclination will enter the man, and he will not be able to join the LORD in heaven after death.

---

[35] Eliezer Ginsburg and Nosson Scherman, *Mishlei: Proverbs = Mishlei: a New Translation with a Commentary Anthologized from Talmudic, Midrashic and Rabbinic Sources* (Brooklyn, NY: Mesorah, 2003).

4. What does verse eight mean? (v. 8)

   This verse is a metaphorical warning not only to stay away from idolatry and heresy but even to avoid comparisons and analogies that may lead to heretical thinking, justifying them as a means to strengthen oneself in Torah.[36]

5. Why will strangers be filled with one's strength? (v. 10)

   Strength refers to money in this verse, which has been accumulated through effort and strength, according to the Sage Metzudos[ix].[37]

6. What is "spurned reproof?" (v. 12)

   This phrase means to be chastised.

7. What does verse fifteen mean?

   This sentence means that one must study the Torah, which was given by the LORD. Torah's knowledge will become like a well, for it will begin to flow onto itself.[38]

8. What does verse sixteen mean?

   The Sage Rashi said that once a person learns Torah, they will have many students who will want to learn Torah from him.[39]

---

[36] IBID.

[37] IBID.

[38] IBID.

[39] IBID.

9. What is the symbolism of verse twenty?

The Sage Malbim explained that the strange woman refers to fields of knowledge that misleads a person. One should study the Torah.[40]

Translation Inconsistencies

1. NAU Prov. 5:3 For the lips of an adulteress drip honey and smoother than oil is her speech;

Targum Prov. 5:3 For the lips of a foreign woman drip honeycomb, and her palate is smoother than oil.

NRSV Prov. 5:3 For the lips of a loose woman drip honey, and her speech is smoother than oil;

כִּי נֹפֶת תִּטֹּפְנָה שִׂפְתֵי זָרָה וְחָלָק מִשֶּׁמֶן חִכָּהּ׃ Prov. 5:3

The difference in the translation because of the word זוּר , which is found in the phrase study. In the Proverbs, this word is translated as "adulteress." It means "stranger."

Phrase Study

1. זוּר *(zûr)* (v. 3) *be a stranger.* (ASV and RSV similar.)

"KB gives the basic meaning as "turn aside." BDB cites the similar but apparently not related root סוּר that has this meaning.

Apart from its participial use, the word appears only four times in Qal, twice in Niphal, and once in Hophal. Typical is Job 19:13, where Job states

____

[40] IBID.

that his former friends have become "estranged" from him. The Niphals and Hophals are passive.

זוּר is principally used in the participial form, זָר, appearing sixty-nine times. It carries the force of a noun, and is so I by KB. It is used for some action strange to the law (Lev 10:1), and for one who is a stranger to another household (Deut 25:5), to another person (Prov 14:10), and to another land (Hos 7:9). The basic thought is of non-acquaintance or non-relatedness. The feminine form, "The Strange Woman," often in Prov is the adulteress."[41]

Thoughts

This chapter can be viewed as a lesson on adultery and a lesson on studying books other than the Torah. It is wrong to be married and to sleep with another woman. It is wrong to study anything that is not directly connected with the Torah. The sayings of the Sages, the other books of the Bible, and commentaries by learned men are all based on the learnings that the LORD gave us in the Torah. It is essential to stick to the Torah.

---

[41] Sniders, L. A., "The Meaning of *zr* in the Old Testament," OTS 10: 1–154.

Chapter Six

Language

New American Standard 1995	Hebrew
[1] My son, if you have become surety for your neighbor, Have given a pledge for a stranger,	בְּנִי אִם־עָרַבְתָּ לְרֵעֶךָ תָּקַעְתָּ לַזָּר כַּפֶּיךָ: 2
[2] *If* you have been snared with the words of your mouth, Have been caught with the words of your mouth,	נוֹקַשְׁתָּ בְאִמְרֵי־פִיךָ נִלְכַּדְתָּ בְּאִמְרֵי־פִיךָ:
[3] Do this then, my son, and deliver yourself; Since you have come into the hand of your neighbor, Go, humble yourself, and importune your neighbor.	3 עֲשֵׂה זֹאת אֵפוֹא בְּנִי וְהִנָּצֵל כִּי בָאתָ בְכַף־רֵעֶךָ לֵךְ הִתְרַפֵּס וּרְהַב רֵעֶיךָ:
[4] Give no sleep to your eyes, Nor slumber to your eyelids;	4 אַל־תִּתֵּן שֵׁנָה לְעֵינֶיךָ וּתְנוּמָה לְעַפְעַפֶּיךָ:
[5] Deliver yourself like a gazelle from *the hunter's* hand And like a bird from the hand of the fowler.	5 הִנָּצֵל כִּצְבִי מִיָּד וּכְצִפּוֹר מִיַּד יָקוּשׁ: פ
[6] Go to the ant, O sluggard, Observe her ways and be wise,	6 לֵךְ־אֶל־נְמָלָה עָצֵל רְאֵה דְרָכֶיהָ וַחֲכָם:
[7] Which, having no chief, Officer or ruler,	7 אֲשֶׁר אֵין־לָהּ קָצִין שֹׁטֵר וּמֹשֵׁל:
[8] Prepares her food in the summer *And* gathers her provision in the harvest.	8 תָּכִין בַּקַּיִץ לַחְמָהּ אָגְרָה בַקָּצִיר מַאֲכָלָהּ:
[9] How long will you lie down, O sluggard? When will you arise from your sleep?	9 עַד־מָתַי עָצֵל תִּשְׁכָּב מָתַי תָּקוּם מִשְּׁנָתֶךָ:
[10] "A little sleep, a little slumber, A little folding of the hands to rest "--	10 מְעַט שֵׁנוֹת מְעַט תְּנוּמוֹת מְעַט חִבֻּק יָדַיִם לִשְׁכָּב:
[11] Your poverty will come in like a vagabond And your need like an armed man.	11 וּבָא־כִמְהַלֵּךְ רֵאשֶׁךָ וּמַחְסֹרְךָ כְּאִישׁ מָגֵן: פ
[12] A worthless person, a wicked man, Is the one who walks with a perverse mouth,	12 אָדָם בְּלִיַּעַל אִישׁ אָוֶן הוֹלֵךְ עִקְּשׁוּת פֶּה:
	13 קֹרֵץ בְּעֵינָו מֹלֵל בְּרַגְלָו מֹרֶה בְּאֶצְבְּעֹתָיו:
	14 תַּהְפֻּכוֹת בְּלִבּוֹ חֹרֵשׁ רָע בְּכָל־עֵת (מִדָנִים) [מִדְיָנִים] יְשַׁלֵּחַ:
	15 עַל־כֵּן פִּתְאֹם יָבוֹא אֵידוֹ פֶּתַע יִשָּׁבֵר וְאֵין מַרְפֵּא: פ
	16 שֶׁשׁ־הֵנָּה שָׂנֵא יְהוָה וְשֶׁבַע (תּוֹעֲבוֹת) [תּוֹעֲבַת] נַפְשׁוֹ:
	17 עֵינַיִם רָמוֹת לְשׁוֹן שָׁקֶר וְיָדַיִם שֹׁפְכוֹת דָּם־נָקִי:
	18 לֵב חֹרֵשׁ מַחְשְׁבוֹת אָוֶן רַגְלַיִם מְמַהֲרוֹת לָרוּץ לָרָעָה:
	19 יָפִיחַ כְּזָבִים עֵד שָׁקֶר וּמְשַׁלֵּחַ מְדָנִים בֵּין אַחִים: פ
	20 נְצֹר בְּנִי מִצְוַת אָבִיךָ וְאַל־תִּטֹּשׁ תּוֹרַת אִמֶּךָ:
	21 קָשְׁרֵם עַל־לִבְּךָ תָמִיד עָנְדֵם עַל־גַּרְגְּרֹתֶךָ:

[13] Who winks with his eyes, who signals with his feet, Who points with his fingers;

[14] Who *with* perversity in his heart continually devises evil, Who spreads strife.

[15] Therefore his calamity will come suddenly; Instantly he will be broken and there will be no healing.

[16] There are six things which the LORD hates, Yes, seven which are an abomination to Him:

[17] Haughty eyes, a lying tongue, And hands that shed innocent blood,

[18] A heart that devises wicked plans, Feet that run rapidly to evil,

[19] A false witness *who* utters lies, And one who spreads strife among brothers.

[20] My son, observe the commandment of your father And do not forsake the teaching of your mother;

[21] Bind them continually on your heart; Tie them around your neck.

[22] When you walk about, they will guide you; When you sleep, they will watch over you; And when you awake, they will talk to you.

[23] For the commandment is a lamp and the teaching is light; And reproofs for discipline are the way of life

[24] To keep you from the evil woman, From the smooth tongue of the adulteress.

[25] Do not desire her beauty in your heart, Nor let her capture you with her eyelids.

[26] For on account of a harlot *one is reduced* to a loaf of bread, And an adulteress hunts for the precious life.

[27] Can a man take fire in his bosom And his clothes not be burned?

בְּהִתְהַלֶּכְךָ תַּנְחֶה אֹתָךְ בְּשָׁכְבְּךָ תִּשְׁמֹר עָלֶיךָ וַהֲקִיצוֹתָ הִיא תְשִׂיחֶךָ: [22]

כִּי נֵר מִצְוָה וְתוֹרָה אוֹר וְדֶרֶךְ חַיִּים תּוֹכְחוֹת מוּסָר: [23]

לִשְׁמָרְךָ מֵאֵשֶׁת רָע מֵחֶלְקַת לָשׁוֹן נָכְרִיָּה: [24]

אַל־תַּחְמֹד יָפְיָהּ בִּלְבָבֶךָ וְאַל־תִּקָּחֲךָ בְּעַפְעַפֶּיהָ: [25]

כִּי בְעַד־אִשָּׁה זוֹנָה עַד־כִּכַּר לָחֶם וְאֵשֶׁת אִישׁ נֶפֶשׁ יְקָרָה תָצוּד: פ [26]

הֲיַחְתֶּה אִישׁ אֵשׁ בְּחֵיקוֹ וּבְגָדָיו לֹא תִשָּׂרַפְנָה: [27]

אִם־יְהַלֵּךְ אִישׁ עַל־הַגֶּחָלִים וְרַגְלָיו לֹא תִכָּוֶינָה: [28]

כֵּן הַבָּא אֶל־אֵשֶׁת רֵעֵהוּ לֹא יִנָּקֶה כָּל־הַנֹּגֵעַ בָּהּ: [29]

לֹא־יָבוּזוּ לַגַּנָּב כִּי יִגְנוֹב לְמַלֵּא נַפְשׁוֹ כִּי יִרְעָב: [30]

וְנִמְצָא יְשַׁלֵּם שִׁבְעָתָיִם אֶת־כָּל־הוֹן בֵּיתוֹ יִתֵּן: [31]

נֹאֵף אִשָּׁה חֲסַר־לֵב מַשְׁחִית נַפְשׁוֹ הוּא יַעֲשֶׂנָּה: [32]

נֶגַע־וְקָלוֹן יִמְצָא וְחֶרְפָּתוֹ לֹא תִמָּחֶה: [33]

כִּי־קִנְאָה חֲמַת־גָּבֶר וְלֹא־יַחְמוֹל בְּיוֹם נָקָם: [34]

לֹא־יִשָּׂא פְּנֵי כָל־כֹּפֶר וְלֹא־יֹאבֶה כִּי תַרְבֶּה־שֹׁחַד: פ [35]

²⁸ Or can a man walk on hot coals And his feet not be scorched?

²⁹ So is the one who goes in to his neighbor's wife; Whoever touches her will not go unpunished.

³⁰ Men do not despise a thief if he steals To satisfy himself when he is hungry;

³¹ But when he is found, he must repay sevenfold; He must give all the substance of his house.

³² The one who commits adultery with a woman is lacking sense; He who would destroy himself does it.

³³ Wounds and disgrace he will find, And his reproach will not be blotted out.

³⁴ For jealousy enrages a man, And he will not spare in the day of vengeance.

³⁵ He will not accept any ransom, Nor will he be satisfied though you give many gifts.

Process of Discovery

Linguistics Section

Linguistic Structure

[**Advice**] [1] My son, if you have become surety for your neighbor, Have given a pledge for a stranger, [2] *If* you have been snared with the words of your mouth, Have been caught with the words of your mouth, [3] Do this then, my son, and deliver yourself; Since you have come into the hand of your neighbor, Go, humble yourself, and importune your neighbor.

[**Advice**] [4] Give no sleep to your eyes, Nor slumber to your eyelids; [5] Deliver yourself like a gazelle from *the hunter's* hand And like a bird from the hand of the fowler. [6] Go to the ant, O sluggard, Observe her ways and be wise, [7] Which, having no chief, Officer or ruler, [8] Prepares her food in the summer *And* gathers her provision in the harvest.

[**Question**] [9] How long will you lie down, O sluggard? When will you arise from your sleep?

[**Answer**] [10] "A little sleep, a little slumber, A little folding of the hands to rest "-- [11] Your poverty will come in like a vagabond And your need like an armed man. [12] A worthless person, a wicked man, Is the one who walks with a perverse mouth, [13] Who winks with his eyes, who signals with his feet, Who points with his fingers; [14] Who *with* perversity in his heart continually devises evil, Who spreads strife. [15] Therefore his calamity will come suddenly; Instantly he will be broken and there will be no healing.

[**Statement**] [16] There are six things which the LORD hates, Yes, seven which are an abomination to Him: [17] Haughty eyes, a lying tongue, And hands that shed innocent blood, [18] A heart that devises wicked plans, Feet that run rapidly to evil, [19] A false witness *who* utters lies, And one who spreads strife among brothers.

[**Advice**] [20] My son, observe the commandment of your father And do not forsake the teaching of your mother; [21] Bind them continually on your heart; Tie them around your neck. [22] When you walk about, they will guide you; When you sleep, they will watch over you; And when you awake, they will talk to you. [23] For the commandment is a lamp and the teaching is light; And reproofs for discipline are the way of life

[**Adultery**] [24] To keep you from the evil woman, From the smooth tongue of the adulteress. [25] Do not desire her beauty in your heart, Nor let her capture you with her eyelids. [26] For on account of a harlot *one is reduced* to a loaf of bread, And an adulteress hunts for the precious life. [27] Can a man take fire in his bosom And his clothes not be burned? [28] Or can a man walk on hot coals And his feet not be scorched? [29] So is the one who goes in to his neighbor's wife; Whoever touches her will not go unpunished. [30] Men do not despise a thief if he steals To satisfy himself when he is hungry; [31] But when he is found, he must repay sevenfold; He must give all the substance of his house. [32] The one who commits adultery with a woman is lacking sense; He who would destroy himself does it. [33] Wounds and disgrace he will find, And his reproach will not be blotted out. [34] For jealousy enrages a man, And he will not spare in the day of vengeance. [35] He will not accept any ransom, Nor will he be satisfied though you give many gifts.

Discussion

Chapter six offers additional advice against laziness and adultery.

Questioning the Passage

1. Why is the guarantor mentioned twice in verse one?

   The verse is referring to a person who has become a cosigner for a loan. The Sage, the Vilna Gaon, said that there are two types of guarantors mentioned. The first is one who pledges to pay back a loan if the borrower defaults. The second one is a cosigner who unconditionally accepts the obligation.[42] The implication is that the first type of cosigner could decide not to accept the payment for a defaulted loan even though he/she accepted the responsibility. The second type of cosigner will offer payments, no matter what happens.

   This verse can be viewed metaphorically. There are two types of leaders in Israel, teachers, and judges. Teachers of the Torah are obligated to educate the people in the LORD's ways through the Torah so that they will not error before the LORD. The Judges are like unconditional guarantors. They get paid for their decisions, thus taking money from people.

---

[42] Eliezer Ginsburg and Nosson Scherman, *Mishlei: Proverbs = Mishlei: a New Translation with a Commentary Anthologized from Talmudic, Midrashic and Rabbinic Sources* (Brooklyn, NY: Mesorah, 2003).

2. Why did King Solomon say that cosigning a loan can be dangerous? (v. 2)

Solomon said to his son that by cosigning a loan for a friend, he might have placed himself into his enemy's hands.[43] It is possible that the friend was lent money by a person who was an enemy of his son. The lender could then raise the interest rate to the point where his friend cannot pay back the loan. If a default occurs, then Solomon's son is responsible for the loan. That could weaken Solomon's son financially. His enemy would be using economic warfare.

3. What does the metaphor of "an ant" mean? (v. 6)

The Sage, the Vilna Gaon, said that there are three characteristics that one can learn from the ant: (1) its good deeds, (2) its fine attributes, (3) its wisdom.[44] If a person is sluggish, they can learn from the ant because it gathers more than it needs to survive. The "ways of the ant" talk about how eager it is to collect a large amount of food and will not touch any food that it did not collect. The ant's wisdom is that it stores food in the lower compartment of the anthill to protect the food from the elements of nature.

4. What is verse eleven referring to?

This verse is connected to verse ten. Poverty will come to a person who does not work. Therefore, a person cannot earn a living. Poverty will set in because the person does not have an income. This verse metaphorically means that

---

[43] Rocco A. Errico and George M. Lamsa, *Aramaic Light on Ezra through the Song of Solomon* (Smyma, GA: Noohra Foundation, 2010).

[44] Eliezer Ginsburg and Nosson Scherman, *Mishlei: Proverbs = Mishlei: a New Translation with a Commentary Anthologized from Talmudic, Midrashic and Rabbinic Sources* (Brooklyn, NY: Mesorah, 2003).

Torah study must be continuous. Stopping the Torah study will disconnect a person from the LORD.[45]

5. What does it mean to bind the mitzvot to the heart and tie them around the neck? (v. 21)

The heart signifies thought. The neck signifies speech.[46]

6. What is verse twenty-five to thirty-five referring to?

This section is a warning against committing adultery.

Phrase Study

1. תְּנוּמָה. (v. 4) "*Slumber, slumberings.* The basic use of the noun in Proverbs is in a figurative sense of laziness and inactivity (23:21; 6:10; 24:33), but the literal sense of sleep or slumber is also found (6:4, there similar to Ps 132:4)."[47] In verse four, it means light sleep. Solomon told his son not to sleep or even relax until he gets himself out of the situation.

Thoughts

This chapter commences by talking about laziness and how it can lead to poverty. The metaphorical interpretation is that if a person does not study the Torah, the person will be influenced by Evil Inclination. The Torah is a shield against the evil in the world. Never neglect to study the LORD's Word for understanding and a good life. The later part of the chapter is a warning against adultery. Marriage is a sacred trust

---

[45] IBID.

[46] IBID.

[47] R. Laird Harris, Gleason L. Archer, and Bruce K. Waltke, *Theological Wordbook of the Old Testament* (Chicago: Moody Press, 2004).

between a man and a woman and should never be broken. It is a violation of the Torah, and the results will be disastrous.

Chapter Seven

Language

New American Standard 1995	Hebrew
[1] My son, keep my words And treasure my commandments within you.	בְּנִי שְׁמֹר אֲמָרֶי וּמִצְוֹתַי תִּצְפֹּן אִתָּךְ: [2]שְׁמֹר
[2] Keep my commandments and live, And my teaching as the apple of your eye.	מִצְוֹתַי וֶחְיֵה וְתוֹרָתִי כְּאִישׁוֹן עֵינֶיךָ:
[3] Bind them on your fingers; Write them on the tablet of your heart.	[3] קָשְׁרֵם עַל־אֶצְבְּעֹתֶיךָ כָּתְבֵם עַל־לוּחַ לִבֶּךָ:
[4] Say to wisdom, "You are my sister," And call understanding *your* intimate friend;	[4] אֱמֹר לַחָכְמָה אֲחֹתִי אָתְּ וּמֹדָע לַבִּינָה תִקְרָא:
[5] That they may keep you from an adulteress, From the foreigner who flatters with her words.	[5] לִשְׁמָרְךָ מֵאִשָּׁה זָרָה מִנָּכְרִיָּה אֲמָרֶיהָ הֶחֱלִיקָה:
[6] For at the window of my house I looked out through my lattice,	[6] כִּי בְּחַלּוֹן בֵּיתִי בְּעַד אֶשְׁנַבִּי נִשְׁקָפְתִּי:
[7] And I saw among the naive, *And* discerned among the youths A young man lacking sense,	[7] וָאֵרֶא בַפְּתָאיִם אָבִינָה בַבָּנִים נַעַר חֲסַר־לֵב:
[8] Passing through the street near her corner; And he takes the way to her house,	[8] עֹבֵר בַּשּׁוּק אֵצֶל פִּנָּהּ וְדֶרֶךְ בֵּיתָהּ יִצְעָד:
[9] In the twilight, in the evening, In the middle of the night and *in* the darkness.	[9] בְּנֶשֶׁף־בְּעֶרֶב יוֹם בְּאִישׁוֹן לַיְלָה וַאֲפֵלָה:
[10] And behold, a woman *comes* to meet him, Dressed as a harlot and cunning of heart.	[10] וְהִנֵּה אִשָּׁה לִקְרָאתוֹ שִׁית זוֹנָה וּנְצֻרַת לֵב:
[11] She is boisterous and rebellious, Her feet do not remain at home;	[11] הֹמִיָּה הִיא וְסֹרָרֶת בְּבֵיתָהּ לֹא־יִשְׁכְּנוּ רַגְלֶיהָ:
[12] *She is* now in the streets, now in the squares, And lurks by every corner.	[12] פַּעַם בַּחוּץ פַּעַם בָּרְחֹבוֹת וְאֵצֶל כָּל־פִּנָּה תֶאֱרֹב:
[13] So she seizes him and kisses him And with a brazen face she says to him:	[13] וְהֶחֱזִיקָה בּוֹ וְנָשְׁקָה־לּוֹ הֵעֵזָה פָנֶיהָ וַתֹּאמַר לוֹ:
[14] "I was due to offer peace offerings; Today I have paid my vows.	[14] זִבְחֵי שְׁלָמִים עָלָי הַיּוֹם שִׁלַּמְתִּי נְדָרָי:
	[15] עַל־כֵּן יָצָאתִי לִקְרָאתֶךָ לְשַׁחֵר פָּנֶיךָ וָאֶמְצָאֶךָּ:
	[16] מַרְבַדִּים רָבַדְתִּי עַרְשִׂי חֲטֻבוֹת אֵטוּן מִצְרָיִם:
	[17] נַפְתִּי מִשְׁכָּבִי מֹר אֲהָלִים וְקִנָּמוֹן:
	[18] לְכָה נִרְוֶה דֹדִים עַד־הַבֹּקֶר נִתְעַלְּסָה בָּאֳהָבִים:
	[19] כִּי אֵין הָאִישׁ בְּבֵיתוֹ הָלַךְ בְּדֶרֶךְ מֵרָחוֹק:
	[20] צְרוֹר־הַכֶּסֶף לָקַח בְּיָדוֹ לְיוֹם הַכֵּסֶא יָבֹא בֵיתוֹ:
	[21] הִטַּתּוּ בְּרֹב לִקְחָהּ בְּחֵלֶק שְׂפָתֶיהָ תַּדִּיחֶנּוּ:

¹⁵ "Therefore I have come out to meet you, To seek your presence earnestly, and I have found you.

¹⁶ "I have spread my couch with coverings, With colored linens of Egypt.

¹⁷ "I have sprinkled my bed With myrrh, aloes and cinnamon.

¹⁸ "Come, let us drink our fill of love until morning; Let us delight ourselves with caresses.

¹⁹ "For my husband is not at home, He has gone on a long journey;

²⁰ He has taken a bag of money with him, At the full moon he will come home."

²¹ With her many persuasions she entices him; With her flattering lips she seduces him.

²² Suddenly he follows her As an ox goes to the slaughter, Or as *one in* fetters to the discipline of a fool,

²³ Until an arrow pierces through his liver; As a bird hastens to the snare, So he does not know that it *will cost him* his life.

²⁴ Now therefore, *my* sons, listen to me, And pay attention to the words of my mouth.

²⁵ Do not let your heart turn aside to her ways, Do not stray into her paths.

²⁶ For many are the victims she has cast down, And numerous are all her slain.

²⁷ Her house is the way to Sheol, Descending to the chambers of death.

הוֹלֵ֣ךְ אַ֭חֲרֶיהָ פִּתְאֹ֑ם כְּ֝שׁ֗וֹר אֶל־טֶ֥בַח יָבֽוֹא וּ֝כְעֶ֗כֶס אֶל־מוּסַ֥ר אֱוִֽיל׃ ²²

עַ֤ד יְפַלַּ֪ח חֵ֡ץ כְּֽבֵ֗דוֹ כְּמַהֵ֣ר צִפּ֣וֹר אֶל־פָּ֑ח וְלֹֽא־יָ֝דַ֗ע כִּֽי־בְנַפְשׁ֥וֹ הֽוּא׃ פ ²³

וְעַתָּ֣ה בָ֭נִים שִׁמְעוּ־לִ֑י וְ֝הַקְשִׁ֗יבוּ לְאִמְרֵי־פִֽי׃ ²⁴

אַל־יֵ֣שְׂטְ אֶל־דְּרָכֶ֣יהָ לִבֶּ֑ךָ אַל־תֵּ֝תַע בִּנְתִיבוֹתֶֽיהָ׃ ²⁵

כִּֽי־רַבִּ֣ים חֲלָלִ֣ים הִפִּ֑ילָה וַ֝עֲצֻמִ֗ים כָּל־הֲרֻגֶֽיהָ׃ ²⁶

דַּרְכֵ֣י שְׁא֣וֹל בֵּיתָ֑הּ יֹ֝רְד֗וֹת אֶל־חַדְרֵי־מָֽוֶת׃ פ ²⁷

Process of Discovery

Linguistics Section

Linguistic Structure

A [1] My son, keep my words And treasure my commandments within you. [2] Keep my commandments and live, And my teaching as the apple of your eye. [3] Bind them on your fingers; Write them on the tablet of your heart. [4] Say to wisdom, "You are my sister," And call understanding *your* intimate friend; [5] That they may keep you from an adulteress, From the foreigner who flatters with her words.

B [6] For at the window of my house I looked out through my lattice, [7] And I saw among the naive, *And* discerned among the youths A young man lacking sense, [8] Passing through the street near her corner; And he takes the way to her house, [9] In the twilight, in the evening, In the middle of the night and *in* the darkness. [10] And behold, a woman *comes* to meet him, Dressed as a harlot and cunning of heart. [11] She is boisterous and rebellious, Her feet do not remain at home; [12] *She is* now in the streets, now in the squares, And lurks by every corner.

C [13] So she seizes him and kisses him And with a brazen face she says to him: [14] "I was due to offer peace offerings; Today I have paid my vows. [15] "Therefore I have come out to meet you, To seek your presence earnestly, and I have found you. [16] "I have spread my couch with coverings, With colored linens of Egypt. [17] "I have sprinkled my bed With myrrh, aloes and cinnamon. [18] "Come, let us drink our fill of love until morning; Let us delight ourselves with caresses. [19] "For my husband is not at home, He has gone on a long journey; [20] He has taken a bag of money with him, At the full moon he will come home."

B' [21] With her many persuasions she entices him; With her flattering lips she seduces him. [22] Suddenly he follows her As an ox goes to the slaughter, Or as *one in* fetters to the discipline of a fool,

A' [23] Until an arrow pierces through his liver; As a bird hastens to the snare, So he does not know that it *will cost him* his life.

[Transition] [24] Now therefore, *my* sons, listen to me, And pay attention to the words of my mouth.

[Final Thoughts] [25] Do not let your heart turn aside to her ways, Do not stray into her paths. [26] For many are the victims she has cast down, And numerous are all her slain. [27] Her house is the way to Sheol, Descending to the chambers of death.

Discussion

This chapter deals with the question of adultery. It has an A-B chiasm and a conclusion statement.

Questioning the Passage

1. What is the "apple of your eye?" (v. 2)

   The Sage Rashi said that this is referring to the pupil of the eye. Rashi also believed that this verse was referring to the night's blackness, which is the pupil because it looks black.[48] It can be surmised that the reference refers to the trouble that occurs when the body takes over the mind.

2. What does verse four mean?

   Wisdom was considered a daughter of the LORD. People are indebted to the LORD for their physical existence. People should also be indebted to Wisdom because the LORD placed wisdom at our side as a helping sister. The example from Scripture is Miriam, who watched over the infant Moses and arranged for his own mother to nurse him.[49]

3. What is verse nine referring to?

   The Vilna Goan explained the four stages of darkness:[50]

   a. Twilight – the period when the day is waning, but it is not night yet

---

48 Eliezer Ginsburg and Nosson Scherman, *Mishlei: Proverbs = Mishlei: a New Translation with a Commentary Anthologized from Talmudic, Midrashic and Rabbinic Sources* (Brooklyn, NY: Mesorah, 2003).
49 IBID.
50 IBID.

    b. Evening – when the stars appear and day and night are mixed

    c. In the darkness of night – refers to the middle of the night when people can only be seen with great difficulty

    d. Pitch darkness – is the predawn hours in the night when the darkness is absolute.

4. What does it mean that "her feet do not dwell at home?" (v. 11)

The Sage Malbin said that a woman not staying in her home violates her modesty.[51]

5. What is the significance of linens from Egypt? (v. 16)

Egypt is the symbol of earthly pleasures, for lust, and is the breeding ground for impurities.[52]

Culture Section

Discussion

Near Eastern women did not speak to unknown men. Therefore, the harlot would have to use body language to lure a man into her bed. She would use her eyes and head nods to attract men.

Questioning the passage

1. What does "bind them upon your fingers" mean? (v. 3)

This phrase is a Near Eastern idiom that means "do not forget them." Near Eastern people would carry amulets containing passages of the Scriptures. They

---

[51] IBID.
[52] IBID.

believed that the amulets would protect them from evil spirits and as a reminder of promises and vows.[53]

Thoughts

This chapter concentrates on one of the many sins that can be done against the LORD. The warning is to stay away from an adulterous woman. A man must understand that there are women who will try to lure him into evil. The chapter tells a man how to recognize the situation and to avoid it.

---

[53] Rocco A. Errico and George M. Lamsa, *Aramaic Light on Ezra through the Song of Solomon* (Smyma, GA: Noohra Foundation, 2010).

Chapter Eight

Language

New American Standard 1995	
[1] Does not wisdom call, And understanding lift up her voice? [2] On top of the heights beside the way, Where the paths meet, she takes her stand; [3] Beside the gates, at the opening to the city, At the entrance of the doors, she cries out: [4] "To you, O men, I call, And my voice is to the sons of men. [5] "O naive ones, understand prudence; And, O fools, understand wisdom. [6] "Listen, for I will speak noble things; And the opening of my lips *will reveal* right things. [7] "For my mouth will utter truth; And wickedness is an abomination to my lips. [8] "All the utterances of my mouth are in righteousness; There is nothing crooked or perverted in them. [9] "They are all straightforward to him who understands, And right to those who find knowledge. [10] "Take my instruction and not silver, And knowledge rather than choicest gold. [11] "For wisdom is better than jewels; And all desirable things cannot compare with her. [12] "I, wisdom, dwell with prudence, And I find knowledge *and* discretion.	הֲלֹא־חָכְמָה תִקְרָא וּתְבוּנָה תִּתֵּן קוֹלָהּ׃ 2בְּרֹאשׁ־מְרוֹמִים עֲלֵי־דָרֶךְ בֵּית נְתִיבוֹת נִצָּבָה׃ 3לְיַד־שְׁעָרִים לְפִי־קָרֶת מְבוֹא פְתָחִים תָּרֹנָּה׃ 4אֲלֵיכֶם אִישִׁים אֶקְרָא וְקוֹלִי אֶל־בְּנֵי אָדָם׃ 5הָבִינוּ פְתָאיִם עָרְמָה וּכְסִילִים הָבִינוּ לֵב׃ 6שִׁמְעוּ כִּי־נְגִידִים אֲדַבֵּר וּמִפְתַּח שְׂפָתַי מֵישָׁרִים׃ 7כִּי־אֱמֶת יֶהְגֶּה חִכִּי וְתוֹעֲבַת שְׂפָתַי רֶשַׁע׃ 8בְּצֶדֶק כָּל־אִמְרֵי־פִי אֵין בָּהֶם נִפְתָּל וְעִקֵּשׁ׃ 9כֻּלָּם נְכֹחִים לַמֵּבִין וִישָׁרִים לְמֹצְאֵי דָעַת׃ 10קְחוּ־מוּסָרִי וְאַל־כָּסֶף וְדַעַת מֵחָרוּץ נִבְחָר׃ 11כִּי־טוֹבָה חָכְמָה מִפְּנִינִים וְכָל־חֲפָצִים לֹא יִשְׁווּ־בָהּ׃ 12אֲנִי־חָכְמָה שָׁכַנְתִּי עָרְמָה וְדַעַת מְזִמּוֹת אֶמְצָא׃ 13יִרְאַת יְהוָֹה שְׂנֹאת רָע גֵּאָה וְגָאוֹן וְדֶרֶךְ רָע וּפִי תַהְפֻּכוֹת שָׂנֵאתִי׃ 14לִי־עֵצָה וְתוּשִׁיָּה אֲנִי בִינָה לִי גְבוּרָה׃

¹³ "The fear of the LORD is to hate evil; Pride and arrogance and the evil way And the perverted mouth, I hate.

¹⁴ "Counsel is mine and sound wisdom; I am understanding, power is mine.

¹⁵ "By me kings reign, And rulers decree justice.

¹⁶ "By me princes rule, and nobles, All who judge rightly.

¹⁷ "I love those who love me; And those who diligently seek me will find me.

¹⁸ "Riches and honor are with me, Enduring wealth and righteousness.

¹⁹ "My fruit is better than gold, even pure gold, And my yield *better* than choicest silver.

²⁰ "I walk in the way of righteousness, In the midst of the paths of justice,

²¹ To endow those who love me with wealth, That I may fill their treasuries.

²² "The LORD possessed me at the beginning of His way, Before His works of old.

²³ "From everlasting I was established, From the beginning, from the earliest times of the earth.

²⁴ "When there were no depths I was brought forth, When there were no springs abounding with water.

²⁵ "Before the mountains were settled, Before the hills I was brought forth;

²⁶ While He had not yet made the earth and the fields, Nor the first dust of the world.

²⁷ "When He established the heavens, I was there, When He inscribed a circle on the face of the deep,

²⁸ When He made firm the skies above, When the springs of the deep became fixed,

בִּי מְלָכִים יִמְלֹכוּ וְרוֹזְנִים יְחֹקְקוּ צֶדֶק: ¹⁵

בִּי שָׂרִים יָשֹׂרוּ וּנְדִיבִים כָּל־שֹׁפְטֵי צֶדֶק: ¹⁶

אֲנִי (אֹהֲבֶיהָ) [אֹהֲבַי] אֵהָב וּמְשַׁחֲרַי יִמְצָאֻנְנִי: ¹⁷

עֹשֶׁר־וְכָבוֹד אִתִּי הוֹן עָתֵק וּצְדָקָה: ¹⁸

טוֹב פִּרְיִי מֵחָרוּץ וּמִפָּז וּתְבוּאָתִי מִכֶּסֶף נִבְחָר: ¹⁹

בְּאֹרַח־צְדָקָה אֲהַלֵּךְ בְּתוֹךְ נְתִיבוֹת מִשְׁפָּט: ²⁰

לְהַנְחִיל אֹהֲבַי יֵשׁ וְאֹצְרֹתֵיהֶם אֲמַלֵּא: פ ²¹

יְהוָה קָנָנִי רֵאשִׁית דַּרְכּוֹ קֶדֶם מִפְעָלָיו מֵאָז: ²²

מֵעוֹלָם נִסַּכְתִּי מֵרֹאשׁ מִקַּדְמֵי־אָרֶץ: ²³

בְּאֵין־תְּהֹמוֹת חוֹלָלְתִּי בְּאֵין מַעְיָנוֹת נִכְבַּדֵּי־מָיִם: ²⁴

בְּטֶרֶם הָרִים הָטְבָּעוּ לִפְנֵי גְבָעוֹת חוֹלָלְתִּי: ²⁵

עַד־לֹא עָשָׂה אֶרֶץ וְחוּצוֹת וְרֹאשׁ עַפְרוֹת תֵּבֵל: ²⁶

בַּהֲכִינוֹ שָׁמַיִם שָׁם אָנִי בְּחוּקוֹ חוּג עַל־פְּנֵי תְהוֹם: ²⁷

בְּאַמְּצוֹ שְׁחָקִים מִמָּעַל בַּעֲזוֹז עִינוֹת תְּהוֹם: ²⁸

בְּשׂוּמוֹ לַיָּם חֻקּוֹ וּמַיִם לֹא יַעַבְרוּ־פִיו בְּחוּקוֹ מוֹסְדֵי אָרֶץ: ²⁹

וָאֶהְיֶה אֶצְלוֹ אָמוֹן וָאֶהְיֶה שַׁעֲשֻׁעִים יוֹם יוֹם מְשַׂחֶקֶת לְפָנָיו בְּכָל־עֵת: ³⁰

מְשַׂחֶקֶת בְּתֵבֵל אַרְצוֹ וְשַׁעֲשֻׁעַי אֶת־בְּנֵי אָדָם: פ ³¹

וְעַתָּה בָנִים שִׁמְעוּ־לִי וְאַשְׁרֵי דְּרָכַי יִשְׁמֹרוּ: ³²

29 When He set for the sea its boundary So that the water would not transgress His command, When He marked out the foundations of the earth;

30 Then I was beside Him, *as* a master workman; And I was daily *His* delight, Rejoicing always before Him,

31 Rejoicing in the world, His earth, And *having* my delight in the sons of men.

32 "Now therefore, *O* sons, listen to me, For blessed are they who keep my ways.

33 "Heed instruction and be wise, And do not neglect *it*.

34 "Blessed is the man who listens to me, Watching daily at my gates, Waiting at my doorposts.

35 "For he who finds me finds life And obtains favor from the LORD.

36 "But he who sins against me injures himself; All those who hate me love death.

33 שִׁמְעוּ מוּסָר וַחֲכָמוּ וְאַל־תִּפְרָעוּ:

34 אַשְׁרֵי אָדָם שֹׁמֵעַ לִי לִשְׁקֹד עַל־דַּלְתֹתַי יוֹם‪|‬יוֹם לִשְׁמֹר מְזוּזֹת פְּתָחָי:

35 כִּי מֹצְאִי (מֹצְאֵי) [מָצָא] חַיִּים וַיָּפֶק רָצוֹן מֵיְהוָה:

36 וְחֹטְאִי חֹמֵס נַפְשׁוֹ כָּל־מְשַׂנְאַי אָהֲבוּ מָוֶת: פ

Process of Discovery

Linguistics Section

Linguistic Structure

[Wisdom calls] [1] Does not wisdom call, And understanding lift up her voice? [2] On top of the heights beside the way, Where the paths meet, she takes her stand; [3] Beside the gates, at the opening to the city, At the entrance of the doors, she cries out: [4] "To you, O men, I call, And my voice is to the sons of men. [5] "O naive ones, understand prudence; And, O fools, understand wisdom.

[Wisdom speaks] [6] "Listen, for I will speak noble things; And the opening of my lips *will reveal* right things. [7] "For my mouth will utter truth; And wickedness is an abomination to my lips.
[8] "All the utterances of my mouth are in righteousness; There is nothing crooked or perverted in them. [9] "They are all straightforward to him who understands, And right to those who find knowledge.

[Wisdom speaks] [10] "Take my instruction and not silver, And knowledge rather than choicest gold. [11] "For wisdom is better than jewels; And all desirable things cannot compare with her. [12] "I, wisdom, dwell with prudence, And I find knowledge *and* discretion.

[Wisdom speaks] [13] "The fear of the LORD is to hate evil; Pride and arrogance and the evil way And the perverted mouth, I hate. [14] "Counsel is mine and sound wisdom; I am understanding, power is mine. [15] "By me kings reign, And rulers decree justice. [16] "By me princes rule, and nobles, All who judge rightly.

[Wisdom speaks] [17] "I love those who love me; And those who diligently seek me will find me. [18] "Riches and honor are with me, Enduring wealth and righteousness. [19] "My fruit is better than gold, even pure gold, And my yield *better* than choicest silver. [20] "I walk in the way of righteousness, In the midst of the paths of justice, [21] To endow those who love me with wealth, That I may fill their treasuries.

[Wisdom speaks] [22] "The LORD possessed me at the beginning of His way, Before His works of old. [23] "From everlasting I was established, From the beginning, from the earliest times of the earth. [24] "When there were no depths I was brought forth, When there were no springs abounding with water. [25] "Before the mountains were settled, Before the hills I was brought forth; [26] While He had not yet made the earth and the fields, Nor the first dust of the world. [27] "When He established the heavens, I was there, When He inscribed a circle on the face of the deep, [28] When He made firm the skies above, When the springs of the deep became fixed, [29] When He set for the sea its boundary So that the water would not transgress His command, When He marked out the foundations of the earth; [30] Then I was beside Him, *as* a master workman; And I was daily *His* delight, Rejoicing always before Him,

[Wisdom speaks] [31] Rejoicing in the world, His earth, And *having* my delight in the sons of men. [32] "Now therefore, *O* sons, listen to me, For blessed are they who keep my ways. [33] "Heed instruction and be wise, And do not neglect *it.*

[Beattitude] [34] "Blessed is the man who listens to me, Watching daily at my gates, Waiting at my doorposts. [35] "For he who finds me finds life And obtains favor from the LORD. [36] "But he who sins against me injures himself; All those who hate me love death.

Discussion

This chapter is about the value of wisdom. The author makes wisdom the

speaker.

Questioning the Passage

1. Why is wisdom feminine? (v. 1)

   The Hebrew word for wisdom is: חָכְמָה

   Grammatically this word is feminine. Since English does not have

   masculine and feminine words, it is more difficult for English speaking

   people to understand this concept. Since wisdom is a feminine noun, the

   author refers to wisdom as a female personification.

2. Where is "on top of the heights beside the way" located? (v. 2)

   It was believed in ancient times that the closer to the firmament (the sky)

   one could be, the closer one was to God. Therefore, wisdom was on the

   top of the heights indicating wisdom was with God. When Moses ascended

   Mount Sinai, he met God on the top of the mountain.

3. Why is wisdom crying out to the sons of men? (v. 4)

   Wisdom is a gift that comes from God. Wisdom crying out could be interpreted as the fact that men's sons do not always call upon wisdom.

4. Several verses use the pronoun "I." Who is "I?"

   The pronoun is the Torah.

5. What are God's works of old? (v. 22)

   God's works of old are found in Genesis chapter 1, the creation story. The oldest works of God in this universe is the creation of the universe. Wisdom was there when creation occurred.

6. Why is wisdom brought up from the depths of a sea that does not exist? (v. 24)

   The author is using parallelism, telling us again that wisdom existed before the creation of the universe. Water was a part of the chaos that existed, according to Genesis. A part of creation was the separation of the waters with the creation of a firmament. Wisdom was there. It is just a reinforcement of this concept.

7. What are the delights in the son of man in verse 31?

   Wisdom wants to help us in our travels through life. Wisdom delights when we call upon her. The question to contemplate is, why don't we?

Definition of Wisdom

Wisdom is a spiritual entity that existed from the beginning of creation. The author emphasizes that point in the parallelism of the passage. Wisdom was on high with the LORD, the master architect of creation. Wisdom was there when the LORD took the chaos of creation and ordered it. Wisdom was there are the structures of the universe unfolded. Also, wisdom is a gift from the LORD to humankind. To call upon the spiritual entity of wisdom is a great thing to do and offers delight to wisdom herself. Why are we not calling upon the wisdom of the LORD? What is blocking our understanding? Each of us is supposed to call upon wisdom.

Phrase Study

1. אָמוֹן *amon*, Meaning: an artificer, architect, master workman (v. 30).

    Interestingly, *amon* is used in Proverbs 8:30 and is translated as "master worker" or "architect." The other usages of the lemma produce different translations. So this word's translation in verse 30 is unique. The master workman is the LORD in this case.

Culture Section

Questioning the narrative culturally

1. What does verse three mean?

    The city gates are where the administrative functions and courts of the city resided. Wisdom was there to assist the administrators and the judges of the city to rule fairly. When they listened to wisdom, they ruled fairly.

Midrash

"The Midrash on Proverbs: Translated from the Hebrew with an Introduction and Annotations by Burton L. Visotzky (New Haven and London: Yale University Press, 1992), p. 46, claims that the divine Wisdom mentioned in Proverbs 8:22ff is the Torah which God created before he brought forth anything else:

"R. Nehemiah said: Come and see what a good thing God has created in His world even before He created the universe. What may this be? It is the Torah!."

We also read:

"What [is the scriptural proof for] Torah? The Lord created me at the beginning of his course, As the first of His works of old (Prov 8:22) . . . At first Torah was in heaven, as it is said, I was with Him as a confidant (Prov 8:30). Later on Moses arose and brought it down to earth to give it to humanity, as it is said, Rejoicing in his inhabited world, Finding delight with mankind (Prov 8:31)."

According to this Midrash on Proverbs, the Torah was "created" prior to the cosmos: it was preexistent. Compare Ecclesiasticus 1:1-4" [54]

Zohar

Chochmah, wisdom, is the second Sefirot in the Kabbalah Tree of Life. Keter, the crown, was the first emanation of Ein Sof (God) and is a transitional realm between Heaven and God. Keter is called the crown because the creation of the universe comes from Keter when commanded. Chochmah is the second Sefirot

---

[54] "Foster's Theological Reflections." : Proverbs 8:22ff (Midrash): Torah Created First? Accessed May 18, 2016. http://fosterheologicalreflections.blogspot.com/2016/05/proverbs-822ff-midrash-torah-created.html.

but is also a first Sefirot of creation. Therefore, Chochmah was with Keter as creation began. Wisdom is a part of the top three Sefirot, which together create the pseudo-sefirot Da'at, which is also called the God-head. In Christian Kabbalah, Keter is considered the Father, Chochmah, the Son, and Binah, the Holy Spirit. Since Yeshua is called Sophia (from the Greek), which means wisdom, it is clear why the early Christian Kabbalists would associate Chochmah with the Messiah Yeshua.

Thoughts

Wisdom is so critical to our existence that the LORD created wisdom before the foundation of the universe. Binah, the third Sefirot, means foundation, and its creation coincides with the LORD, creating structure out of chaos. Wisdom is a gift that the LORD gives to us. The question is, why are we not using wisdom as we should? Why are people not calling upon the LORD's wisdom to be bestowed upon them? The results of asking the LORD for wisdom can be seen in the life of King Solomon. He prayed for Wisdom, and he received it (1 Kings 3). Wisdom stands ready to be with us. All we have to do is to follow the ways of the Torah and ask the LORD to send His Chochmah to us.

84

Chapter Nine

Language

New American Standard 1995	Hebrew
[1] Wisdom has built her house, She has hewn out her seven pillars; [2] She has prepared her food, she has mixed her wine; She has also set her table; [3] She has sent out her maidens, she calls From the tops of the heights of the city: [4] "Whoever is naive, let him turn in here!" To him who lacks understanding she says, [5] "Come, eat of my food And drink of the wine I have mixed. [6] "Forsake *your* folly and live, And proceed in the way of understanding." [7] He who corrects a scoffer gets dishonor for himself, And he who reproves a wicked man *gets* insults for himself. [8] Do not reprove a scoffer, or he will hate you, Reprove a wise man and he will love you. [9] Give *instruction* to a wise man and he will be still wiser, Teach a righteous man and he will increase *his* learning. [10] The fear of the LORD is the beginning of wisdom, And the knowledge of the Holy One is understanding. [11] For by me your days will be multiplied, And years of life will be added to you. [12] If you are wise, you are wise for yourself, And if you scoff, you alone will bear it. [13] The woman of folly is boisterous, *She is* naive and knows nothing.	חָכְמוֹת בָּנְתָה בֵיתָהּ חָצְבָה עַמּוּדֶיהָ שִׁבְעָה: [2] טָבְחָה טִבְחָהּ מָסְכָה יֵינָהּ אַף עָרְכָה שֻׁלְחָנָהּ: [3] שָׁלְחָה נַעֲרֹתֶיהָ תִקְרָא עַל־גַּפֵּי מְרֹמֵי קָרֶת: [4] מִי־פֶתִי יָסֻר הֵנָּה חֲסַר־לֵב אָמְרָה לּוֹ: [5] לְכוּ לַחֲמוּ בְלַחֲמִי וּשְׁתוּ בְּיַיִן מָסָכְתִּי: [6] עִזְבוּ פְתָאיִם וִחְיוּ וְאִשְׁרוּ בְּדֶרֶךְ בִּינָה: [7] יֹסֵר לֵץ לֹקֵחַ לוֹ קָלוֹן וּמוֹכִיחַ לְרָשָׁע מוּמוֹ: [8] אַל־תּוֹכַח לֵץ פֶּן־יִשְׂנָאֶךָּ הוֹכַח לְחָכָם וְיֶאֱהָבֶךָּ: [9] תֵּן לְחָכָם וְיֶחְכַּם־עוֹד הוֹדַע לְצַדִּיק וְיוֹסֶף לֶקַח: פ [10] תְּחִלַּת חָכְמָה יִרְאַת יְהוָה וְדַעַת קְדֹשִׁים בִּינָה: [11] כִּי־בִי יִרְבּוּ יָמֶיךָ וְיוֹסִיפוּ לְּךָ שְׁנוֹת חַיִּים: [12] אִם־חָכַמְתָּ חָכַמְתָּ לָּךְ וְלַצְתָּ לְבַדְּךָ תִשָּׂא: [13] אֵשֶׁת כְּסִילוּת הֹמִיָּה פְּתַיּוּת וּבַל־יָדְעָה מָּה: [14] וְיָשְׁבָה לְפֶתַח בֵּיתָהּ עַל־כִּסֵּא מְרֹמֵי קָרֶת: [15] לִקְרֹא לְעֹבְרֵי־דָרֶךְ הַמְיַשְּׁרִים אֹרְחוֹתָם: [16] מִי־פֶתִי יָסֻר הֵנָּה וַחֲסַר־לֵב וְאָמְרָה לּוֹ:

<table>
<tr>
<td>

14 She sits at the doorway of her house, On a seat by the high places of the city,

15 Calling to those who pass by, Who are making their paths straight:

16 "Whoever is naive, let him turn in here," And to him who lacks understanding she says,

17 "Stolen water is sweet; And bread *eaten* in secret is pleasant."

18 But he does not know that the dead are there, *That* her guests are in the depths of Sheol.

</td>
<td>

מַיִם־גְּנוּבִים יִמְתָּקוּ וְלֶחֶם סְתָרִים יִנְעָם: 17

וְלֹא־יָדַע כִּי־רְפָאִים שָׁם בְּעִמְקֵי שְׁאוֹל קְרֻאֶיהָ: פ 18

</td>
</tr>
</table>

Process of Discovery

Linguistics Section

Linguistic Structure

[Wisdom's Works] [1] Wisdom has built her house, She has hewn out her seven pillars; [2] She has prepared her food, she has mixed her wine; She has also set her table; [3] She has sent out her maidens, she calls From the tops of the heights of the city: [4] "Whoever is naive, let him turn in here!" To him who lacks understanding she says, [5] "Come, eat of my food And drink of the wine I have mixed. [6] "Forsake *your* folly and live, And proceed in the way of understanding."

A [7] He who corrects a scoffer gets dishonor for himself, And he who reproves a wicked man *gets* insults for himself.

> **B** [8] Do not reprove a scoffer, or he will hate you, Reprove a wise man and he will love you.

A' [9] Give *instruction* to a wise man and he will be still wiser, Teach a righteous man and he will increase *his* learning.

[Reverence and Knowledge] [10] The fear of the LORD is the beginning of wisdom, And the knowledge of the Holy One is understanding. [11] For by me your days will be multiplied, And years of life will be added to you. [12] If you are wise, you are wise for yourself, And if you scoff, you alone will bear it.

[Woman of Folly] [13] The woman of folly is boisterous, *She is* naive and knows nothing. [14] She sits at the doorway of her house, On a seat by the high places of the city, [15] Calling to those who pass by, Who are making their paths straight: [16] "Whoever is naive, let him turn in here," And to him who lacks understanding she says, [17] "Stolen water is sweet; And bread *eaten* in secret is pleasant." [18] But he does not know that the dead are there, *That* her guests are in the depths of Sheol.

Discussion

King Solomon continues imparting his wisdom.

Questioning the Passage

1. What do the seven pillars represent? (v. 1)

    The seven pillars represent the seven days of creation. The entire universe, the structure of the house, was completed at that time. Wisdom is based on Creation. "Wisdom has built her house" is referring to the Torah. The Torah is the blueprint that the LORD used to create the Universe in seven days. The Torah came into existence before Creation had begun.

2. What does verse two mean?

    The Sage Rashi said that this verse refers to creating all solids and liquids in the Universe. In the Near East, the wine was always mixed with water because it was powerful (high alcohol content). The Vilna Goan said that the food being prepared was the Torah. The Torah needed to be prepared for the Hebrew people to accept it at Mount Sinai when it was right.[55]

3. Can wisdom add days and years to one's life? (v. 11)

    This verse refers to days that are dedicated and consecrated to the LORD and His service. Studying the Torah will increase one's days and years on Earth.

---

[55] Eliezer Ginsburg and Nosson Scherman, *Mishlei: Proverbs = Mishlei: a New Translation with a Commentary Anthologized from Talmudic, Midrashic and Rabbinic Sources* (Brooklyn, NY: Mesorah, 2003).

Culture Section

Discussion

Questioning the passage

1. What is the meaning of verse seventeen?

   In the Near East, water was and is scarce. Water was sold in the marketplaces. During droughts, sheep and cattle would die of thirst. People would often steal water. Water was usually stored in a skin that was hung on a pole in one's tent. Water was also hidden under bed clothing. Stolen water was sweet because it quenched the person's thirst for stealing it, and it was not paid for it.

   This expression was not about water but rather is a metaphor about stolen love. It is about men who neglected their wives and satisfied their desires by secretly loving the wives of other men. Anything that is stolen may taste sweet when obtained, but sooner or later, it turns bitter.[56]

Thoughts

Wisdom was created when the seven days of Creation occurred. She is always with us. Wisdom can be felt through the Shekinah, who resides in the realm of Malkhut. It is smart to follow Wisdom. She will lead the righteous to a life of Torah study. This study will lead to success in the material and spiritual world.

---

[56] Rocco A. Errico and George M. Lamsa, *Aramaic Light on Ezra through the Song of Solomon* (Smyma, GA: Noohra Foundation, 2010).

Chapter Ten

Language

New American Standard 1995	Hebrew
[1] The proverbs of Solomon. A wise son makes a father glad, But a foolish son is a grief to his mother. [2] Ill-gotten gains do not profit, But righteousness delivers from death. [3] The LORD will not allow the righteous to hunger, But He will reject the craving of the wicked. [4] Poor is he who works with a negligent hand, But the hand of the diligent makes rich. [5] He who gathers in summer is a son who acts wisely, *But* he who sleeps in harvest is a son who acts shamefully. [6] Blessings are on the head of the righteous, But the mouth of the wicked conceals violence. [7] The memory of the righteous is blessed, But the name of the wicked will rot. [8] The wise of heart will receive commands, But a babbling fool will be ruined. [9] He who walks in integrity walks securely, But he who perverts his ways will be found out. [10] He who winks the eye causes trouble, And a babbling fool will be ruined. [11] The mouth of the righteous is a fountain of life, But the mouth of the wicked conceals violence. [12] Hatred stirs up strife, But love covers all transgressions.	מִשְׁלֵי שְׁלֹמֹה פ בֵּן חָכָם יְשַׂמַּח־אָב וּבֵן כְּסִיל תּוּגַת אִמּוֹ: [2] לֹא־יוֹעִילוּ אוֹצְרוֹת רֶשַׁע וּצְדָקָה תַּצִּיל מִמָּוֶת: [3] לֹא־יַרְעִיב יְהוָה נֶפֶשׁ צַדִּיק וְהַוַּת רְשָׁעִים יֶהְדֹּף: [4] רָאשׁ עֹשֶׂה כַף־רְמִיָּה וְיַד חָרוּצִים תַּעֲשִׁיר: [5] אֹגֵר בַּקַּיִץ בֵּן מַשְׂכִּיל נִרְדָּם בַּקָּצִיר בֵּן מֵבִישׁ: [6] בְּרָכוֹת לְרֹאשׁ צַדִּיק וּפִי רְשָׁעִים יְכַסֶּה חָמָס: [7] זֵכֶר צַדִּיק לִבְרָכָה וְשֵׁם רְשָׁעִים יִרְקָב: [8] חֲכַם־לֵב יִקַּח מִצְוֹת וֶאֱוִיל שְׂפָתַיִם יִלָּבֵט: [9] הוֹלֵךְ בַּתֹּם יֵלֶךְ בֶּטַח וּמְעַקֵּשׁ דְּרָכָיו יִוָּדֵעַ: [10] קֹרֵץ עַיִן יִתֵּן עַצָּבֶת וֶאֱוִיל שְׂפָתַיִם יִלָּבֵט: [11] מְקוֹר חַיִּים פִּי צַדִּיק וּפִי רְשָׁעִים יְכַסֶּה חָמָס: [12] שִׂנְאָה תְּעוֹרֵר מְדָנִים וְעַל כָּל־פְּשָׁעִים תְּכַסֶּה אַהֲבָה: [13] בְּשִׂפְתֵי נָבוֹן תִּמָּצֵא חָכְמָה וְשֵׁבֶט לְגֵו חֲסַר־לֵב: [14] חֲכָמִים יִצְפְּנוּ־דָעַת וּפִי־אֱוִיל מְחִתָּה קְרֹבָה: [15] הוֹן עָשִׁיר קִרְיַת עֻזּוֹ מְחִתַּת דַּלִּים רֵישָׁם:

¹³ On the lips of the discerning, wisdom is found, But a rod is for the back of him who lacks understanding.

¹⁴ Wise men store up knowledge, But with the mouth of the foolish, ruin is at hand.

¹⁵ The rich man's wealth is his fortress, The ruin of the poor is their poverty.

¹⁶ The wages of the righteous is life, The income of the wicked, punishment.

¹⁷ He is *on* the path of life who heeds instruction, But he who ignores reproof goes astray.

¹⁸ He who conceals hatred *has* lying lips, And he who spreads slander is a fool.

¹⁹ When there are many words, transgression is unavoidable, But he who restrains his lips is wise.

²⁰ The tongue of the righteous is *as* choice silver, The heart of the wicked is *worth* little.

²¹ The lips of the righteous feed many, But fools die for lack of understanding.

²² It is the blessing of the LORD that makes rich, And He adds no sorrow to it.

²³ Doing wickedness is like sport to a fool, And *so is* wisdom to a man of understanding.

²⁴ What the wicked fears will come upon him, But the desire of the righteous will be granted.

²⁵ When the whirlwind passes, the wicked is no more, But the righteous *has* an everlasting foundation.

²⁶ Like vinegar to the teeth and smoke to the eyes, So is the lazy one to those who send him.

²⁷ The fear of the LORD prolongs life, But the years of the wicked will be shortened.

פְּעֻלַּת צַדִּיק לְחַיִּים תְּבוּאַת רָשָׁע לְחַטָּאת: ¹⁶

אֹרַח לְחַיִּים שֹׁמֵר מוּסָר וְעוֹזֵב תּוֹכַחַת מַתְעֶה: ¹⁷

מְכַסֶּה שִׂנְאָה שִׂפְתֵי־שָׁקֶר וּמוֹצִא דִבָּה הוּא כְסִיל: ¹⁸

בְּרֹב דְּבָרִים לֹא יֶחְדַּל־פָּשַׁע וְחֹשֵׂךְ שְׂפָתָיו מַשְׂכִּיל: ¹⁹

כֶּסֶף נִבְחָר לְשׁוֹן צַדִּיק לֵב רְשָׁעִים כִּמְעָט: ²⁰

שִׂפְתֵי צַדִּיק יִרְעוּ רַבִּים וֶאֱוִילִים בַּחֲסַר־לֵב יָמוּתוּ: ²¹

בִּרְכַּת יְהוָה הִיא תַעֲשִׁיר וְלֹא־יוֹסִף עֶצֶב עִמָּהּ: ²²

כִּשְׂחוֹק לִכְסִיל עֲשׂוֹת זִמָּה וְחָכְמָה לְאִישׁ תְּבוּנָה: ²³

מְגוֹרַת רָשָׁע הִיא תְבוֹאֶנּוּ וְתַאֲוַת צַדִּיקִים יִתֵּן: ²⁴

כַּעֲבוֹר סוּפָה וְאֵין רָשָׁע וְצַדִּיק יְסוֹד עוֹלָם: ²⁵

כַּחֹמֶץ לַשִּׁנַּיִם וְכֶעָשָׁן לָעֵינָיִם כֵּן הֶעָצֵל לְשֹׁלְחָיו: ²⁶

יִרְאַת יְהוָה תּוֹסִיף יָמִים וּשְׁנוֹת רְשָׁעִים תִּקְצֹרְנָה: ²⁷

תּוֹחֶלֶת צַדִּיקִים שִׂמְחָה וְתִקְוַת רְשָׁעִים תֹּאבֵד: ²⁸

מָעוֹז לַתֹּם דֶּרֶךְ יְהוָה וּמְחִתָּה לְפֹעֲלֵי אָוֶן: ²⁹

צַדִּיק לְעוֹלָם בַּל־יִמּוֹט וּרְשָׁעִים לֹא יִשְׁכְּנוּ־אָרֶץ: ³⁰

פִּי־צַדִּיק יָנוּב חָכְמָה וּלְשׁוֹן תַּהְפֻּכוֹת תִּכָּרֵת: ³¹

שִׂפְתֵי צַדִּיק יֵדְעוּן רָצוֹן וּפִי רְשָׁעִים תַּהְפֻּכוֹת: ³²

[28] The hope of the righteous is gladness, But the expectation of the wicked perishes. [29] The way of the LORD is a stronghold to the upright, But ruin to the workers of iniquity. [30] The righteous will never be shaken, But the wicked will not dwell in the land. [31] The mouth of the righteous flows with wisdom, But the perverted tongue will be cut out. [32] The lips of the righteous bring forth what is acceptable, But the mouth of the wicked what is perverted.	

Process of Discovery

Linguistics Section

Linguistic Structure

[1] The proverbs of Solomon. A wise son makes a father glad, But a foolish son is a grief to his mother.

[2] Ill-gotten gains do not profit, But righteousness delivers from death. [3] The LORD will not allow the righteous to hunger, But He will reject the craving of the wicked. [4] Poor is he who works with a negligent hand, But the hand of the diligent makes rich. [5] He who gathers in summer is a son who acts wisely, *But* he who sleeps in harvest is a son who acts shamefully. [6] Blessings are on the head of the righteous, But the mouth of the wicked conceals violence.

[7] The memory of the righteous is blessed, But the name of the wicked will rot. [8] The wise of heart will receive commands, But a babbling fool will be ruined. [9] He who walks in integrity walks securely, But he who perverts his ways will be found out. [10] He who winks the eye causes trouble, And a babbling fool will be ruined. [11] The mouth of the righteous is a fountain of life, But the mouth of the wicked conceals violence. [12] Hatred stirs up strife, But love covers all transgressions. [13] On the lips of the discerning, wisdom is found, But a rod is for the back of him who lacks understanding.

[14] Wise men store up knowledge, But with the mouth of the foolish, ruin is at hand. [15] The rich man's wealth is his fortress, The ruin of the poor is their poverty. [16] The wages of the righteous is life, The income of the wicked, punishment. [17] He is *on* the path of life who heeds instruction, But he who ignores reproof goes astray.

[18] He who conceals hatred *has* lying lips, And he who spreads slander is a fool. [19] When there are many words, transgression is unavoidable, But he who restrains his lips is wise.

[20] The tongue of the righteous is *as* choice silver, The heart of the wicked is *worth* little. [21] The lips of the righteous feed many, But fools die for lack of understanding. [22] It is the blessing of the LORD that makes rich, And He adds no sorrow to it. [23] Doing wickedness is like sport to a fool, And *so is* wisdom to a man of understanding. [24] What the wicked fears will come upon him, But the desire of the righteous will be granted. [25] When the whirlwind passes, the wicked is no more, But the righteous *has* an everlasting foundation.

[26] Like vinegar to the teeth and smoke to the eyes, So is the lazy one to those who send him. [27] The fear of the LORD prolongs life, But the years of the wicked will be shortened. [28] The hope of the righteous is gladness, But the expectation of the wicked

perishes. [29] The way of the LORD is a stronghold to the upright, But ruin to the workers of iniquity. [30] The righteous will never be shaken, But the wicked will not dwell in the land. [31] The mouth of the righteous flows with wisdom, But the perverted tongue will be cut out [32] The lips of the righteous bring forth what is acceptable, But the mouth of the wicked what is perverted.

Discussion

This chapter is a grouping of saying from King Solomon.

Questioning the Passage

1. What does verse three mean?

Droughts were common in biblical times. The reference means that the LORD will always provide for righteous people who follow the LORD in good and bad times.

2. What does verse eleven mean?

The righteous one's mouth is a fountain of life, which means that the righteous one teaching the Torah offers the mitzvot to his/her students. The performance of the mitzvot is a source of life for all. Wicked people conceal their evil by using the words of the Torah to appear to be righteous. One must be on guard against such people.[57]

3. What does the reference to a rod in verse thirteen mean?

A rod is necessary to hit a person who will not listen to the words of the LORD. Pharaoh in Egypt did not listen to the LORD and was hit with a rod of ten plagues.

---

[57] Eliezer Ginsburg and Nosson Scherman, *Mishlei: Proverbs = Mishlei: a New Translation with a Commentary Anthologized from Talmudic, Midrashic and Rabbinic Sources* (Brooklyn, NY: Mesorah, 2003).

4. What does verse fifteen mean?

    A person's wealth can protect them in the same way a citadel and a wall protects a city. In this verse, "wealth" is a metaphor for "wisdom." People must understand that it is not their wealth that defined them, but rather ways of righteousness define them.[58]

5. What does silver mean in verse twenty?

    The rebuke from a righteous person is like silver because pure silver does not have impurities. A righteous person's rebuke is done positively.

Thoughts

This chapter is a continuation of wisdom that King Solomon wanted to impart to us. The concept of good and evil is clearly laid out in this chapter. The LORD loves righteous people and hates the wicked. It behooves all people to repent and become righteous people. The Torah offers the instruction that one needs to become righteous.

---

[58] IBID.

Chapter Eleven

Language

New American Standard 1995	Hebrew
[1] A false balance is an abomination to the LORD, But a just weight is His delight. [2] When pride comes, then comes dishonor, But with the humble is wisdom. [3] The integrity of the upright will guide them, But the crookedness of the treacherous will destroy them. [4] Riches do not profit in the day of wrath, But righteousness delivers from death. [5] The righteousness of the blameless will smooth his way, But the wicked will fall by his own wickedness. [6] The righteousness of the upright will deliver them, But the treacherous will be caught by *their own* greed. [7] When a wicked man dies, *his* expectation will perish, And the hope of strong men perishes. [8] The righteous is delivered from trouble, But the wicked takes his place. [9] With *his* mouth the godless man destroys his neighbor, But through knowledge the righteous will be delivered. [10] When it goes well with the righteous, the city rejoices, And when the wicked perish, there is joyful shouting. [11] By the blessing of the upright a city is exalted, But by the mouth of the wicked it is torn down. [12] He who despises his neighbor lacks sense, But a man of understanding keeps silent.	מֹאזְנֵי מִרְמָה תּוֹעֲבַת יְהוָה וְאֶבֶן שְׁלֵמָה רְצוֹנוֹ: [2] בָּא־זָדוֹן וַיָּבֹא קָלוֹן וְאֶת־צְנוּעִים חָכְמָה: [3] תֻּמַּת יְשָׁרִים תַּנְחֵם וְסֶלֶף בּוֹגְדִים (וְשַׁדָּם) [יְשָׁדֵּם]: [4] לֹא־יוֹעִיל הוֹן בְּיוֹם עֶבְרָה וּצְדָקָה תַּצִּיל מִמָּוֶת: [5] צִדְקַת תָּמִים תְּיַשֵּׁר דַּרְכּוֹ וּבְרִשְׁעָתוֹ יִפֹּל רָשָׁע: [6] צִדְקַת יְשָׁרִים תַּצִּילֵם וּבְהַוַּת בֹּגְדִים יִלָּכֵדוּ: [7] בְּמוֹת אָדָם רָשָׁע תֹּאבַד תִּקְוָה וְתוֹחֶלֶת אוֹנִים אָבָדָה: [8] צַדִּיק מִצָּרָה נֶחֱלָץ וַיָּבֹא רָשָׁע תַּחְתָּיו: [9] בְּפֶה חָנֵף יַשְׁחִת רֵעֵהוּ וּבְדַעַת צַדִּיקִים יֵחָלֵצוּ: [10] בְּטוּב צַדִּיקִים תַּעֲלֹץ קִרְיָה וּבַאֲבֹד רְשָׁעִים רִנָּה: [11] בְּבִרְכַּת יְשָׁרִים תָּרוּם קָרֶת וּבְפִי רְשָׁעִים תֵּהָרֵס: [12] בָּז־לְרֵעֵהוּ חֲסַר־לֵב וְאִישׁ תְּבוּנוֹת יַחֲרִישׁ: [13] הוֹלֵךְ רָכִיל מְגַלֶּה־סּוֹד וְנֶאֱמַן־רוּחַ מְכַסֶּה דָבָר: [14] בְּאֵין תַּחְבֻּלוֹת יִפָּל־עָם וּתְשׁוּעָה בְּרֹב יוֹעֵץ: [15] רַע־יֵרוֹעַ כִּי־עָרַב זָר וְשֹׂנֵא תֹקְעִים בּוֹטֵחַ:

13 He who goes about as a talebearer reveals secrets, But he who is trustworthy conceals a matter.

14 Where there is no guidance the people fall, But in abundance of counselors there is victory.

15 He who is guarantor for a stranger will surely suffer for it, But he who hates being a guarantor is secure.

16 A gracious woman attains honor, And ruthless men attain riches.

17 The merciful man does himself good, But the cruel man does himself harm.

18 The wicked earns deceptive wages, But he who sows righteousness *gets* a true reward.

19 He who is steadfast in righteousness *will attain* to life, And he who pursues evil *will bring about* his own death.

20 The perverse in heart are an abomination to the LORD, But the blameless in *their* walk are His delight.

21 Assuredly, the evil man will not go unpunished, But the descendants of the righteous will be delivered.

22 *As* a ring of gold in a swine's snout *So is* a beautiful woman who lacks discretion.

23 The desire of the righteous is only good, *But* the expectation of the wicked is wrath.

24 There is one who scatters, and *yet* increases all the more, And there is one who withholds what is justly due, *and yet it results* only in want.

25 The generous man will be prosperous, And he who waters will himself be watered.

26 He who withholds grain, the people will curse him, But blessing will be on the head of him who sells *it*.

אֵשֶׁת־חֵן תִּתְמֹךְ כָּבוֹד וְעָרִיצִים 16 יִתְמְכוּ־עֹשֶׁר:

גֹּמֵל נַפְשׁוֹ אִישׁ חָסֶד וְעֹכֵר שְׁאֵרוֹ 17 אַכְזָרִי:

רָשָׁע עֹשֶׂה פְעֻלַּת־שָׁקֶר וְזֹרֵעַ צְדָקָה 18 שֶׂכֶר אֱמֶת:

כֵּן־צְדָקָה לְחַיִּים וּמְרַדֵּף רָעָה 19 לְמוֹתוֹ:

תּוֹעֲבַת יְהוָה עִקְּשֵׁי־לֵב וּרְצוֹנוֹ 20 תְמִימֵי דָרֶךְ:

יָד לְיָד לֹא־יִנָּקֶה רָּע וְזֶרַע צַדִּיקִים 21 נִמְלָט:

נֶזֶם זָהָב בְּאַף חֲזִיר אִשָּׁה יָפָה 22 וְסָרַת טָעַם:

תַּאֲוַת צַדִּיקִים אַךְ־טוֹב תִּקְוַת 23 רְשָׁעִים עֶבְרָה:

יֵשׁ מְפַזֵּר וְנוֹסָף עוֹד וְחוֹשֵׂךְ מִיֹּשֶׁר 24 אַךְ־לְמַחְסוֹר:

נֶפֶשׁ־בְּרָכָה תְדֻשָּׁן וּמַרְוֶה גַּם־הוּא 25 יוֹרֶא:

מֹנֵעַ בָּר יִקְּבֻהוּ לְאוֹם וּבְרָכָה לְרֹאשׁ 26 מַשְׁבִּיר:

שֹׁחֵר טוֹב יְבַקֵּשׁ רָצוֹן וְדֹרֵשׁ רָעָה 27 תְבוֹאֶנּוּ:

בּוֹטֵחַ בְּעָשְׁרוֹ הוּא יִפֹּל וְכֶעָלֶה 28 צַדִּיקִים יִפְרָחוּ:

עוֹכֵר בֵּיתוֹ יִנְחַל־רוּחַ וְעֶבֶד אֱוִיל 29 לַחֲכַם־לֵב:

פְּרִי־צַדִּיק עֵץ חַיִּים וְלֹקֵחַ נְפָשׁוֹת 30 חָכָם:

הֵן צַדִּיק בָּאָרֶץ יְשֻׁלָּם אַף כִּי־רָשָׁע 31 וְחוֹטֵא:

²⁷ He who diligently seeks good seeks favor, But he who seeks evil, evil will come to him.

²⁸ He who trusts in his riches will fall, But the righteous will flourish like the *green* leaf.

²⁹ He who troubles his own house will inherit wind, And the foolish will be servant to the wisehearted.

³⁰ The fruit of the righteous is a tree of life, And he who is wise wins souls.

³¹ If the righteous will be rewarded in the earth, How much more the wicked and the sinner!

Process of Discovery

Linguistics Section

Linguistic Structure

[1] A false balance is an abomination to the LORD, But a just weight is His delight. [2] When pride comes, then comes dishonor, But with the humble is wisdom. [3] The integrity of the upright will guide them, But the crookedness of the treacherous will destroy them. [4] Riches do not profit in the day of wrath, But righteousness delivers from death.

A [5] The righteousness of the blameless will smooth his way, But the wicked will fall by his own wickedness.

> **B** [6] The righteousness of the upright will deliver them, But the treacherous will be caught by *their own* greed.

> **B'** [7] When a wicked man dies, *his* expectation will perish, And the hope of strong men perishes.

A' [8] The righteous is delivered from trouble, But the wicked takes his place.

[9] With *his* mouth the godless man destroys his neighbor, But through knowledge the righteous will be delivered. [10] When it goes well with the righteous, the city rejoices, And when the wicked perish, there is joyful shouting.

[11] By the blessing of the upright a city is exalted, But by the mouth of the wicked it is torn down.

[12] He who despises his neighbor lacks sense, But a man of understanding keeps silent. [13] He who goes about as a talebearer reveals secrets, But he who is trustworthy conceals a matter.

[14] Where there is no guidance the people fall, But in abundance of counselors there is victory. [15] He who is guarantor for a stranger will surely suffer for it, But he who hates being a guarantor is secure.

[16] A gracious woman attains honor, And ruthless men attain riches. [17] The merciful man does himself good, But the cruel man does himself harm. [18] The wicked earns deceptive wages, But he who sows righteousness *gets* a true reward.

[19] He who is steadfast in righteousness *will attain* to life, And he who pursues evil *will bring about* his own death.

[20] The perverse in heart are an abomination to the LORD, But the blameless in *their* walk are His delight. [21] Assuredly, the evil man will not go unpunished, But the descendants of the righteous will be delivered.

[22] *As* a ring of gold in a swine's snout *So is* a beautiful woman who lacks discretion. [23] The desire of the righteous is only good, *But* the expectation of the wicked is wrath. [24] There is one who scatters, and *yet* increases all the more, And there is one who withholds what is justly due, *and yet it results* only in want.

[25] The generous man will be prosperous, And he who waters will himself be watered. [26] He who withholds grain, the people will curse him, But blessing will be on the head of him who sells *it*. [27] He who diligently seeks good seeks favor, But he who seeks evil, evil will come to him.

[28] He who trusts in his riches will fall, But the righteous will flourish like the *green* leaf. [29] He who troubles his own house will inherit wind, And the foolish will be servant to the wisehearted. [30] The fruit of the righteous is a tree of life, And he who is wise wins souls. [31] If the righteous will be rewarded in the earth, How much more the wicked and the sinner!

Discussion

There is a small chiasm in verses five to eight. The rest of the chapter talks about righteousness and wickedness.

Questioning the Passage

1. What does a false balance mean? (v. 1)

   The "balance" is a scale. The LORD abhors merchants who use scales that incorrectly measure products in order to cheat their customers. Therefore, when the scale is perfectly balanced, the LORD is pleased. In other words, the LORD gets angered by cheaters.

Translation Inconsistencies

1. **Proverbs 11:7** [WTT] בְּמוֹת אָדָם רָשָׁע תֹּאבַד תִּקְוָה וְתוֹחֶלֶת אוֹנִים אָבָדָה:

[NAU] **Proverbs 11:7** When a wicked man dies, *his* expectation will perish, And the hope of strong men perishes.

[NIV] **Proverbs 11:7** Hopes placed in mortals die with them; all the promise of their power comes to nothing.

[NRS] **Proverbs 11:7** When the wicked die, their hope perishes, and the expectation of the godless comes to nothing.

[KJV] **Proverbs 11:7** When a wicked man dieth, *his* expectation shall perish: and the hope of unjust *men* perisheth.

[NAS] **Proverbs 11:7** When a wicked man dies, *his* expectation will perish, And the hope of strong men perishes.

[TNIV] **Proverbs 11:7** Hopes placed in mortals die with them; all the promise of their power comes to nothing.

[TNK] **Proverbs 11:7** At death the hopes of a wicked man are doomed, And the ambition of evil men comes to nothing.

There are several different translations for verse seven. The NAU appears to be the closest to the original Hebrew. The Targum says that "when a wicked man dies his hopes perish and the hope of those who do wrong perish."[59]

Culture Section

Questioning the passage

1. What is the day of wrath? (v. 4)

   The day of wrath is the "Day of the LORD." On this day, humans will be rewarded according to their deeds. It is the day of reckoning.[60]

2. Who are the counselors? (v. 14)

   The counselors are exemplary leaders of Israel. The nation of Israel is portrayed as a flock of sheep without a shepherd. When the nation does not have an excellent leader, she will not defend herself against invaders. Exile, poverty, and death cannot be stopped when the attacks come from outside the nation.

3. What is the meaning of verse seventeen?

   A pious person does good deeds because it is a part of his character. An evil person destroys his/her own body by depraved behavior.[61]

---

[59] Mangan Céline. *The Targum of Job.: the Targum of Proverbs U.a.* Liturgical Press, 1987.

[60] Rocco A. Errico and George M. Lamsa, *Aramaic Light on Ezra through the Song of Solomon* (Smyma, GA: Noohra Foundation, 2010).

[61] IBID.

Thoughts

The wisdom of Solomon continues in this chapter. The righteous will be attended to by the LORD because of their righteous acts. The LORD will condemn wicked people because of their evil acts. It is a bad thing to rid oneself of the ways of the LORD.

Chapter Twelve

Language

New American Standard 1995	Hebrew
[1] Whoever loves discipline loves knowledge, But he who hates reproof is stupid.	אֹהֵב מוּסָר אֹהֵב דָּעַת וְשֹׂנֵא תוֹכַחַת בָּעַר: [2]טוֹב יָפִיק רָצוֹן מֵיְהוָה וְאִישׁ מְזִמּוֹת יַרְשִׁיעַ:
[2] A good man will obtain favor from the LORD, But He will condemn a man who devises evil.	[3]לֹא־יִכּוֹן אָדָם בְּרֶשַׁע וְשֹׁרֶשׁ צַדִּיקִים בַּל־יִמּוֹט:
[3] A man will not be established by wickedness, But the root of the righteous will not be moved.	[4]אֵשֶׁת־חַיִל עֲטֶרֶת בַּעְלָהּ וּכְרָקָב בְּעַצְמוֹתָיו מְבִישָׁה:
[4] An excellent wife is the crown of her husband, But she who shames *him* is like rottenness in his bones.	[5]מַחְשְׁבוֹת צַדִּיקִים מִשְׁפָּט תַּחְבֻּלוֹת רְשָׁעִים מִרְמָה:
[5] The thoughts of the righteous are just, *But* the counsels of the wicked are deceitful.	[6]דִּבְרֵי רְשָׁעִים אֱרָב־דָּם וּפִי יְשָׁרִים יַצִּילֵם:
[6] The words of the wicked lie in wait for blood, But the mouth of the upright will deliver them.	[7]הָפוֹךְ רְשָׁעִים וְאֵינָם וּבֵית צַדִּיקִים יַעֲמֹד:
[7] The wicked are overthrown and are no more, But the house of the righteous will stand.	[8]לְפִי־שִׂכְלוֹ יְהֻלַּל־אִישׁ וְנַעֲוֵה־לֵב יִהְיֶה לָבוּז:
[8] A man will be praised according to his insight, But one of perverse mind will be despised.	[9]טוֹב נִקְלֶה וְעֶבֶד לוֹ מִמְּתַכַּבֵּד וַחֲסַר־לָחֶם:
[9] Better is he who is lightly esteemed and has a servant Than he who honors himself and lacks bread.	[10]יוֹדֵעַ צַדִּיק נֶפֶשׁ בְּהֶמְתּוֹ וְרַחֲמֵי רְשָׁעִים אַכְזָרִי:
[10] A righteous man has regard for the life of his animal, But *even* the compassion of the wicked is cruel.	[11]עֹבֵד אַדְמָתוֹ יִשְׂבַּע־לָחֶם וּמְרַדֵּף רֵיקִים חֲסַר־לֵב:
[11] He who tills his land will have plenty of bread, But he who pursues worthless *things* lacks sense.	[12]חָמַד רָשָׁע מְצוֹד רָעִים וְשֹׁרֶשׁ צַדִּיקִים יִתֵּן: [13]בְּפֶשַׁע שְׂפָתַיִם מוֹקֵשׁ רָע וַיֵּצֵא מִצָּרָה צַדִּיק: [14]מִפְּרִי פִי־אִישׁ יִשְׂבַּע־טוֹב וּגְמוּל יְדֵי־אָדָם (יָשׁוּב) [יָשִׁיב] לוֹ:

¹² The wicked man desires the booty of evil men, But the root of the righteous yields *fruit*.

¹³ An evil man is ensnared by the transgression of his lips, But the righteous will escape from trouble.

¹⁴ A man will be satisfied with good by the fruit of his words, And the deeds of a man's hands will return to him.

¹⁵ The way of a fool is right in his own eyes, But a wise man is he who listens to counsel.

¹⁶ A fool's anger is known at once, But a prudent man conceals dishonor.

¹⁷ He who speaks truth tells what is right, But a false witness, deceit.

¹⁸ There is one who speaks rashly like the thrusts of a sword, But the tongue of the wise brings healing.

¹⁹ Truthful lips will be established forever, But a lying tongue is only for a moment.

²⁰ Deceit is in the heart of those who devise evil, But counselors of peace have joy.

²¹ No harm befalls the righteous, But the wicked are filled with trouble.

²² Lying lips are an abomination to the LORD, But those who deal faithfully are His delight.

²³ A prudent man conceals knowledge, But the heart of fools proclaims folly.

²⁴ The hand of the diligent will rule, But the slack *hand* will be put to forced labor.

²⁵ Anxiety in a man's heart weighs it down, But a good word makes it glad.

²⁶ The righteous is a guide to his neighbor, But the way of the wicked leads them astray.

דֶּרֶךְ אֱוִיל יָשָׁר בְּעֵינָיו וְשֹׁמֵעַ לְעֵצָה חָכָם: ¹⁵

אֱוִיל בַּיּוֹם יִוָּדַע כַּעְסוֹ וְכֹסֶה קָלוֹן עָרוּם: ¹⁶

יָפִיחַ אֱמוּנָה יַגִּיד צֶדֶק וְעֵד שְׁקָרִים מִרְמָה: ¹⁷

יֵשׁ בּוֹטֶה כְּמַדְקְרוֹת חָרֶב וּלְשׁוֹן חֲכָמִים מַרְפֵּא: ¹⁸

שְׂפַת־אֱמֶת תִּכּוֹן לָעַד וְעַד־אַרְגִּיעָה לְשׁוֹן שָׁקֶר: ¹⁹

מִרְמָה בְּלֶב־חֹרְשֵׁי רָע וּלְיֹעֲצֵי שָׁלוֹם שִׂמְחָה: ²⁰

לֹא־יְאֻנֶּה לַצַּדִּיק כָּל־אָוֶן וּרְשָׁעִים מָלְאוּ רָע: ²¹

תּוֹעֲבַת יְהוָה שִׂפְתֵי־שָׁקֶר וְעֹשֵׂי אֱמוּנָה רְצוֹנוֹ: ²²

אָדָם עָרוּם כֹּסֶה דָּעַת וְלֵב כְּסִילִים יִקְרָא אִוֶּלֶת: ²³

יַד־חָרוּצִים תִּמְשׁוֹל וּרְמִיָּה תִּהְיֶה לָמַס: ²⁴

דְּאָגָה בְלֶב־אִישׁ יַשְׁחֶנָּה וְדָבָר טוֹב יְשַׂמְּחֶנָּה: ²⁵

יָתֵר מֵרֵעֵהוּ צַדִּיק וְדֶרֶךְ רְשָׁעִים תַּתְעֵם: ²⁶

לֹא־יַחֲרֹךְ רְמִיָּה צֵידוֹ וְהוֹן־אָדָם יָקָר חָרוּץ: ²⁷

בְּאֹרַח־צְדָקָה חַיִּים וְדֶרֶךְ נְתִיבָה אַל־מָוֶת: ²⁸

| ²⁷ A lazy man does not roast his prey, But the precious possession of a man *is* diligence.
²⁸ In the way of righteousness is life, And in *its* pathway there is no death. | |

Process of Discovery

Linguistics Section

Linguistic Structure

¹ Whoever loves discipline loves knowledge, But he who hates reproof is stupid. ² A good man will obtain favor from the LORD, But He will condemn a man who devises evil. ³ A man will not be established by wickedness, But the root of the righteous will not be moved. ⁴ An excellent wife is the crown of her husband, But she who shames *him* is like rottenness in his bones. ⁵ The thoughts of the righteous are just, *But* the counsels of the wicked are deceitful. ⁶ The words of the wicked lie in wait for blood, But the mouth of the upright will deliver them. ⁷ The wicked are overthrown and are no more, But the house of the righteous will stand. ⁸ A man will be praised according to his insight, But one of perverse mind will be despised. ⁹ Better is he who is lightly esteemed and has a servant Than he who honors himself and lacks bread. ¹⁰ A righteous man has regard for the life of his animal, But *even* the compassion of the wicked is cruel. ¹¹ He who tills his land will have plenty of bread, But he who pursues worthless *things* lacks sense. ¹² The wicked man desires the booty of evil men, But the root of the righteous yields *fruit.* ¹³ An evil man is ensnared by the transgression of his lips, But the righteous will escape from trouble. ¹⁴ A man will be satisfied with good by the fruit of his words, And the deeds of a man's hands will return to him. ¹⁵ The way of a fool is right in his own eyes, But a wise man is he who listens to counsel. ¹⁶ A fool's anger is known at once, But a prudent man conceals dishonor. ¹⁷ He who speaks truth tells what is right, But a false witness, deceit. ¹⁸ There is one who speaks rashly like the thrusts of a sword, But the tongue of the wise brings healing. ¹⁹ Truthful lips will be established forever, But a lying tongue is only for a moment. ²⁰ Deceit is in the heart of those who devise evil, But counselors of peace have joy. ²¹ No harm befalls the righteous, But the wicked are filled with trouble. ²² Lying lips are an abomination to the LORD, But those who deal faithfully are His delight. ²³ A prudent man conceals knowledge, But the heart of fools proclaims folly. ²⁴ The hand of the diligent will rule, But the slack *hand* will be put to forced labor. ²⁵ Anxiety in a man's heart weighs it down, But a good word makes it glad. ²⁶ The righteous is a guide to his neighbor, But the way of the wicked leads them astray. ²⁷ A lazy man does not roast his prey, But the precious possession of a man *is* diligence. ²⁸ In the way of righteousness is life, And in *its* pathway there is no death.

Discussion

This chapter is a string of twenty-eight sayings of King Solomon.

Questioning the Passage

1. What does it mean that a woman is the crown of her husband? (v. 4)

   Like a crown, a wife becomes the source of dignity and pride in the eyes of others.[62] (See phrase study אֵשֶׁת־חַיִל)

2. What does it mean to beware of a shameful woman? (v. 4)

   A shameful wife is one who is evil and wicked. A wife is considered a part of her husband's bones (from the Genesis story of how the LORD created Eve); therefore, it is as if part of the husband's has rottened when she acts shamefully. The verse says that a man must investigate whom he should choose for his wife. [63]

   An interesting note on verse four is that in Solomon's day, marriage is arranged in some Jewish sects. How does the husband control the woman he married when it was his father who makes that determination?

3. Why did the Sages connect Noah to verse thirteen?

   The generation of the Flood spoke against the LORD. They claimed that there was no benefit to serve Him. The Flood was a snare that removed their evil and wickedness from the Earth. Noah was spared from this distress because he believed in the LORD.[64]

---

[62] Eliezer Ginsburg and Nosson Scherman, *Mishlei: Proverbs = Mishlei: a New Translation with a Commentary Anthologized from Talmudic, Midrashic and Rabbinic Sources* (Brooklyn, NY: Mesorah, 2003).
[63] IBID.
[64] IBID.

4. What is verse eighteen referring to?

A person can invoke violence against another person by the words he/she uses. That violence could result in death.

Phrase Study

1. אֵשֶׁת־חַיִל - this phrase is translated as a "woman of strength." It is used to describe a woman who is:

   a. Diligent in her actions

   b. A woman who can acquire wealth for her husband. She is honored like a queen by her king.

   c. A woman who protects her husband so that nothing happens to him.

   d. A virtuous woman.

Thoughts

Like the previous chapter, this chapter is a collection of statements of wisdom. For the most part, they are not connected. If one lived by the wisdom of this chapter and other chapters, the LORD would always be pleased with him/her.

Chapter Thirteen

Language

New American Standard 1995	Hebrew
[1] A wise son *accepts his* father's discipline, But a scoffer does not listen to rebuke. [2] From the fruit of a man's mouth he enjoys good, But the desire of the treacherous is violence. [3] The one who guards his mouth preserves his life; The one who opens wide his lips comes to ruin. [4] The soul of the sluggard craves and *gets* nothing, But the soul of the diligent is made fat. [5] A righteous man hates falsehood, But a wicked man acts disgustingly and shamefully. [6] Righteousness guards the one whose way is blameless, But wickedness subverts the sinner. [7] There is one who pretends to be rich, but has nothing; *Another* pretends to be poor, but has great wealth. [8] The ransom of a man's life is his wealth, But the poor hears no rebuke. [9] The light of the righteous rejoices, But the lamp of the wicked goes out. [10] Through insolence comes nothing but strife, But wisdom is with those who receive counsel. [11] Wealth *obtained* by fraud dwindles, But the one who gathers by labor increases *it*. [12] Hope deferred makes the heart sick, But desire fulfilled is a tree of life. [13] The one who despises the word will be in debt to it, But the one who fears the commandment will be rewarded.	בֵּן חָכָם מוּסַר אָב וְלֵץ לֹא־שָׁמַע גְּעָרָה: [2] מִפְּרִי פִי־אִישׁ יֹאכַל טוֹב וְנֶפֶשׁ בֹּגְדִים חָמָס: [3] נֹצֵר פִּיו שֹׁמֵר נַפְשׁוֹ פֹּשֵׂק שְׂפָתָיו מְחִתָּה־לוֹ: [4] מִתְאַוָּה וָאַיִן נַפְשׁוֹ עָצֵל וְנֶפֶשׁ חָרֻצִים תְּדֻשָּׁן: [5] דְּבַר־שֶׁקֶר יִשְׂנָא צַדִּיק וְרָשָׁע יַבְאִישׁ וְיַחְפִּיר: [6] צְדָקָה תִּצֹּר תָּם־דָּרֶךְ וְרִשְׁעָה תְּסַלֵּף חַטָּאת: [7] יֵשׁ מִתְעַשֵּׁר וְאֵין כֹּל מִתְרוֹשֵׁשׁ וְהוֹן רָב: [8] כֹּפֶר נֶפֶשׁ־אִישׁ עָשְׁרוֹ וְרָשׁ לֹא־שָׁמַע גְּעָרָה: [9] אוֹר־צַדִּיקִים יִשְׂמָח וְנֵר רְשָׁעִים יִדְעָךְ: [10] רַק־בְּזָדוֹן יִתֵּן מַצָּה וְאֶת־נוֹעָצִים חָכְמָה: [11] הוֹן מֵהֶבֶל יִמְעָט וְקֹבֵץ עַל־יָד יַרְבֶּה: [12] תּוֹחֶלֶת מְמֻשָּׁכָה מַחֲלָה־לֵב וְעֵץ חַיִּים תַּאֲוָה בָאָה: [13] בָּז לְדָבָר יֵחָבֶל לוֹ וִירֵא מִצְוָה הוּא יְשֻׁלָּם: [14] תּוֹרַת חָכָם מְקוֹר חַיִּים לָסוּר מִמֹּקְשֵׁי מָוֶת: [15] שֵׂכֶל־טוֹב יִתֶּן־חֵן וְדֶרֶךְ בֹּגְדִים אֵיתָן: [16] כָּל־עָרוּם יַעֲשֶׂה בְדָעַת וּכְסִיל יִפְרֹשׂ אִוֶּלֶת:

111

14 The teaching of the wise is a fountain of life, To turn aside from the snares of death.

15 Good understanding produces favor, But the way of the treacherous is hard.

16 Every prudent man acts with knowledge, But a fool displays folly.

17 A wicked messenger falls into adversity, But a faithful envoy *brings* healing.

18 Poverty and shame *will come* to him who neglects discipline, But he who regards reproof will be honored.

19 Desire realized is sweet to the soul, But it is an abomination to fools to turn away from evil.

20 He who walks with wise men will be wise, But the companion of fools will suffer harm.

21 Adversity pursues sinners, But the righteous will be rewarded with prosperity.

22 A good man leaves an inheritance to his children's children, And the wealth of the sinner is stored up for the righteous.

23 Abundant food *is in* the fallow ground of the poor, But it is swept away by injustice.

24 He who withholds his rod hates his son, But he who loves him disciplines him diligently.

25 The righteous has enough to satisfy his appetite, But the stomach of the wicked is in need.

מַלְאָךְ רָשָׁע יִפֹּל בְּרָע וְצִיר אֱמוּנִים מַרְפֵּא: 17

רֵישׁ וְקָלוֹן פּוֹרֵעַ מוּסָר וְשׁוֹמֵר תּוֹכַחַת יְכֻבָּד: 18

תַּאֲוָה נִהְיָה תֶּעֱרַב לְנָפֶשׁ וְתוֹעֲבַת כְּסִילִים סוּר מֵרָע: 19

(הָלוֹךְ) [הוֹלֵךְ] אֶת־חֲכָמִים (וַחֲכָם) [יֶחְכָּם] וְרֹעֶה כְסִילִים יֵרוֹעַ: 20

חַטָּאִים תְּרַדֵּף רָעָה וְאֶת־צַדִּיקִים יְשַׁלֶּם־טוֹב: 21

טוֹב יַנְחִיל בְּנֵי־בָנִים וְצָפוּן לַצַּדִּיק חֵיל חוֹטֵא: 22

רָב־אֹכֶל נִיר רָאשִׁים וְיֵשׁ נִסְפֶּה בְּלֹא מִשְׁפָּט: 23

חוֹשֵׂךְ שִׁבְטוֹ שׂוֹנֵא בְנוֹ וְאֹהֲבוֹ שִׁחֲרוֹ מוּסָר: 24

צַדִּיק אֹכֵל לְשֹׂבַע נַפְשׁוֹ וּבֶטֶן רְשָׁעִים תֶּחְסָר: פ 25

Process of Discovery

Linguistics Section

Linguistic Structure

[1] A wise son *accepts his* father's discipline, But a scoffer does not listen to rebuke. [2] From the fruit of a man's mouth he enjoys good, But the desire of the treacherous is violence [3] The one who guards his mouth preserves his life; The one who opens wide his lips comes to ruin.

[4] The soul of the sluggard craves and *gets* nothing, But the soul of the diligent is made fat.

[5] A righteous man hates falsehood, But a wicked man acts disgustingly and shamefully. [6] Righteousness guards the one whose way is blameless, But wickedness subverts the sinner.

[7] There is one who pretends to be rich, but has nothing; *Another* pretends to be poor, but has great wealth. [8] The ransom of a man's life is his wealth, But the poor hears no rebuke.

[9] The light of the righteous rejoices, But the lamp of the wicked goes out. [10] Through insolence comes nothing but strife, But wisdom is with those who receive counsel. [11] Wealth *obtained* by fraud dwindles, But the one who gathers by labor increases *it*.

[12] Hope deferred makes the heart sick, But desire fulfilled is a tree of life. [13] The one who despises the word will be in debt to it, But the one who fears the commandment will be rewarded. [14] The teaching of the wise is a fountain of life, To turn aside from the snares of death. [15] Good understanding produces favor, But the way of the treacherous is hard. [16] Every prudent man acts with knowledge, But a fool displays folly. [17] A wicked messenger falls into adversity, But a faithful envoy *brings* healing. [18] Poverty and shame *will come* to him who neglects discipline, But he who regards reproof will be honored. [19] Desire realized is sweet to the soul, But it is an abomination to fools to turn away from evil. [20] He who walks with wise men will be wise, But the companion of fools will suffer harm. [21] Adversity pursues sinners, But the righteous will be rewarded with prosperity. [22] A good man leaves an inheritance to his children's children, And the wealth of the sinner is stored up for the righteous.

[23] Abundant food *is in* the fallow ground of the poor, But it is swept away by injustice. [24] He who withholds his rod hates his son, But he who loves him disciplines him diligently. [25] The righteous has enough to satisfy his appetite, But the stomach of the wicked is in need.

Discussion

This chapter is a listing of wisdom from King Solomon.

Questioning the Passage

1. What does it mean to guard one's mouth? (v. 3)

   A person must be on guard not to say anything that is forbidden or against the LORD.

2. What does it mean that the soul of the diligent is made fat? (v. 4)

   In a spiritual sense, a person who wearies his/her body through diligent pursuit of wisdom will have his/her soul gratified by blessings from Heaven.[65]

3. What does verse seven mean?

   The Chafetz Chaim[x] offers the following explanation. A person may be rich but have nothing in the World to Come, for his concern was about material wealth and not spiritual wealth. A person may be lacking in the material world but has stored up treasures in Heaven.

---

[65] Eliezer Ginsburg and Nosson Scherman, *Mishlei: Proverbs = Mishlei: a New Translation with a Commentary Anthologized from Talmudic, Midrashic and Rabbinic Sources* (Brooklyn, NY: Mesorah, 2003).

4. What "word" is being referred to in verse thirteen?

The word being referred to is the Torah.

5. What does verse twenty-three mean?

The Sage Rashi said that there is much grain produced through the plowing of poor people. The harvest will suffer if the owner fails to separate the required tithes and gifts to the poor.[66]

In a spiritual sense, the verse is saying that if one studies and learns Torah but does not apply it to their life, then learnings are useless.

6. What does verse twenty-four mean?

A parent who does not rebuke and correct a child is doing a disservice to the child. The child will never learn the difference between good and evil, nor morality and good ethics. The child will turn to evil because the teachings of the LORD were omitted.

Culture Section

Questioning the passage

1. What does it mean that the lamp of the wicked goes out? (v. 9)

"Light" in this verse means "posterity." The lamp is a metaphor for an heir. The verse says that the posterity (the children) of the righteous shall rejoice in the LORD. The posterity of the wicked will become extinct. It is a Near Eastern custom to say "God has given him a lamp" and "May God preserve

---

[66] IBID.

your lamp" which means that God has given righteous offspring. An example is:[67]

> [4] But for David's sake the LORD his God gave him a lamp in Jerusalem, to raise up his son after him and to establish Jerusalem; (1 Ki. 15:4 NAU)

Thoughts

The majority of wisdom in this chapter is on righteousness and the obligation that parents have to raise their children to know the LORD. They are to be raised to study, learn and apply the Torah to their lives.

---

[67] Rocco A. Errico and George M. Lamsa, *Aramaic Light on Ezra through the Song of Solomon* (Smyma, GA: Noohra Foundation, 2010).

Chapter Fourteen

Language

New American Standard 1995	Hebrew
[1] The wise woman builds her house, But the foolish tears it down with her own hands.	חַכְמוֹת נָשִׁים בָּנְתָה בֵיתָהּ וְאִוֶּלֶת בְּיָדֶיהָ תֶהֶרְסֶנּוּ: [2] הוֹלֵךְ בְּיָשְׁרוֹ יְרֵא יְהוָה וּנְלוֹז דְּרָכָיו בּוֹזֵהוּ:
[2] He who walks in his uprightness fears the LORD, But he who is devious in his ways despises Him.	[3] בְּפִי־אֱוִיל חֹטֶר גַּאֲוָה וְשִׂפְתֵי חֲכָמִים תִּשְׁמוּרֵם:
[3] In the mouth of the foolish is a rod for *his* back, But the lips of the wise will protect them.	[4] בְּאֵין אֲלָפִים אֵבוּס בָּר וְרָב־תְּבוּאוֹת בְּכֹחַ שׁוֹר:
[4] Where no oxen are, the manger is clean, But much revenue *comes* by the strength of the ox.	[5] עֵד אֱמוּנִים לֹא יְכַזֵּב וְיָפִיחַ כְּזָבִים עֵד שָׁקֶר:
[5] A trustworthy witness will not lie, But a false witness utters lies.	[6] בִּקֶּשׁ־לֵץ חָכְמָה וָאָיִן וְדַעַת לְנָבוֹן נָקָל:
[6] A scoffer seeks wisdom and *finds* none, But knowledge is easy to one who has understanding.	[7] לֵךְ מִנֶּגֶד לְאִישׁ כְּסִיל וּבַל־יָדַעְתָּ שִׂפְתֵי־דָעַת:
[7] Leave the presence of a fool, Or you will not discern words of knowledge.	[8] חָכְמַת עָרוּם הָבִין דַּרְכּוֹ וְאִוֶּלֶת כְּסִילִים מִרְמָה:
[8] The wisdom of the sensible is to understand his way, But the foolishness of fools is deceit.	[9] אֱוִלִים יָלִיץ אָשָׁם וּבֵין יְשָׁרִים רָצוֹן:
[9] Fools mock at sin, But among the upright there is good will.	[10] לֵב יוֹדֵעַ מָרַּת נַפְשׁוֹ וּבְשִׂמְחָתוֹ לֹא־יִתְעָרַב זָר:
[10] The heart knows its own bitterness, And a stranger does not share its joy.	[11] בֵּית רְשָׁעִים יִשָּׁמֵד וְאֹהֶל יְשָׁרִים יַפְרִיחַ:
[11] The house of the wicked will be destroyed, But the tent of the upright will flourish.	[12] יֵשׁ דֶּרֶךְ יָשָׁר לִפְנֵי־אִישׁ וְאַחֲרִיתָהּ דַּרְכֵי־מָוֶת:
[12] There is a way *which seems* right to a man, But its end is the way of death.	[13] גַּם־בִּשְׂחוֹק יִכְאַב־לֵב וְאַחֲרִיתָהּ שִׂמְחָה תוּגָה:
[13] Even in laughter the heart may be in pain, And the end of joy may be grief.	[14] מִדְּרָכָיו יִשְׂבַּע סוּג לֵב וּמֵעָלָיו אִישׁ טוֹב:
	[15] פֶּתִי יַאֲמִין לְכָל־דָּבָר וְעָרוּם יָבִין לַאֲשֻׁרוֹ:
	[16] חָכָם יָרֵא וְסָר מֵרָע וּכְסִיל מִתְעַבֵּר וּבוֹטֵחַ:
	[17] קְצַר־אַפַּיִם יַעֲשֶׂה אִוֶּלֶת וְאִישׁ מְזִמּוֹת יִשָּׂנֵא:
	[18] נָחֲלוּ פְתָאיִם אִוֶּלֶת וַעֲרוּמִים יַכְתִּרוּ דָעַת:
	[19] שַׁחוּ רָעִים לִפְנֵי טוֹבִים וּרְשָׁעִים עַל־שַׁעֲרֵי צַדִּיק:
	[20] גַּם־לְרֵעֵהוּ יִשָּׂנֵא רָשׁ וְאֹהֲבֵי עָשִׁיר רַבִּים:

14 The backslider in heart will have his fill of his own ways, But a good man will *be satisfied* with his.

15 The naive believes everything, But the sensible man considers his steps.

16 A wise man is cautious and turns away from evil, But a fool is arrogant and careless.

17 A quick-tempered man acts foolishly, And a man of evil devices is hated.

18 The naive inherit foolishness, But the sensible are crowned with knowledge.

19 The evil will bow down before the good, And the wicked at the gates of the righteous.

20 The poor is hated even by his neighbor, But those who love the rich are many.

21 He who despises his neighbor sins, But happy is he who is gracious to the poor.

22 Will they not go astray who devise evil? But kindness and truth *will be to* those who devise good.

23 In all labor there is profit, But mere talk *leads* only to poverty.

24 The crown of the wise is their riches, *But* the folly of fools is foolishness.

25 A truthful witness saves lives, But he who utters lies is treacherous.

26 In the fear of the LORD there is strong confidence, And his children will have refuge.

27 The fear of the LORD is a fountain of life, That one may avoid the snares of death.

28 In a multitude of people is a king's glory, But in the dearth of people is a prince's ruin.

21 בָּז־לְרֵעֵהוּ חוֹטֵא וּמְחוֹנֵן (עֲנָיִים) [עֲנָוִים] אַשְׁרָיו:

22 הֲלוֹא־יִתְעוּ חֹרְשֵׁי רָע וְחֶסֶד וֶאֱמֶת חֹרְשֵׁי טוֹב:

23 בְּכָל־עֶצֶב יִהְיֶה מוֹתָר וּדְבַר־שְׂפָתַיִם אַךְ־לְמַחְסוֹר:

24 עֲטֶרֶת חֲכָמִים עָשְׁרָם אִוֶּלֶת כְּסִילִים אִוֶּלֶת:

25 מַצִּיל נְפָשׁוֹת עֵד אֱמֶת וְיָפַח כְּזָבִים מִרְמָה:

26 בְּיִרְאַת יְהוָה מִבְטַח־עֹז וּלְבָנָיו יִהְיֶה מַחְסֶה:

27 יִרְאַת יְהוָה מְקוֹר חַיִּים לָסוּר מִמֹּקְשֵׁי מָוֶת:

28 בְּרָב־עָם הַדְרַת־מֶלֶךְ וּבְאֶפֶס לְאֹם מְחִתַּת רָזוֹן:

29 אֶרֶךְ אַפַּיִם רַב־תְּבוּנָה וּקְצַר־רוּחַ מֵרִים אִוֶּלֶת:

30 חַיֵּי בְשָׂרִים לֵב מַרְפֵּא וּרְקַב עֲצָמוֹת קִנְאָה:

31 עֹשֵׁק־דָּל חֵרֵף עֹשֵׂהוּ וּמְכַבְּדוֹ חֹנֵן אֶבְיוֹן:

32 בְּרָעָתוֹ יִדָּחֶה רָשָׁע וְחֹסֶה בְמוֹתוֹ צַדִּיק:

33 בְּלֵב נָבוֹן תָּנוּחַ חָכְמָה וּבְקֶרֶב כְּסִילִים תִּוָּדֵעַ:

34 צְדָקָה תְרוֹמֵם־גּוֹי וְחֶסֶד לְאֻמִּים חַטָּאת:

35 רְצוֹן־מֶלֶךְ לְעֶבֶד מַשְׂכִּיל וְעֶבְרָתוֹ תִּהְיֶה מֵבִישׁ:

²⁹ He who is slow to anger has great understanding, But he who is quick-tempered exalts folly.
³⁰ A tranquil heart is life to the body, But passion is rottenness to the bones.
³¹ He who oppresses the poor taunts his Maker, But he who is gracious to the needy honors Him.
³² The wicked is thrust down by his wrongdoing, But the righteous has a refuge when he dies.
³³ Wisdom rests in the heart of one who has understanding, But in the hearts of fools it is made known.
³⁴ Righteousness exalts a nation, But sin is a disgrace to *any* people.
³⁵ The king's favor is toward a servant who acts wisely, But his anger is toward him who acts shamefully.

Process of Discovery

Linguistics Section

Linguistic Structure

[1] The wise woman builds her house, But the foolish tears it down with her own hands.

[2] He who walks in his uprightness fears the LORD, But he who is devious in his ways despises Him.

[3] In the mouth of the foolish is a rod for *his* back, But the lips of the wise will protect them.

[4] Where no oxen are, the manger is clean, But much revenue *comes* by the strength of the ox.

[5] A trustworthy witness will not lie, But a false witness utters lies.

[6] A scoffer seeks wisdom and *finds* none, But knowledge is easy to one who has understanding.

[7] Leave the presence of a fool, Or you will not discern words of knowledge.

[8] The wisdom of the sensible is to understand his way, But the foolishness of fools is deceit.

[9] Fools mock at sin, But among the upright there is good will.

[10] The heart knows its own bitterness, And a stranger does not share its joy.

[11] The house of the wicked will be destroyed, But the tent of the upright will flourish.

[12] There is a way *which seems* right to a man, But its end is the way of death.

[13] Even in laughter the heart may be in pain, And the end of joy may be grief.

[14] The backslider in heart will have his fill of his own ways, But a good man will *be satisfied* with his.

[15] The naive believes everything, But the sensible man considers his steps.

[16] A wise man is cautious and turns away from evil, But a fool is arrogant and careless.

[17] A quick-tempered man acts foolishly, And a man of evil devices is hated.

[18] The naive inherit foolishness, But the sensible are crowned with knowledge.

[19] The evil will bow down before the good, And the wicked at the gates of the righteous.

[20] The poor is hated even by his neighbor, But those who love the rich are many.

[21] He who despises his neighbor sins, But happy is he who is gracious to the poor.

[22] Will they not go astray who devise evil? But kindness and truth *will be to* those who devise good.

[23] In all labor there is profit, But mere talk *leads* only to poverty.

[24] The crown of the wise is their riches, *But* the folly of fools is foolishness.

[25] A truthful witness saves lives, But he who utters lies is treacherous.

[26] In the fear of the LORD there is strong confidence, And his children will have refuge.

[27] The fear of the LORD is a fountain of life, That one may avoid the snares of death.

[28] In a multitude of people is a king's glory, But in the dearth of people is a prince's ruin.

[29] He who is slow to anger has great understanding, But he who is quick-tempered exalts folly.

[30] A tranquil heart is life to the body, But passion is rottenness to the bones.

[31] He who oppresses the poor taunts his Maker, But he who is gracious to the needy honors Him.

[32] The wicked is thrust down by his wrongdoing, But the righteous has a refuge when he dies.

[33] Wisdom rests in the heart of one who has understanding, But in the hearts of fools it is made known.

[34] Righteousness exalts a nation, But sin is a disgrace to *any* people.

[35] The king's favor is toward a servant who acts wisely, But his anger is toward him who acts shamefully.

Discussion

These verses are wise sayings of King Solomon.

Questioning the Passage

1. What does it mean that a wise woman builds her house? (v. 1)

   The wife was responsible in ancient times to take care of the household. She needed knowledge, sight, abilities, skills, and moral and spiritual excellence to execute her task.[68]

2. What does it mean to have a rod in one's mouth? (v. 3)

   The rod is pride and arrogance.

3. What is the bitterness of the heart? (v. 10)

   This verse means that only the person knows the depth of his/her sorrow.

---

[68] Eliezer Ginsburg and Nosson Scherman, *Mishlei: Proverbs = Mishlei: a New Translation with a Commentary Anthologized from Talmudic, Midrashic and Rabbinic Sources* (Brooklyn, NY: Mesorah, 2003).

4. What is the aching of the heart? (v. 13)

    The aching of the heart refers to the pain of knowing that one has sinned and has not repented.

5. What is the dross of the heart? (v. 14)

    This phrase is a person who turns away from the LORD.[69]

Culture Section

Questioning the passage

1. What does the "house" mean in verse eleven?

    In this instance, "house" is referring to a household. Near Eastern overlords had large households consisting of many servants. They enriched themselves by their private tax collectors and armies, which exploited the poor. When the wicked (overlords) houses are overthrown, then the poor (the upright) will flourish.[70]

2. What does "their riches" mean in verse twenty-four?

    "Their riches" is referring to wisdom, intelligence, and understanding. In the Near East, not all wise men are blessed with material goods. Many times a wise man would neglect his business or his trade and generally become poor. They overlooked the material world to learn as much as they could about the spiritual world.[71]

---

[69] IBID.

[70] Rocco A. Errico and George M. Lamsa, *Aramaic Light on Ezra through the Song of Solomon* (Smyma, GA: Noohra Foundation, 2010).

[71] IBID.

3. Why are people important? (v. 28)

   This verse is referring to the increase in the population of the nation. When famines and plagues strike the land, many people perish, which weakens the kingdom. The king becomes impoverished when this happens.[72] There are fewer people to tax and fewer men for the armies of the King.

4. What is verse thirty saying?

   People who can control their answers will heal their hearts. Anger kills people.

5. What is verse thirty-two saying?

   Righteous people know that after death, they will be exalted in the next world while the wicked will be driven away from the world to come because of their wickedness.

Thoughts

This chapter consists of more sayings of King Solomon.

---

[72] IBID.

Chapter Fifteen

Language

New American Standard 1995	Hebrew
[1] A gentle answer turns away wrath, But a harsh word stirs up anger.	מַעֲנֶה־רַּךְ יָשִׁיב חֵמָה וּדְבַר־עֶצֶב יַעֲלֶה־ אָף׃ [2]
[2] The tongue of the wise makes knowledge acceptable, But the mouth of fools spouts folly.	לְשׁוֹן חֲכָמִים תֵּיטִיב דָּעַת וּפִי כְסִילִים יַבִּיעַ אִוֶּלֶת׃
[3] The eyes of the LORD are in every place, Watching the evil and the good.	[3] בְּכָל־מָקוֹם עֵינֵי יְהוָה צֹפוֹת רָעִים וְטוֹבִים׃
[4] A soothing tongue is a tree of life, But perversion in it crushes the spirit.	[4] מַרְפֵּא לָשׁוֹן עֵץ חַיִּים וְסֶלֶף בָּהּ שֶׁבֶר בְּרוּחַ׃
[5] A fool rejects his father's discipline, But he who regards reproof is prudent.	[5] אֱוִיל יִנְאַץ מוּסַר אָבִיו וְשֹׁמֵר תּוֹכַחַת יַעְרִם׃
[6] Much wealth is *in* the house of the righteous, But trouble is in the income of the wicked.	[6] בֵּית צַדִּיק חֹסֶן רָב וּבִתְבוּאַת רָשָׁע נֶעְכָּרֶת׃
[7] The lips of the wise spread knowledge, But the hearts of fools are not so.	[7] שִׂפְתֵי חֲכָמִים יְזָרוּ דָעַת וְלֵב כְּסִילִים לֹא־ כֵן׃
[8] The sacrifice of the wicked is an abomination to the LORD, But the prayer of the upright is His delight.	[8] זֶבַח רְשָׁעִים תּוֹעֲבַת יְהוָה וּתְפִלַּת יְשָׁרִים רְצוֹנוֹ׃
[9] The way of the wicked is an abomination to the LORD, But He loves him who pursues righteousness.	[9] תּוֹעֲבַת יְהוָה דֶּרֶךְ רָשָׁע וּמְרַדֵּף צְדָקָה יֶאֱהָב׃
[10] Stern discipline is for him who forsakes the way; He who hates reproof will die.	[10] מוּסָר רָע לְעֹזֵב אֹרַח שׂוֹנֵא תוֹכַחַת יָמוּת׃
[11] Sheol and Abaddon *lie open* before the LORD, How much more the hearts of men!	[11] שְׁאוֹל וַאֲבַדּוֹן נֶגֶד יְהוָה אַף כִּי־לִבּוֹת בְּנֵי־ אָדָם׃
[12] A scoffer does not love one who reproves him, He will not go to the wise.	[12] לֹא יֶאֱהַב־לֵץ הוֹכֵחַ לוֹ אֶל־חֲכָמִים לֹא יֵלֵךְ׃
[13] A joyful heart makes a cheerful face, But when the heart is sad, the spirit is broken.	[13] לֵב שָׂמֵחַ יֵיטִב פָּנִים וּבְעַצְּבַת־לֵב רוּחַ נְכֵאָה׃
	[14] לֵב נָבוֹן יְבַקֶּשׁ־דָּעַת (וּפְנֵי) [וּפִי] כְסִילִים יִרְעֶה אִוֶּלֶת׃
	[15] כָּל־יְמֵי עָנִי רָעִים וְטוֹב־לֵב מִשְׁתֶּה תָמִיד׃
	[16] טוֹב־מְעַט בְּיִרְאַת יְהוָה מֵאוֹצָר רָב וּמְהוּמָה בוֹ׃
	[17] טוֹב אֲרֻחַת יָרָק וְאַהֲבָה־שָׁם מִשּׁוֹר אָבוּס וְשִׂנְאָה־בוֹ׃
	[18] אִישׁ חֵמָה יְגָרֶה מָדוֹן וְאֶרֶךְ אַפַּיִם יַשְׁקִיט רִיב׃
	[19] דֶּרֶךְ עָצֵל כִּמְשֻׂכַת חָדֶק וְאֹרַח יְשָׁרִים סְלֻלָה׃
	[20] בֵּן חָכָם יְשַׂמַּח־אָב וּכְסִיל אָדָם בּוֹזֶה אִמּוֹ׃

¹⁴ The mind of the intelligent seeks knowledge, But the mouth of fools feeds on folly.

¹⁵ All the days of the afflicted are bad, But a cheerful heart *has* a continual feast.

¹⁶ Better is a little with the fear of the LORD, Than great treasure and turmoil with it.

¹⁷ Better is a dish of vegetables where love is, Than a fattened ox and hatred with it.

¹⁸ A hot-tempered man stirs up strife, But the slow to anger pacifies contention.

¹⁹ The way of the sluggard is as a hedge of thorns, But the path of the upright is a highway.

²⁰ A wise son makes a father glad, But a foolish man despises his mother.

²¹ Folly is joy to him who lacks sense, But a man of understanding walks straight.

²² Without consultation, plans are frustrated, But with many counselors they succeed.

²³ A man has joy in an apt answer, And how delightful is a timely word!

²⁴ The path of life *leads* upward for the wise, That he may keep away from Sheol below.

²⁵ The LORD will tear down the house of the proud, But He will establish the boundary of the widow.

²⁶ Evil plans are an abomination to the LORD, But pleasant words are pure.

²⁷ He who profits illicitly troubles his own house, But he who hates bribes will live.

²⁸ The heart of the righteous ponders how to answer, But the mouth of the wicked pours out evil things.

אִוֶּלֶת שִׂמְחָה לַחֲסַר־לֵב וְאִישׁ תְּבוּנָה יְיַשֶּׁר־לָכֶת: ²¹

הָפֵר מַחֲשָׁבוֹת בְּאֵין סוֹד וּבְרֹב יוֹעֲצִים תָּקוּם: ²²

שִׂמְחָה לָאִישׁ בְּמַעֲנֵה־פִיו וְדָבָר בְּעִתּוֹ מַה־טּוֹב: ²³

אֹרַח חַיִּים לְמַעְלָה לְמַשְׂכִּיל לְמַעַן סוּר מִשְּׁאוֹל מָטָּה: ²⁴

בֵּית גֵּאִים יִסַּח יְהוָה וְיַצֵּב גְּבוּל אַלְמָנָה: ²⁵

תּוֹעֲבַת יְהוָה מַחְשְׁבוֹת רָע וּטְהֹרִים אִמְרֵי־נֹעַם: ²⁶

עֹכֵר בֵּיתוֹ בּוֹצֵעַ בָּצַע וְשׂוֹנֵא מַתָּנֹת יִחְיֶה: ²⁷

לֵב צַדִּיק יֶהְגֶּה לַעֲנוֹת וּפִי רְשָׁעִים יַבִּיעַ רָעוֹת: ²⁸

רָחוֹק יְהוָה מֵרְשָׁעִים וּתְפִלַּת צַדִּיקִים יִשְׁמָע: ²⁹

מְאוֹר־עֵינַיִם יְשַׂמַּח־לֵב שְׁמוּעָה טוֹבָה תְּדַשֶּׁן־עָצֶם: ³⁰

אֹזֶן שֹׁמַעַת תּוֹכַחַת חַיִּים בְּקֶרֶב חֲכָמִים תָּלִין: ³¹

פּוֹרֵעַ מוּסָר מוֹאֵס נַפְשׁוֹ וְשׁוֹמֵעַ תּוֹכַחַת קוֹנֶה לֵּב: ³²

יִרְאַת יְהוָה מוּסַר חָכְמָה וְלִפְנֵי כָבוֹד עֲנָוָה: ³³

29 The LORD is far from the wicked, But He hears the prayer of the righteous. 30 Bright eyes gladden the heart; Good news puts fat on the bones. 31 He whose ear listens to the life-giving reproof Will dwell among the wise. 32 He who neglects discipline despises himself, But he who listens to reproof acquires understanding. 33 The fear of the LORD is the instruction for wisdom, And before honor *comes* humility.	

Process of Discovery

Linguistics Section

Linguistic Structure

[More saying of King Solomon][1] A gentle answer turns away wrath, But a harsh word stirs up anger.

[2] The tongue of the wise makes knowledge acceptable, But the mouth of fools spouts folly.

[3] The eyes of the LORD are in every place, Watching the evil and the good.

[4] A soothing tongue is a tree of life, But perversion in it crushes the spirit.

[5] A fool rejects his father's discipline, But he who regards reproof is prudent.

[6] Much wealth is *in* the house of the righteous, But trouble is in the income of the wicked.

[7] The lips of the wise spread knowledge, But the hearts of fools are not so.

[8] The sacrifice of the wicked is an abomination to the LORD, But the prayer of the upright is His delight.

[9] The way of the wicked is an abomination to the LORD, But He loves him who pursues righteousness.

[10] Stern discipline is for him who forsakes the way; He who hates reproof will die.

[11] Sheol and Abaddon *lie open* before the LORD, How much more the hearts of men!

[12] A scoffer does not love one who reproves him, He will not go to the wise.

[13] A joyful heart makes a cheerful face, But when the heart is sad, the spirit is broken.

[14] The mind of the intelligent seeks knowledge, But the mouth of fools feeds on folly.

[15] All the days of the afflicted are bad, But a cheerful heart *has* a continual feast.

[16] Better is a little with the fear of the LORD, Than great treasure and turmoil with it.

[17] Better is a dish of vegetables where love is, Than a fattened ox and hatred with it.

[18] A hot-tempered man stirs up strife, But the slow to anger pacifies contention.

[19] The way of the sluggard is as a hedge of thorns, But the path of the upright is a highway.

[20] A wise son makes a father glad, But a foolish man despises his mother.

[21] Folly is joy to him who lacks sense, But a man of understanding walks straight.

[22] Without consultation, plans are frustrated, But with many counselors they succeed.

[23] A man has joy in an apt answer, And how delightful is a timely word!

[24] The path of life *leads* upward for the wise, That he may keep away from Sheol below.

[25] The LORD will tear down the house of the proud, But He will establish the boundary of the widow.

[26] Evil plans are an abomination to the LORD, But pleasant words are pure.

[27] He who profits illicitly troubles his own house, But he who hates bribes will live.

[28] The heart of the righteous ponders how to answer, But the mouth of the wicked pours out evil things.

[29] The LORD is far from the wicked, But He hears the prayer of the righteous.

[30] Bright eyes gladden the heart; Good news puts fat on the bones.

[31] He whose ear listens to the life-giving reproof Will dwell among the wise.

[32] He who neglects discipline despises himself, But he who listens to reproof acquires understanding.

[33] The fear of the LORD is the instruction for wisdom, And before honor *comes* humility.

Discussion

More sayings of King Solomon

Questioning the Passage

1. What does the reference to a smooth tongue mean in verse three?

   The Sage Ibn Ezra[xi] said that a smooth tongue is the words of *mussar*[xii]. Those words heal the "illness" of foolishness. Just as a person eats from the tree of life enjoys longevity, so too is a person who learns the *mussar.*

2. What is the sacrifice of the wicked that it is abhorrent to the LORD? (v. 8)

   The LORD abhors any sacrifice offered if the item being sacrificed was stolen.[73] Only sacrifices that are made through the work of the person are acceptable.

3. What is Abaddon? (v. 11)

   The Zohar says that Abaddon is a place in Hell where the Ruach (spirit of the person) can repent for sins that the person did not repent for during their life. When complete, the person can enter Heaven as righteous.

---

[73] Eliezer Ginsburg and Nosson Scherman, *Mishlei: Proverbs = Mishlei: a New Translation with a Commentary Anthologized from Talmudic, Midrashic and Rabbinic Sources* (Brooklyn, NY: Mesorah, 2003).

4. What does verse sixteen mean?

    It is better to gain a little material (or money) through reverence to the Laws of the LORD than it is to accumulate treasure through ways that are not pleasing to the LORD.[74]

5. What does "the boundary of the widow" mean? (v. 25)

    If a man marries a widow to take advantage of her dead husband's wealth, he has violated her boundary. The LORD protects widows from these types of men.

6. What does it mean that "good news puts fat on bones?" (v. 30)

    Good news brings happiness to the heart. Fat on the bones is another way of saying the same thing.

Culture Section

Questioning the passage

1. What does verse seventeen mean?

    Poor people ate vegetables because they could not afford meat. Wealthy people slaughtered animals to have meat. Wealthy people did not eat vegetables. "Eat turnips" was a saying that the wealthy used when angry at their neighbors. King Solomon said that it is better to be poor and have loved than it was to be rich and not have love. Love is the most valuable thing a person can have.[75]

---

[74] IBID.

[75] Rocco A. Errico and George M. Lamsa, *Aramaic Light on Ezra through the Song of Solomon* (Smyma, GA: Noohra Foundation, 2010).

Thoughts

This chapter is more saying of King Solomon.

Chapter Sixteen

Language

New American Standard 1995	Hebrew
[1] The plans of the heart belong to man, But the answer of the tongue is from the LORD.	[2] לְאָדָם מַעַרְכֵי־לֵב וּמֵיהוָה מַעֲנֵה לָשׁוֹן:[1]
[2] All the ways of a man are clean in his own sight, But the LORD weighs the motives.	כָּל־דַּרְכֵי־אִישׁ זַךְ בְּעֵינָיו וְתֹכֵן רוּחוֹת יְהוָה:
[3] Commit your works to the LORD, And your plans will be established.	גֹּל אֶל־יְהוָה מַעֲשֶׂיךָ וְיִכֹּנוּ מַחְשְׁבֹתֶיךָ:[3]
[4] The LORD has made everything for its own purpose, Even the wicked for the day of evil.	כֹּל פָּעַל יְהוָה לַמַּעֲנֵהוּ וְגַם־רָשָׁע לְיוֹם רָעָה:[4]
[5] Everyone who is proud in heart is an abomination to the LORD; Assuredly, he will not be unpunished.	תּוֹעֲבַת יְהוָה כָּל־גְּבַהּ־לֵב יָד לְיָד לֹא יִנָּקֶה:[5]
[6] By lovingkindness and truth iniquity is atoned for, And by the fear of the LORD one keeps away from evil.	בְּחֶסֶד וֶאֱמֶת יְכֻפַּר עָוֹן וּבְיִרְאַת יְהוָה סוּר מֵרָע:[6]
[7] When a man's ways are pleasing to the LORD, He makes even his enemies to be at peace with him.	בִּרְצוֹת יְהוָה דַּרְכֵי־אִישׁ גַּם־אוֹיְבָיו יַשְׁלִם אִתּוֹ:[7]
[8] Better is a little with righteousness Than great income with injustice.	טוֹב־מְעַט בִּצְדָקָה מֵרֹב תְּבוּאוֹת בְּלֹא מִשְׁפָּט:[8]
[9] The mind of man plans his way, But the LORD directs his steps.	לֵב אָדָם יְחַשֵּׁב דַּרְכּוֹ וַיהוָה יָכִין צַעֲדוֹ:[9]
[10] A divine decision is in the lips of the king; His mouth should not err in judgment.	קֶסֶם עַל־שִׂפְתֵי־מֶלֶךְ בְּמִשְׁפָּט לֹא יִמְעַל־פִּיו:[10]
[11] A just balance and scales belong to the LORD; All the weights of the bag are His concern.	פֶּלֶס וּמֹאזְנֵי מִשְׁפָּט לַיהוָה מַעֲשֵׂהוּ כָּל־אַבְנֵי־כִיס:[11]
[12] It is an abomination for kings to commit wickedness, For a throne is established on righteousness.	תּוֹעֲבַת מְלָכִים עֲשׂוֹת רֶשַׁע כִּי בִּצְדָקָה יִכּוֹן כִּסֵּא:[12]
	רְצוֹן מְלָכִים שִׂפְתֵי־צֶדֶק וְדֹבֵר יְשָׁרִים יֶאֱהָב:[13]
	חֲמַת־מֶלֶךְ מַלְאֲכֵי־מָוֶת וְאִישׁ חָכָם יְכַפְּרֶנָּה:[14]
	בְּאוֹר־פְּנֵי־מֶלֶךְ חַיִּים וּרְצוֹנוֹ כְּעָב מַלְקוֹשׁ:[15]
	קְנֹה־חָכְמָה מַה־טּוֹב מֵחָרוּץ וּקְנוֹת בִּינָה נִבְחָר מִכָּסֶף:[16]
	מְסִלַּת יְשָׁרִים סוּר מֵרָע שֹׁמֵר נַפְשׁוֹ נֹצֵר דַּרְכּוֹ:[17]
	לִפְנֵי־שֶׁבֶר גָּאוֹן וְלִפְנֵי כִשָּׁלוֹן גֹּבַהּ רוּחַ:[18]
	טוֹב שְׁפַל־רוּחַ אֶת־(עֲנָיִו) [עֲנָוִים] מֵחַלֵּק שָׁלָל אֶת־גֵּאִים:[19]
	מַשְׂכִּיל עַל־דָּבָר יִמְצָא־טוֹב וּבוֹטֵחַ בַּיהוָה אַשְׁרָיו:[20]

¹³ Righteous lips are the delight of kings, And he who speaks right is loved.

¹⁴ The wrath of a king is *as* messengers of death, But a wise man will appease it.

¹⁵ In the light of a king's face is life, And his favor is like a cloud with the spring rain.

¹⁶ How much better it is to get wisdom than gold! And to get understanding is to be chosen above silver.

¹⁷ The highway of the upright is to depart from evil; He who watches his way preserves his life.

¹⁸ Pride *goes* before destruction, And a haughty spirit before stumbling.

¹⁹ It is better to be of a humble spirit with the lowly, Than to divide the spoil with the proud.

²⁰ He who gives attention to the word shall find good, And blessed is he who trusts in the LORD.

²¹ The wise in heart will be called discerning, And sweetness of speech increases persuasiveness.

²² Understanding is a fountain of life to him who has it, But the discipline of fools is folly.

²³ The heart of the wise teaches his mouth, And adds persuasiveness to his lips.

²⁴ Pleasant words are a honeycomb, Sweet to the soul and healing to the bones.

²⁵ There is a way *which seems* right to a man, But its end is the way of death.

²⁶ A worker's appetite works for him, For his hunger urges him *on*.

²⁷ A worthless man digs up evil, While his words are as a scorching fire.

²¹ לְחֲכַם־לֵב יִקָּרֵא נָבוֹן וּמֶתֶק שְׂפָתַיִם יֹסִיף לֶקַח:

²² מְקוֹר חַיִּים שֵׂכֶל בְּעָלָיו וּמוּסַר אֱוִלִים אִוֶּלֶת:

²³ לֵב חָכָם יַשְׂכִּיל פִּיהוּ וְעַל־שְׂפָתָיו יֹסִיף לֶקַח:

²⁴ צוּף־דְּבַשׁ אִמְרֵי־נֹעַם מָתוֹק לַנֶּפֶשׁ וּמַרְפֵּא לָעָצֶם:

²⁵ יֵשׁ דֶּרֶךְ יָשָׁר לִפְנֵי־אִישׁ וְאַחֲרִיתָהּ דַּרְכֵי־מָוֶת:

²⁶ נֶפֶשׁ עָמֵל עָמְלָה לּוֹ כִּי־אָכַף עָלָיו פִּיהוּ:

²⁷ אִישׁ בְּלִיַּעַל כֹּרֶה רָעָה וְעַל־(שְׂפָתָיו) [שְׂפָתוֹ] כְּאֵשׁ צָרָבֶת:

²⁸ אִישׁ תַּהְפֻּכוֹת יְשַׁלַּח מָדוֹן וְנִרְגָּן מַפְרִיד אַלּוּף:

²⁹ אִישׁ חָמָס יְפַתֶּה רֵעֵהוּ וְהוֹלִיכוֹ בְּדֶרֶךְ לֹא־טוֹב:

³⁰ עֹצֶה עֵינָיו לַחְשֹׁב תַּהְפֻּכוֹת קֹרֵץ שְׂפָתָיו כִּלָּה רָעָה:

³¹ עֲטֶרֶת תִּפְאֶרֶת שֵׂיבָה בְּדֶרֶךְ צְדָקָה תִּמָּצֵא:

³² טוֹב אֶרֶךְ אַפַּיִם מִגִּבּוֹר וּמֹשֵׁל בְּרוּחוֹ מִלֹּכֵד עִיר:

³³ בַּחֵיק יוּטַל אֶת־הַגּוֹרָל וּמֵיְהֹוָה כָּל־מִשְׁפָּטוֹ:

<table>
<tr><td>

²⁸ A perverse man spreads strife, And a slanderer separates intimate friends.

²⁹ A man of violence entices his neighbor, And leads him in a way that is not good.

³⁰ He who winks his eyes *does so* to devise perverse things; He who compresses his lips brings evil to pass.

³¹ A gray head is a crown of glory; It is found in the way of righteousness.

³² He who is slow to anger is better than the mighty, And he who rules his spirit, than he who captures a city.

³³ The lot is cast into the lap, But its every decision is from the LORD.

</td><td></td></tr>
</table>

Process of Discovery

Linguistics Section

Linguistic Structure

[1] The plans of the heart belong to man, But the answer of the tongue is from the LORD.
[2] All the ways of a man are clean in his own sight, But the LORD weighs the motives.
[3] Commit your works to the LORD, And your plans will be established.
[4] The LORD has made everything for its own purpose, Even the wicked for the day of evil.
[5] Everyone who is proud in heart is an abomination to the LORD; Assuredly, he will not be unpunished.
[6] By lovingkindness and truth iniquity is atoned for, And by the fear of the LORD one keeps away from evil.
[7] When a man's ways are pleasing to the LORD, He makes even his enemies to be at peace with him.
[8] Better is a little with righteousness Than great income with injustice.
[9] The mind of man plans his way, But the LORD directs his steps.
[10] A divine decision is in the lips of the king; His mouth should not err in judgment.
[11] A just balance and scales belong to the LORD; All the weights of the bag are His concern.
[12] It is an abomination for kings to commit wickedness, For a throne is established on righteousness.
[13] Righteous lips are the delight of kings, And he who speaks right is loved.
[14] The wrath of a king is *as* messengers of death, But a wise man will appease it.
[15] In the light of a king's face is life, And his favor is like a cloud with the spring rain.
[16] How much better it is to get wisdom than gold! And to get understanding is to be chosen above silver.
[17] The highway of the upright is to depart from evil; He who watches his way preserves his life.
[18] Pride *goes* before destruction, And a haughty spirit before stumbling.
[19] It is better to be of a humble spirit with the lowly, Than to divide the spoil with the proud.
[20] He who gives attention to the word shall find good, And blessed is he who trusts in the LORD.
[21] The wise in heart will be called discerning, And sweetness of speech increases persuasiveness.
[22] Understanding is a fountain of life to him who has it, But the discipline of fools is folly.
[23] The heart of the wise teaches his mouth, And adds persuasiveness to his lips.
[24] Pleasant words are a honeycomb, Sweet to the soul and healing to the bones.

[25] There is a way *which seems* right to a man, But its end is the way of death.

[26] A worker's appetite works for him, For his hunger urges him *on*.

[27] A worthless man digs up evil, While his words are as a scorching fire.

[28] A perverse man spreads strife, And a slanderer separates intimate friends.

[29] A man of violence entices his neighbor, And leads him in a way that is not good.

[30] He who winks his eyes *does so* to devise perverse things; He who compresses his lips brings evil to pass.

[31] A gray head is a crown of glory; It is found in the way of righteousness.

[32] He who is slow to anger is better than the mighty, And he who rules his spirit, than he who captures a city.

[33] The lot is cast into the lap, But its every decision is from the LORD.

Discussion

More sayings of King Solomon.

Questioning the Passage

1. What does it mean that the answer of the tongue is from the LORD? (v. 1) A person has the ability to organize their thoughts. The ability to express these thoughts requires the LORD's help. Therefore, a person must be cautious about what he/she is about to say so that it exemplifies the LORD.

2. What does it mean that the LORD created everything for His sake? (v. 2) Everything the LORD created in the Universe to give honor and praise to Him.[76]

---

[76] Eliezer Ginsburg and Nosson Scherman, *Mishlei: Proverbs = Mishlei: a New Translation with a Commentary Anthologized from Talmudic, Midrashic and Rabbinic Sources* (Brooklyn, NY: Mesorah, 2003) Volume Two.

3. What does it mean to have a proud heart? (v. 5)

    This means that the person is a bragger. The LORD does not like it when a person brags about the gifts and graces that the LORD has given to them. When one does this, it is easy to upset other people.

4. What does verse nine mean?

    The Targum says, "The heart of man ponders his ways, but the LORD directs his steps."[77] This verse teaches that a person is not entirely in charge of their destiny. A person can make plans, but the ultimate plan is from the LORD.

5. What does verse eleven mean?

    The LORD created scales and balances. This phrase is used as a metaphor that the LORD will balance a person's good deeds versus evil deeds when the day of judgment arrives.

6. Why is the anger of a king like messengers of death? (v. 14)

    When a king gets angry, he can use his power to have his subjects put to death. Therefore, it is wise not to anger the king and stay out of his way.

7. What does verse fifteen mean?

    This verse says that it is best to be in the king's favor. When this is combined with verse fourteen, it says that it is best to be a king's favored subject than not.

---

[77] Mangan Céline and Martin McNamara, *The Aramaic Bible: the Targums* (Edinburgh: Clark, 1991).

8. What is verse twenty-four referring to?

   Honey is sweet for the body and because it contains sugar, it energizes the person. King Solomon said that pleasant words energize a person as must as sugar does.

9. What does verse thirty-three mean?

   It is better to follow the ways of the LORD and His path than it is to randomly select your own ways.

Thoughts

This chapter is more saying of King Solomon.

Chapter Seventeen

Language

New American Standard 1995	Hebrew
[1] Better is a dry morsel and quietness with it Than a house full of feasting with strife.	טוֹב פַּת חֲרֵבָה וְשַׁלְוָה־בָהּ מִבַּיִת מָלֵא זִבְחֵי־רִיב: [2] עֶבֶד־מַשְׂכִּיל יִמְשֹׁל בְּבֵן מֵבִישׁ וּבְתוֹךְ אַחִים יַחֲלֹק נַחֲלָה:
[2] A servant who acts wisely will rule over a son who acts shamefully, And will share in the inheritance among brothers.	[3] מַצְרֵף לַכֶּסֶף וְכוּר לַזָּהָב וּבֹחֵן לִבּוֹת יְהוָה:
[3] The refining pot is for silver and the furnace for gold, But the LORD tests hearts.	[4] מֵרַע מַקְשִׁיב עַל־שְׂפַת־אָוֶן שֶׁקֶר מֵזִין עַל־לְשׁוֹן הַוֹּת:
[4] An evildoer listens to wicked lips; A liar pays attention to a destructive tongue.	[5] לֹעֵג לָרָשׁ חֵרֵף עֹשֵׂהוּ שָׂמֵחַ לְאֵיד לֹא יִנָּקֶה:
[5] He who mocks the poor taunts his Maker; He who rejoices at calamity will not go unpunished.	[6] עֲטֶרֶת זְקֵנִים בְּנֵי בָנִים וְתִפְאֶרֶת בָּנִים אֲבוֹתָם:
[6] Grandchildren are the crown of old men, And the glory of sons is their fathers.	[7] לֹא־נָאוָה לְנָבָל שְׂפַת־יֶתֶר אַף כִּי־לְנָדִיב שְׂפַת־שָׁקֶר:
[7] Excellent speech is not fitting for a fool, Much less are lying lips to a prince.	[8] אֶבֶן־חֵן הַשֹּׁחַד בְּעֵינֵי בְעָלָיו אֶל־כָּל־אֲשֶׁר יִפְנֶה יַשְׂכִּיל:
[8] A bribe is a charm in the sight of its owner; Wherever he turns, he prospers.	[9] מְכַסֶּה־פֶּשַׁע מְבַקֵּשׁ אַהֲבָה וְשֹׁנֶה בְדָבָר מַפְרִיד אַלּוּף:
[9] He who conceals a transgression seeks love, But he who repeats a matter separates intimate friends.	[10] תֵּחַת גְּעָרָה בְמֵבִין מֵהַכּוֹת כְּסִיל מֵאָה:
[10] A rebuke goes deeper into one who has understanding Than a hundred blows into a fool.	[11] אַךְ־מְרִי יְבַקֶּשׁ־רָע וּמַלְאָךְ אַכְזָרִי יְשֻׁלַּח־בּוֹ:
[11] A rebellious man seeks only evil, So a cruel messenger will be sent against him.	[12] פָּגוֹשׁ דֹּב שַׁכּוּל בְּאִישׁ וְאַל־כְּסִיל בְּאִוַּלְתּוֹ:
[12] Let a man meet a bear robbed of her cubs, Rather than a fool in his folly.	[13] מֵשִׁיב רָעָה תַּחַת טוֹבָה לֹא־(תָמִישׁ) [תָמוּשׁ] רָעָה מִבֵּיתוֹ:

¹³ He who returns evil for good, Evil will not depart from his house.

¹⁴ The beginning of strife is *like* letting out water, So abandon the quarrel before it breaks out.

¹⁵ He who justifies the wicked and he who condemns the righteous, Both of them alike are an abomination to the LORD.

¹⁶ Why is there a price in the hand of a fool to buy wisdom, When he has no sense?

¹⁷ A friend loves at all times, And a brother is born for adversity.

¹⁸ A man lacking in sense pledges And becomes guarantor in the presence of his neighbor.

¹⁹ He who loves transgression loves strife; He who raises his door seeks destruction.

²⁰ He who has a crooked mind finds no good, And he who is perverted in his language falls into evil.

²¹ He who sires a fool *does so* to his sorrow, And the father of a fool has no joy.

²² A joyful heart is good medicine, But a broken spirit dries up the bones.

²³ A wicked man receives a bribe from the bosom To pervert the ways of justice.

²⁴ Wisdom is in the presence of the one who has understanding, But the eyes of a fool are on the ends of the earth.

²⁵ A foolish son is a grief to his father And bitterness to her who bore him.

²⁶ It is also not good to fine the righteous, *Nor* to strike the noble for *their* uprightness.

¹⁴ פּוֹטֵר מַיִם רֵאשִׁית מָדוֹן וְלִפְנֵי הִתְגַּלַּע הָרִיב נְטוֹשׁ׃

¹⁵ מַצְדִּיק רָשָׁע וּמַרְשִׁיעַ צַדִּיק תּוֹעֲבַת יְהוָה גַּם־שְׁנֵיהֶם׃

¹⁶ לָמָּה־זֶּה מְחִיר בְּיַד־כְּסִיל לִקְנוֹת חָכְמָה וְלֶב־אָיִן׃

¹⁷ בְּכָל־עֵת אֹהֵב הָרֵעַ וְאָח לְצָרָה יִוָּלֵד׃

¹⁸ אָדָם חֲסַר־לֵב תּוֹקֵעַ כָּף עֹרֵב עֲרֻבָּה לִפְנֵי רֵעֵהוּ׃

¹⁹ אֹהֵב פֶּשַׁע אֹהֵב מַצָּה מַגְבִּיהַּ פִּתְחוֹ מְבַקֶּשׁ־שָׁבֶר׃

²⁰ עִקֶּשׁ־לֵב לֹא יִמְצָא־טוֹב וְנֶהְפָּךְ בִּלְשׁוֹנוֹ יִפּוֹל בְּרָעָה׃

²¹ יֹלֵד כְּסִיל לְתוּגָה לוֹ וְלֹא־יִשְׂמַח אֲבִי נָבָל׃

²² לֵב שָׂמֵחַ יֵיטִב גֵּהָה וְרוּחַ נְכֵאָה תְּיַבֶּשׁ־גָּרֶם׃

²³ שֹׁחַד מֵחֵיק רָשָׁע יִקָּח לְהַטּוֹת אָרְחוֹת מִשְׁפָּט׃

²⁴ אֶת־פְּנֵי מֵבִין חָכְמָה וְעֵינֵי כְסִיל בִּקְצֵה־אָרֶץ׃

²⁵ כַּעַס לְאָבִיו בֵּן כְּסִיל וּמֶמֶר לְיוֹלַדְתּוֹ׃

²⁶ גַּם עֲנוֹשׁ לַצַּדִּיק לֹא־טוֹב לְהַכּוֹת נְדִיבִים עַל־יֹשֶׁר׃

²⁷ חוֹשֵׂךְ אֲמָרָיו יוֹדֵעַ דָּעַת (וְקַר־)[יְקַר־]רוּחַ אִישׁ תְּבוּנָה׃

²⁸ גַּם אֱוִיל מַחֲרִישׁ חָכָם יֵחָשֵׁב אֹטֵם שְׂפָתָיו נָבוֹן׃

[27] He who restrains his words has knowledge, And he who has a cool spirit is a man of understanding. [28] Even a fool, when he keeps silent, is considered wise; When he closes his lips, he is *considered* prudent.	

Process of Discovery

Linguistics Section

Linguistic Structure

[1] Better is a dry morsel and quietness with it Than a house full of feasting with strife.

[2] A servant who acts wisely will rule over a son who acts shamefully, And will share in the inheritance among brothers.

[3] The refining pot is for silver and the furnace for gold, But the LORD tests hearts.

[4] An evildoer listens to wicked lips; A liar pays attention to a destructive tongue.

[5] He who mocks the poor taunts his Maker; He who rejoices at calamity will not go unpunished.

[6] Grandchildren are the crown of old men, And the glory of sons is their fathers.

[7] Excellent speech is not fitting for a fool, Much less are lying lips to a prince.

[8] A bribe is a charm in the sight of its owner; Wherever he turns, he prospers.

[9] He who conceals a transgression seeks love, But he who repeats a matter separates intimate friends.

[10] A rebuke goes deeper into one who has understanding Than a hundred blows into a fool.

[11] A rebellious man seeks only evil, So a cruel messenger will be sent against him.

[12] Let a man meet a bear robbed of her cubs, Rather than a fool in his folly.

[13] He who returns evil for good, Evil will not depart from his house.

[14] The beginning of strife is *like* letting out water, So abandon the quarrel before it breaks out.

[15] He who justifies the wicked and he who condemns the righteous, Both of them alike are an abomination to the LORD.

[16] Why is there a price in the hand of a fool to buy wisdom, When he has no sense?

[17] A friend loves at all times, And a brother is born for adversity.

[18] A man lacking in sense pledges And becomes guarantor in the presence of his neighbor.

[19] He who loves transgression loves strife; He who raises his door seeks destruction.

[20] He who has a crooked mind finds no good, And he who is perverted in his language falls into evil.

[21] He who sires a fool *does so* to his sorrow, And the father of a fool has no joy.

[22] A joyful heart is good medicine, But a broken spirit dries up the bones.

[23] A wicked man receives a bribe from the bosom To pervert the ways of justice.

[24] Wisdom is in the presence of the one who has understanding, But the eyes of a fool are on the ends of the earth.

[25] A foolish son is a grief to his father And bitterness to her who bore him.

[26] It is also not good to fine the righteous, *Nor* to strike the noble for *their* uprightness.
[27] He who restrains his words has knowledge, And he who has a cool spirit is a man of understanding.
[28] Even a fool, when he keeps silent, is considered wise; When he closes his lips, he is *considered* prudent.

Discussion

This chapter is another list of King Solomon's sayings.

Questioning the Passage

1. What does verse two mean?

   Two lessons can be derived from this saying. A father should instruct his children to use their minds; otherwise, a shrewd servant will find a way to steal their material possessions. The other is that a father may think that his child understands his business but does not. By the time the child gains competency, an outsider may have already taken control of the business.[78]

2. What does verse five mean?

   The Targum says that a person who denounced a pauper committed blasphemy. The LORD will punish a person who rejoices at the loss of a neighbor.[79]

---

[78] Eliezer Ginsburg and Nosson Scherman, *Mishlei: Proverbs = Mishlei: a New Translation with a Commentary Anthologized from Talmudic, Midrashic and Rabbinic Sources* (Brooklyn, NY: Mesorah, 2003) Volume Two.

[79] Mangan Céline. *The Targum of Job.: the Targum of Proverbs U.a.* Liturgical Press, 1987.

3. How is a bride like a charming gem? (v. 8)

    The Midrash Tanchuma (Parashas Toldos 8) explains that a bride can be compared to a precious stone because just as the stone can smash whatever it falls upon, so does bribery destroy whatever it happens to fall upon.[80]

4. What does verse ten mean?

    If a person is open to criticism, one sharp word of reproof can influence that person than a fool who has been whipped one-hundred times.[81]

5. What does verse twelve mean?

    A fool is a person who tries to pull a student away from the Torah. That is more dangerous than being attached by a bear who is protecting her cubs. The death of the soul is worse than the death of the body.

6. What does verse fourteen mean?

    The Targum says, "He who spills blood like water stirs up strife, and before an accident, he leads justice astray."[82]

7. What does verse sixteen mean?

    It is a waste of money for a fool to purchase wisdom because the fool will not know what to do with it.

---

[80] Eliezer Ginsburg and Nosson Scherman, *Mishlei: Proverbs = Mishlei: a New Translation with a Commentary Anthologized from Talmudic, Midrashic and Rabbinic Sources* (Brooklyn, NY: Mesorah, 2003) Volume Two.
[81] IBID.

[82] Mangan Céline. *The Targum of Job.: the Targum of Proverbs U.a.* Liturgical Press, 1987.

8. What does verse twenty-four mean?

A foolish person is usually convinced that wisdom is out of his/her reach. A wise man learns something from every person he/she comes in contact with.

Culture Section

Questioning the passage

1. What does verse one mean?

In the Near East, when people were blessed, and their materialism multiplied, they would offer sacrifices to display their wealth. They might slaughter a sheep or oxen and hold a feast to distribute some of the meat to the people who lived around them. Poor people seldom offered sacrifices because they had little to offer, nor did they entertain.

There was a lot of quarreling and strife in the homes of the rich. Many rich men married more than one woman. This situation caused strife and rivalry between women and jealous children.

"Peace of mind is more important than riches, for without peace, there is no contentment, and life becomes meaningless. Peace and harmony can create wealth, but riches cannot buy peace."[83]

Thoughts

This chapter is like the previous one. It is a list of King Solomon's proverbs.

---

[83] Rocco A. Errico and George M. Lamsa, *Aramaic Light on Ezra through the Song of Solomon* (Smyma, GA: Noohra Foundation, 2010).

Chapter Eighteen

Language

New American Standard 1995	Hebrew
[1] He who separates himself seeks *his own* desire, He quarrels against all sound wisdom.	לְתַאֲוָה יְבַקֵּשׁ נִפְרָד בְּכָל־תּוּשִׁיָּה יִתְגַּלָּע׃ [2] לֹא־יַחְפֹּץ כְּסִיל בִּתְבוּנָה כִּי אִם־בְּהִתְגַּלּוֹת לִבּוֹ׃
[2] A fool does not delight in understanding, But only in revealing his own mind.	[3] בְּבוֹא־רָשָׁע בָּא גַם־בּוּז וְעִם־קָלוֹן חֶרְפָּה׃
[3] When a wicked man comes, contempt also comes, And with dishonor *comes* scorn.	[4] מַיִם עֲמֻקִּים דִּבְרֵי פִי־אִישׁ נַחַל נֹבֵעַ מְקוֹר חָכְמָה׃
[4] The words of a man's mouth are deep waters; The fountain of wisdom is a bubbling brook.	[5] שְׂאֵת פְּנֵי־רָשָׁע לֹא־טוֹב לְהַטּוֹת צַדִּיק בַּמִּשְׁפָּט׃
[5] To show partiality to the wicked is not good, *Nor* to thrust aside the righteous in judgment.	[6] שִׂפְתֵי כְסִיל יָבֹאוּ בְרִיב וּפִיו לְמַהֲלֻמוֹת יִקְרָא׃
[6] A fool's lips bring strife, And his mouth calls for blows.	[7] פִּי־כְסִיל מְחִתָּה־לוֹ וּשְׂפָתָיו מוֹקֵשׁ נַפְשׁוֹ׃
[7] A fool's mouth is his ruin, And his lips are the snare of his soul.	[8] דִּבְרֵי נִרְגָּן כְּמִתְלַהֲמִים וְהֵם יָרְדוּ חַדְרֵי־בָטֶן׃
[8] The words of a whisperer are like dainty morsels, And they go down into the innermost parts of the body.	[9] גַּם מִתְרַפֶּה בִמְלַאכְתּוֹ אָח הוּא לְבַעַל מַשְׁחִית׃
[9] He also who is slack in his work Is brother to him who destroys.	[10] מִגְדַּל־עֹז שֵׁם יְהוָה בּוֹ־יָרוּץ צַדִּיק וְנִשְׂגָּב׃
[10] The name of the LORD is a strong tower; The righteous runs into it and is safe.	[11] הוֹן עָשִׁיר קִרְיַת עֻזּוֹ וּכְחוֹמָה נִשְׂגָּבָה בְּמַשְׂכִּיתוֹ׃
[11] A rich man's wealth is his strong city, And like a high wall in his own imagination.	[12] לִפְנֵי־שֶׁבֶר יִגְבַּהּ לֵב־אִישׁ וְלִפְנֵי כָבוֹד עֲנָוָה׃
[12] Before destruction the heart of man is haughty, But humility *goes* before honor.	[13] מֵשִׁיב דָּבָר בְּטֶרֶם יִשְׁמָע אִוֶּלֶת הִיא־לוֹ וּכְלִמָּה׃
[13] He who gives an answer before he hears, It is folly and shame to him.	[14] רוּחַ־אִישׁ יְכַלְכֵּל מַחֲלֵהוּ וְרוּחַ נְכֵאָה מִי יִשָּׂאֶנָּה׃
	[15] לֵב נָבוֹן יִקְנֶה־דָּעַת וְאֹזֶן חֲכָמִים תְּבַקֶּשׁ־דָּעַת׃
	[16] מַתָּן אָדָם יַרְחִיב לוֹ וְלִפְנֵי גְדֹלִים יַנְחֶנּוּ׃
	[17] צַדִּיק הָרִאשׁוֹן בְּרִיבוֹ (יָבֹא־)[וּבָא־]רֵעֵהוּ וַחֲקָרוֹ׃
	[18] מִדְיָנִים יַשְׁבִּית הַגּוֹרָל וּבֵין עֲצוּמִים יַפְרִיד׃
	[19] אָח נִפְשָׁע מִקִּרְיַת־עֹז (וּמְדוֹנִים) [וּמִדְיָנִים] כִּבְרִיחַ אַרְמוֹן׃

[14] The spirit of a man can endure his sickness, But *as for* a broken spirit who can bear it?

[15] The mind of the prudent acquires knowledge, And the ear of the wise seeks knowledge.

[16] A man's gift makes room for him And brings him before great men.

[17] The first to plead his case *seems* right, *Until* another comes and examines him.

[18] The *cast* lot puts an end to strife And decides between the mighty ones.

[19] A brother offended *is harder to be won* than a strong city, And contentions are like the bars of a citadel.

[20] With the fruit of a man's mouth his stomach will be satisfied; He will be satisfied *with* the product of his lips.

[21] Death and life are in the power of the tongue, And those who love it will eat its fruit.

[22] He who finds a wife finds a good thing And obtains favor from the LORD.

[23] The poor man utters supplications, But the rich man answers roughly.

[24] A man of *too many* friends *comes* to ruin, But there is a friend who sticks closer than a brother.

מִפְּרִי פִי־אִישׁ תִּשְׂבַּע בִּטְנוֹ תְּבוּאַת שְׂפָתָיו יִשְׂבָּע׃ 20

מָוֶת וְחַיִּים בְּיַד־לָשׁוֹן וְאֹהֲבֶיהָ יֹאכַל פִּרְיָהּ׃ 21

מָצָא אִשָּׁה מָצָא טוֹב וַיָּפֶק רָצוֹן מֵיְהוָה׃ 22

תַּחֲנוּנִים יְדַבֶּר־רָשׁ וְעָשִׁיר יַעֲנֶה עַזּוֹת׃ 23

אִישׁ רֵעִים לְהִתְרֹעֵעַ וְיֵשׁ אֹהֵב דָּבֵק מֵאָח׃ 24

Process of Discovery

Linguistics Section

Linguistic Structure

[1] He who separates himself seeks *his own* desire, He quarrels against all sound wisdom.
[2] A fool does not delight in understanding, But only in revealing his own mind.
[3] When a wicked man comes, contempt also comes, And with dishonor *comes* scorn.
[4] The words of a man's mouth are deep waters; The fountain of wisdom is a bubbling brook.
[5] To show partiality to the wicked is not good, *Nor* to thrust aside the righteous in judgment.
[6] A fool's lips bring strife, And his mouth calls for blows.
[7] A fool's mouth is his ruin, And his lips are the snare of his soul.
[8] The words of a whisperer are like dainty morsels, And they go down into the innermost parts of the body.
[9] He also who is slack in his work Is brother to him who destroys.
[10] The name of the LORD is a strong tower; The righteous runs into it and is safe.
[11] A rich man's wealth is his strong city, And like a high wall in his own imagination.
[12] Before destruction the heart of man is haughty, But humility *goes* before honor.
[13] He who gives an answer before he hears, It is folly and shame to him.
[14] The spirit of a man can endure his sickness, But *as for* a broken spirit who can bear it?
[15] The mind of the prudent acquires knowledge, And the ear of the wise seeks knowledge.
[16] A man's gift makes room for him And brings him before great men.
[17] The first to plead his case *seems* right, *Until* another comes and examines him.
[18] The *cast* lot puts an end to strife And decides between the mighty ones.
[19] A brother offended *is harder to be won* than a strong city, And contentions are like the bars of a citadel.
[20] With the fruit of a man's mouth his stomach will be satisfied; He will be satisfied *with* the product of his lips.
[21] Death and life are in the power of the tongue, And those who love it will eat its fruit.
[22] He who finds a wife finds a good thing And obtains favor from the LORD.
[23] The poor man utters supplications, But the rich man answers roughly.
[24] A man of *too many* friends *comes* to ruin, But there is a friend who sticks closer than a brother.

Discussion

This chapter is more saying of King Solomon.

Questioning the Passage

1. What does verse one mean?

    The Sage Rashi explained that this verse is referring to a person who separated themselves from the LORD. By doing this, the person has decided not to pursue the Mitzvot of the Torah but rather his heart's desires.[84]

2. What does verse two mean?

    A fool is a person who is not well versed in the Torah. When his/her ignorance is revealed, the person will want to start learning the Torah.

3. What does the metaphor in verse four mean?

    Deep waters can cause a person to drown. In the same way, deceitful words of a person may cause that person's difficulties and sorry. A pious person does not respect the words of a wicked person. A word is a compelling thing. Words of wisdom and truth are gentle like a spring of water and are refreshing to listen to as a spring of water quenches one's thirst.[85]

---

[84] Eliezer Ginsburg and Nosson Scherman, *Mishlei: Proverbs = Mishlei: a New Translation with a Commentary Anthologized from Talmudic, Midrashic and Rabbinic Sources* (Brooklyn, NY: Mesorah, 2003) Volume Two.

[85] Rocco A. Errico and George M. Lamsa, *Aramaic Light on Ezra through the Song of Solomon* (Smyma, GA: Noohra Foundation, 2010).

4. What does verse five mean?

   The Targum says that one should not take the side of a wicked person nor to pervert justice against a righteous person.[86]

5. What does verse eight mean?

   The Targum says that the idle man's words make him weary and bring him down to the depths of Sheol.[87]

6. What does verse eleven mean?

   A wealthy person places his/her trust in their wealth. This person also assumes that wealth will last forever. Worshiping wealth can cause one's downfall. The high wall is a metaphor for wealth because it may be necessary to use it as a ransom.[88]

Culture Section

Questioning the passage

1. What is a man's gift? (v. 16)

   In biblical times the term "gift" is another name for a bribe.[89] Judges were bribed because they did not receive a salary. They made their income through bribes.

Thoughts

This is another chapter of King Solomon's sayings.

---

86 Mangan Céline. *The Targum of Job.: the Targum of Proverbs U.a.* Liturgical Press, 1987.

87 IBID.

88 Eliezer Ginsburg and Nosson Scherman, *Mishlei: Proverbs = Mishlei: a New Translation with a Commentary Anthologized from Talmudic, Midrashic and Rabbinic Sources* (Brooklyn, NY: Mesorah, 2003) Volume Two.

89 Rocco A. Errico and George M. Lamsa, *Aramaic Light on Ezra through the Song of Solomon* (Smyma, GA: Noohra Foundation, 2010).

154

Chapter Nineteen

Language

New American Standard 1995	Hebrew
[1] Better is a poor man who walks in his integrity Than he who is perverse in speech and is a fool.	טֽוֹב־רָ֭שׁ הוֹלֵ֣ךְ בְּתֻמּ֑וֹ מֵעִקֵּ֥שׁ שְׂ֝פָתָ֗יו וְה֣וּא כְסִֽיל׃ [2] גַּ֤ם בְּלֹא־דַ֣עַת נֶ֣פֶשׁ לֹא־ט֑וֹב וְאָ֖ץ בְּרַגְלַ֣יִם חוֹטֵֽא׃ [3] אִוֶּ֣לֶת אָ֭דָם תְּסַלֵּ֣ף דַּרְכּ֑וֹ וְעַל־יְ֝הוָ֗ה יִזְעַ֥ף לִבּֽוֹ׃ [4] ה֗וֹן יֹ֭סִיף רֵעִ֣ים רַבִּ֑ים וְ֝דָ֗ל מֵרֵעֵ֥הוּ יִפָּרֵֽד׃ [5] עֵ֣ד שְׁ֭קָרִים לֹ֣א יִנָּקֶ֑ה וְיָפִ֥יחַ כְּ֝זָבִ֗ים לֹ֣א יִמָּלֵֽט׃ [6] רַ֭בִּים יְחַלּ֣וּ פְנֵֽי־נָדִ֑יב וְכָל־הָ֝רֵ֗עַ לְאִ֣ישׁ מַתָּֽן׃ [7] כָּ֥ל אֲחֵי־רָ֨שׁ׀ שְֽׂנֵאֻ֗הוּ אַ֤ף כִּ֣י מְ֭רֵעֵהוּ רָחֲק֣וּ מִמֶּ֑נּוּ מְרַדֵּ֖ף אֲמָרִ֣ים (לֹא־)[ל֥וֹ־] הֵֽמָּה׃ [8] קֹֽנֶה־לֵּ֭ב אֹהֵ֣ב נַפְשׁ֑וֹ שֹׁמֵ֥ר תְּ֝בוּנָ֗ה לִמְצֹא־טֽוֹב׃ [9] עֵ֣ד שְׁ֭קָרִים לֹ֣א יִנָּקֶ֑ה וְיָפִ֖יחַ כְּזָבִ֣ים יֹאבֵֽד׃ פ [10] לֹֽא־נָאוֶ֣ה לִכְסִ֣יל תַּעֲנ֑וּג אַ֝֗ף כִּֽי־לְעֶ֤בֶד׀ מְשֹׁ֬ל בְּשָׂרִֽים׃ [11] שֵׂ֣כֶל אָ֭דָם הֶאֱרִ֣יךְ אַפּ֑וֹ וְ֝תִפְאַרְתּ֗וֹ עֲבֹ֣ר עַל־פָּֽשַׁע׃ [12] נַ֣הַם כַּ֭כְּפִיר זַ֣עַף מֶ֑לֶךְ וּכְטַ֖ל עַל־עֵ֣שֶׂב רְצוֹנֽוֹ׃ [13] הַוֺּ֣ת לְ֭אָבִיו בֵּ֣ן כְּסִ֑יל וְדֶ֥לֶף טֹ֝רֵ֗ד מִדְיְנֵ֥י אִשָּֽׁה׃ [14] בַּ֤יִת וָה֗וֹן נַחֲלַ֥ת אָב֑וֹת וּ֝מֵיְהוָ֗ה אִשָּׁ֥ה מַשְׂכָּֽלֶת׃
[2] Also it is not good for a person to be without knowledge, And he who hurries his footsteps errs.	
[3] The foolishness of man ruins his way, And his heart rages against the LORD.	
[4] Wealth adds many friends, But a poor man is separated from his friend.	
[5] A false witness will not go unpunished, And he who tells lies will not escape.	
[6] Many will seek the favor of a generous man, And every man is a friend to him who gives gifts.	
[7] All the brothers of a poor man hate him; How much more do his friends abandon him! He pursues *them with* words, *but* they are gone.	
[8] He who gets wisdom loves his own soul; He who keeps understanding will find good.	
[9] A false witness will not go unpunished, And he who tells lies will perish.	
[10] Luxury is not fitting for a fool; Much less for a slave to rule over princes.	
[11] A man's discretion makes him slow to anger, And it is his glory to overlook a transgression.	
[12] The king's wrath is like the roaring of a lion, But his favor is like dew on the grass.	

13 A foolish son is destruction to his father, And the contentions of a wife are a constant dripping.
14 House and wealth are an inheritance from fathers, But a prudent wife is from the LORD.
15 Laziness casts into a deep sleep, And an idle man will suffer hunger.
16 He who keeps the commandment keeps his soul, *But* he who is careless of conduct will die.
17 One who is gracious to a poor man lends to the LORD, And He will repay him for his good deed.
18 Discipline your son while there is hope, And do not desire his death.
19 *A man of* great anger will bear the penalty, For if you rescue *him*, you will only have to do it again.
20 Listen to counsel and accept discipline, That you may be wise the rest of your days.
21 Many plans are in a man's heart, But the counsel of the LORD will stand.
22 What is desirable in a man is his kindness, And *it is* better to be a poor man than a liar.
23 The fear of the LORD *leads* to life, So that one may sleep satisfied, untouched by evil.
24 The sluggard buries his hand in the dish, *But* will not even bring it back to his mouth.
25 Strike a scoffer and the naive may become shrewd, But reprove one who has understanding and he will gain knowledge.
26 He who assaults *his* father *and* drives *his* mother away Is a shameful and disgraceful son.

15 עַצְלָה תַּפִּיל תַּרְדֵּמָה וְנֶפֶשׁ רְמִיָּה תִרְעָב:

16 שֹׁמֵר מִצְוָה שֹׁמֵר נַפְשׁוֹ בּוֹזֵה דְרָכָיו (יוּמָת) [יָמוּת]:

17 מַלְוֵה יְהוָה חוֹנֵן דָּל וּגְמֻלוֹ יְשַׁלֶּם־לוֹ:

18 יַסֵּר בִּנְךָ כִּי־יֵשׁ תִּקְוָה וְאֶל־הֲמִיתוֹ אַל־תִּשָּׂא נַפְשֶׁךָ:

19 (גְּרָל־)[גְּדָל־]חֵמָה נֹשֵׂא עֹנֶשׁ כִּי אִם־תַּצִּיל וְעוֹד תּוֹסִף:

20 שְׁמַע עֵצָה וְקַבֵּל מוּסָר לְמַעַן תֶּחְכַּם בְּאַחֲרִיתֶךָ:

21 רַבּוֹת מַחֲשָׁבוֹת בְּלֶב־אִישׁ וַעֲצַת יְהוָה הִיא תָקוּם:

22 תַּאֲוַת אָדָם חַסְדּוֹ וְטוֹב־רָשׁ מֵאִישׁ כָּזָב:

23 יִרְאַת יְהוָה לְחַיִּים וְשָׂבֵעַ יָלִין בַּל־יִפָּקֶד רָע:

24 טָמַן עָצֵל יָדוֹ בַּצַּלָּחַת גַּם־אֶל־פִּיהוּ לֹא יְשִׁיבֶנָּה:

25 לֵץ תַּכֶּה וּפֶתִי יַעְרִם וְהוֹכִיחַ לְנָבוֹן יָבִין דָּעַת:

26 מְשַׁדֶּד־אָב יַבְרִיחַ אֵם בֵּן מֵבִישׁ וּמַחְפִּיר:

27 חֲדַל־בְּנִי לִשְׁמֹעַ מוּסָר לִשְׁגּוֹת מֵאִמְרֵי־דָעַת:

28 עֵד בְּלִיַּעַל יָלִיץ מִשְׁפָּט וּפִי רְשָׁעִים יְבַלַּע־אָוֶן:

29 נָכוֹנוּ לַלֵּצִים שְׁפָטִים וּמַהֲלֻמוֹת לְגֵו כְּסִילִים:

[27] Cease listening, my son, to discipline, *And you will* stray from the words of knowledge. [28] A rascally witness makes a mockery of justice, And the mouth of the wicked spreads iniquity. [29] Judgments are prepared for scoffers, And blows for the back of fools.	

Process of Discovery

Linguistics Section

Linguistic Structure

¹ Better is a poor man who walks in his integrity Than he who is perverse in speech and is a fool.

² Also it is not good for a person to be without knowledge, And he who hurries his footsteps errs.

³ The foolishness of man ruins his way, And his heart rages against the LORD.

⁴ Wealth adds many friends, But a poor man is separated from his friend.

⁵ A false witness will not go unpunished, And he who tells lies will not escape.

⁶ Many will seek the favor of a generous man, And every man is a friend to him who gives gifts.

⁷ All the brothers of a poor man hate him; How much more do his friends abandon him! He pursues *them with* words, *but* they are gone.

⁸ He who gets wisdom loves his own soul; He who keeps understanding will find good.

⁹ A false witness will not go unpunished, And he who tells lies will perish.

¹⁰ Luxury is not fitting for a fool; Much less for a slave to rule over princes.

¹¹ A man's discretion makes him slow to anger, And it is his glory to overlook a transgression.

¹² The king's wrath is like the roaring of a lion, But his favor is like dew on the grass.

¹³ A foolish son is destruction to his father, And the contentions of a wife are a constant dripping.

¹⁴ House and wealth are an inheritance from fathers, But a prudent wife is from the LORD.

¹⁵ Laziness casts into a deep sleep, And an idle man will suffer hunger.

¹⁶ He who keeps the commandment keeps his soul, *But* he who is careless of conduct will die.

¹⁷ One who is gracious to a poor man lends to the LORD, And He will repay him for his good deed.

¹⁸ Discipline your son while there is hope, And do not desire his death.

¹⁹ *A man of* great anger will bear the penalty, For if you rescue *him*, you will only have to do it again.

²⁰ Listen to counsel and accept discipline, That you may be wise the rest of your days.

²¹ Many plans are in a man's heart, But the counsel of the LORD will stand.

²² What is desirable in a man is his kindness, And *it is* better to be a poor man than a liar.

²³ The fear of the LORD *leads* to life, So that one may sleep satisfied, untouched by evil.

²⁴ The sluggard buries his hand in the dish, *But* will not even bring it back to his mouth.

²⁵ Strike a scoffer and the naive may become shrewd, But reprove one who has understanding and he will gain knowledge.

²⁶ He who assaults *his* father *and* drives *his* mother away Is a shameful and disgraceful son.

²⁷ Cease listening, my son, to discipline, *And you will* stray from the words of knowledge.

²⁸ A rascally witness makes a mockery of justice, And the mouth of the wicked spreads iniquity.

²⁹ Judgments are prepared for scoffers, And blows for the back of fools.

Discussion

This chapter contains more statements of wisdom from King Solomon.

Questioning the Passage

1. What does it mean to have a raging heart against the LORD? (v. 3)

   When a person makes a mistake and retribution come that is not to the person's liking, the person may wonder why the LORD treated him/her poorly. The person does not realize that it was his/her action that caused the retribution.[90]

2. Why is a poor person separated from friends? (v. 4)

   Wealth tends to attract friends. The friends have the opportunity to share in the wealth. A poor person has few friends because he/she has little to nothing to share.

3. What does verse eight mean?

   A person who seeks wisdom will enrich his/her soul. A person who receives wisdom and understands it will be able to use the understanding for good.

---

[90] Eliezer Ginsburg and Nosson Scherman, *Mishlei: Proverbs = Mishlei: a New Translation with a Commentary Anthologized from Talmudic, Midrashic and Rabbinic Sources* (Brooklyn, NY: Mesorah, 2003) Volume Two.

4. What does verse ten mean?

   The Targum says, "tender treatment does not suit a fool, nor indeed does it suit a servant that he should rule over princes." The pleasures of life were created for a purpose. A foot does not use these pleasures properly. A servant will not rule over princes and thus should not use the pleasures of life in an attempt to do so.[91]

5. What does verse thirteen mean?

   A contentious wife will drive the husband to leave home. In ancient days divorce was not acceptable for a contentious wife. The husband had to live with her. Therefore, he would find any reason to leave the house.

6. What does verse twenty-four mean?

   King Solomon discussed the person who has become lazy. It is not acceptable to become lazy. This verse says that a lazy person will place their hand on food on a plate but will not take the food to his/her mouth even if starving. Laziness is not suitable for people.

Culture Section

Questioning the passage

1. What does it mean to hurry one's footsteps? (v. 2)

   A person needs to examine themselves before passing judgment on others. A person with "hasty feet" is a person who is ready to commit a crime or do some other kind of evil thing.[92]

---

[91] Mangan Céline. *The Targum of Job.: the Targum of Proverbs U.a.* Liturgical Press, 1987.

[92] Rocco A. Errico and George M. Lamsa, *Aramaic Light on Ezra through the Song of Solomon* (Smyma, GA: Noohra Foundation, 2010).

2. Why is it better to be poor than be a liar? (v. 22)

   A poor man makes an honest living while a rich man makes his living cheating others. Many rich vendors would up their prices in the markets when a poor person came to their stand. Besides, the vendor would try to cheat the buyer by using incorrect weight measurements.[93]

Thoughts

This chapter contains more sayings of King Solomon.

---

[93] IBID.

162

Chapter Twenty

Language

New American Standard 1995	Hebrew
[1] Wine is a mocker, strong drink a brawler, And whoever is intoxicated by it is not wise. [2] The terror of a king is like the growling of a lion; He who provokes him to anger forfeits his own life. [3] Keeping away from strife is an honor for a man, But any fool will quarrel. [4] The sluggard does not plow after the autumn, So he begs during the harvest and has nothing. [5] A plan in the heart of a man is *like* deep water, But a man of understanding draws it out. [6] Many a man proclaims his own loyalty, But who can find a trustworthy man? [7] A righteous man who walks in his integrity-- How blessed are his sons after him. [8] A king who sits on the throne of justice Disperses all evil with his eyes. [9] Who can say, "I have cleansed my heart, I am pure from my sin "? [10] Differing weights and differing measures, Both of them are abominable to the LORD. [11] It is by his deeds that a lad distinguishes himself If his conduct is pure and right. [12] The hearing ear and the seeing eye, The LORD has made both of them. [13] Do not love sleep, or you will become poor; Open your eyes, *and* you will be satisfied with food. [14] "Bad, bad," says the buyer, But when he goes his way, then he boasts.	לֵץ הַיַּיִן הֹמֶה שֵׁכָר וְכָל־שֹׁגֶה בּוֹ לֹא יֶחְכָּם: [2] נַהַם כַּכְּפִיר אֵימַת מֶלֶךְ מִתְעַבְּרוֹ חוֹטֵא נַפְשׁוֹ: [3] כָּבוֹד לָאִישׁ שֶׁבֶת מֵרִיב וְכָל־אֱוִיל יִתְגַּלָּע: [4] מֵחֹרֶף עָצֵל לֹא־יַחֲרֹשׁ (יִשְׁאַל) [וְשָׁאַל] בַּקָּצִיר וָאָיִן: [5] מַיִם עֲמֻקִּים עֵצָה בְלֶב־אִישׁ וְאִישׁ תְּבוּנָה יִדְלֶנָּה: [6] רָב־אָדָם יִקְרָא אִישׁ חַסְדּוֹ וְאִישׁ אֱמוּנִים מִי יִמְצָא: [7] מִתְהַלֵּךְ בְּתֻמּוֹ צַדִּיק אַשְׁרֵי בָנָיו אַחֲרָיו: [8] מֶלֶךְ יוֹשֵׁב עַל־כִּסֵּא־דִין מְזָרֶה בְעֵינָיו כָּל־רָע: [9] מִי־יֹאמַר זִכִּיתִי לִבִּי טָהַרְתִּי מֵחַטָּאתִי: [10] אֶבֶן וָאֶבֶן אֵיפָה וְאֵיפָה תּוֹעֲבַת יְהוָה גַּם־שְׁנֵיהֶם: [11] גַּם בְּמַעֲלָלָיו יִתְנַכֶּר־נָעַר אִם־זַךְ וְאִם־יָשָׁר פָּעֳלוֹ: [12] אֹזֶן שֹׁמַעַת וְעַיִן רֹאָה יְהוָה עָשָׂה גַּם־שְׁנֵיהֶם: [13] אַל־תֶּאֱהַב שֵׁנָה פֶּן־תִּוָּרֵשׁ פְּקַח עֵינֶיךָ שְׂבַע־לָחֶם: [14] רַע רַע יֹאמַר הַקּוֹנֶה וְאֹזֵל לוֹ אָז יִתְהַלָּל: [15] יֵשׁ זָהָב וְרָב־פְּנִינִים וּכְלִי יְקָר שִׂפְתֵי־דָעַת:

¹⁵ There is gold, and an abundance of jewels; But the lips of knowledge are a more precious thing.

¹⁶ Take his garment when he becomes surety for a stranger; And for foreigners, hold him in pledge.

¹⁷ Bread obtained by falsehood is sweet to a man, But afterward his mouth will be filled with gravel.

¹⁸ Prepare plans by consultation, And make war by wise guidance.

¹⁹ He who goes about as a slanderer reveals secrets, Therefore do not associate with a gossip.

²⁰ He who curses his father or his mother, His lamp will go out in time of darkness.

²¹ An inheritance gained hurriedly at the beginning Will not be blessed in the end.

²² Do not say, "I will repay evil"; Wait for the LORD, and He will save you.

²³ Differing weights are an abomination to the LORD, And a false scale is not good.

²⁴ Man's steps are *ordained* by the LORD, How then can man understand his way?

²⁵ It is a trap for a man to say rashly, "It is holy!" And after the vows to make inquiry.

²⁶ A wise king winnows the wicked, And drives the *threshing* wheel over them.

²⁷ The spirit of man is the lamp of the LORD, Searching all the innermost parts of his being.

²⁸ Loyalty and truth preserve the king, And he upholds his throne by righteousness.

²⁹ The glory of young men is their strength, And the honor of old men is their gray hair.

לָקַח־בִּגְדוֹ כִּי־עָרַב זָר וּבְעַד (נָכְרִים) ¹⁶
[נָכְרִיָּה] חַבְלֵהוּ:

עָרֵב לָאִישׁ לֶחֶם שָׁקֶר וְאַחַר יִמָּלֵא־ ¹⁷
פִיהוּ חָצָץ:

מַחֲשָׁבוֹת בְּעֵצָה תִכּוֹן וּבְתַחְבֻּלוֹת ¹⁸
עֲשֵׂה מִלְחָמָה:

גּוֹלֶה־סּוֹד הוֹלֵךְ רָכִיל וּלְפֹתֶה שְׂפָתָיו ¹⁹
לֹא תִתְעָרָב:

מְקַלֵּל אָבִיו וְאִמּוֹ יִדְעַךְ נֵרוֹ (בֶּאֱשׁוּן) ²⁰
[בֶּאֱשׁוּן] חֹשֶׁךְ:

נַחֲלָה (מְבֻחֶלֶת) [מְבֹהֶלֶת] בָּרִאשֹׁנָה ²¹
וְאַחֲרִיתָהּ לֹא תְבֹרָךְ:

אַל־תֹּאמַר אֲשַׁלְּמָה־רָע קַוֵּה לַיהוָה ²²
וְיֹשַׁע לָךְ:

תּוֹעֲבַת יְהוָה אֶבֶן וָאָבֶן וּמֹאזְנֵי ²³
מִרְמָה לֹא־טוֹב:

מֵיהוָה מִצְעֲדֵי־גָבֶר וְאָדָם מַה־יָּבִין ²⁴
דַּרְכּוֹ:

מוֹקֵשׁ אָדָם יָלַע קֹדֶשׁ וְאַחַר נְדָרִים ²⁵
לְבַקֵּר:

מְזָרֶה רְשָׁעִים מֶלֶךְ חָכָם וַיָּשֶׁב ²⁶
עֲלֵיהֶם אוֹפָן:

נֵר יְהוָה נִשְׁמַת אָדָם חֹפֵשׂ כָּל־ ²⁷
חַדְרֵי־בָטֶן:

חֶסֶד וֶאֱמֶת יִצְּרוּ־מֶלֶךְ וְסָעַד בַּחֶסֶד ²⁸
כִּסְאוֹ:

תִּפְאֶרֶת בַּחוּרִים כֹּחָם וַהֲדַר זְקֵנִים ²⁹
שֵׂיבָה:

חַבֻּרוֹת פֶּצַע (תַּמְרִיק) [תַּמְרוּק] ³⁰
בְּרָע וּמַכּוֹת חַדְרֵי־בָטֶן:

| ³⁰ Stripes that wound scour away evil, And strokes *reach* the innermost parts. | |

Process of Discovery

Linguistics Section

Linguistic Structure

[1] Wine is a mocker, strong drink a brawler, And whoever is intoxicated by it is not wise.

[2] The terror of a king is like the growling of a lion; He who provokes him to anger forfeits his own life.

[3] Keeping away from strife is an honor for a man, But any fool will quarrel.

[4] The sluggard does not plow after the autumn, So he begs during the harvest and has nothing.

[5] A plan in the heart of a man is *like* deep water, But a man of understanding draws it out.

[6] Many a man proclaims his own loyalty, But who can find a trustworthy man?

[7] A righteous man who walks in his integrity-- How blessed are his sons after him.

[8] A king who sits on the throne of justice Disperses all evil with his eyes.

[9] Who can say, "I have cleansed my heart, I am pure from my sin "?

[10] Differing weights and differing measures, Both of them are abominable to the LORD.

[11] It is by his deeds that a lad distinguishes himself If his conduct is pure and right.

[12] The hearing ear and the seeing eye, The LORD has made both of them.

[13] Do not love sleep, or you will become poor; Open your eyes, *and* you will be satisfied with food.

[14] "Bad, bad," says the buyer, But when he goes his way, then he boasts.

[15] There is gold, and an abundance of jewels; But the lips of knowledge are a more precious thing.

[16] Take his garment when he becomes surety for a stranger; And for foreigners, hold him in pledge.

[17] Bread obtained by falsehood is sweet to a man, But afterward his mouth will be filled with gravel.

[18] Prepare plans by consultation, And make war by wise guidance.

[19] He who goes about as a slanderer reveals secrets, Therefore do not associate with a gossip.

[20] He who curses his father or his mother, His lamp will go out in time of darkness.

[21] An inheritance gained hurriedly at the beginning Will not be blessed in the end.

[22] Do not say, "I will repay evil"; Wait for the LORD, and He will save you.

[23] Differing weights are an abomination to the LORD, And a false scale is not good.

[24] Man's steps are *ordained* by the LORD, How then can man understand his way?

[25] It is a trap for a man to say rashly, "It is holy!" And after the vows to make inquiry.

[26] A wise king winnows the wicked, And drives the *threshing* wheel over them.

[27] The spirit of man is the lamp of the LORD, Searching all the innermost parts of his being.
[28] Loyalty and truth preserve the king, And he upholds his throne by righteousness.
[29] The glory of young men is their strength, And the honor of old men is their gray hair.
[30] Stripes that wound scour away evil, And strokes *reach* the innermost parts.

Discussion

This chapter is more wisdom from King Solomon.

Questioning the Passage

1. What do different weights and measures mean? (v. 10)

    Merchants tended to cheat customers by using invalid weights and measurements. For example, going to a butcher and purchasing a pound of meat. When at home, the meat weighed 14 ounces. The buyer was cheated because the merchant used a "lite" weight on the balance scale.

2. What is the meaning of verse twelve?

    A person who sleeps too much will not be able to earn a living. In addition to being awake, a person has to be on the lookout for employment opportunities.

3. What does verse fourteen mean?

    When a buyer wants to purchase an item, negotiations commence. The buyer will downgrade what the seller is selling in order to get a better price. When a deal is struck, the buyer will tell his/her friends of the great deal they received. This verse is an allegory for learning the Torah. A person may lose sleep and have other life difficulties because they expend their energy on Torah study. However, the pain of learning Torah is well worth it because the student can become a counselor to other persons who want to know what the Torah says.[94]

Culture Section

Questioning the passage

1. Why is wine a mocker? (v. 1)

   A general rule in the Near East was that people who drank wine did not drink excessively. However, when they attended banquets, feasts, and weddings, they would drink wine until they were dead drunk. After the festivities, the drunkards would stumble down the streets cursing and uttering shameful remarks. A drunk would be mocked by the sober people while walking down the street.[95]

2. What does it mean to have gravel in your mouth? (v. 17)

   In the Near East, people would become surety for bandits, murderers, and men of bad reputation and credit. They took the risk because they received money or for political reasons. Sometimes they had to pay for the evil the person did. "To have a mouth filled with gravel" is a Semitic expression meaning that a person could not give an answer or exonerate him/herself from an evil deed. Bread often had gravel and small stones in it. The wheat that came from the threshing floor could contain gravel and dirt. The gravel and dirt caused people to choke.[96] The expression became synonymous with having to pay for someone else's sins.

---

[94] Eliezer Ginsburg and Nosson Scherman, *Mishlei: Proverbs = Mishlei: a New Translation with a Commentary Anthologized from Talmudic, Midrashic and Rabbinic Sources* (Brooklyn, NY: Mesorah, 2003) Volume Two.
[95] Rocco A. Errico and George M. Lamsa, *Aramaic Light on Ezra through the Song of Solomon* (Smyma, GA: Noohra Foundation, 2010).
[96] IBID.

3. What does it mean that a lamp will be put out in obscure darkness if parents are cursed? (v. 20)

   Cursing one's parents was considered a capital crime. The word "lamp" is a metaphor meaning "prosperity or heir." The LORD disapproved of wicked people, and it was believed that He would take their prosperity away.[97]

4. What does verse twenty-five mean?

   The Scripture admonished Israelites to fulfill their vows as soon as possible. Vowes were reminders of the LORD's favor and blessings. For example, when a person vowed to help the poor, it was essential to perform the vow. The LORD did not need the charity, but the poor person did.[98]

5. What does verse thirty mean?

   It was believed that wounds and other alignments were caused by evil. The person performing evil acts would eventually suffer physical discomforts.

Thoughts

This chapter is a continuation of wisdom from King Solomon.

---

[97] IBID.
[98] IBID.

Chapter Twenty-One

Language

New American Standard 1995	Hebrew
[1] The king's heart is *like* channels of water in the hand of the LORD; He turns it wherever He wishes. [2] Every man's way is right in his own eyes, But the LORD weighs the hearts. [3] To do righteousness and justice Is desired by the LORD more than sacrifice. [4] Haughty eyes and a proud heart, The lamp of the wicked, is sin. [5] The plans of the diligent *lead* surely to advantage, But everyone who is hasty *comes* surely to poverty. [6] The acquisition of treasures by a lying tongue Is a fleeting vapor, the pursuit of death. [7] The violence of the wicked will drag them away, Because they refuse to act with justice. [8] The way of a guilty man is crooked, But as for the pure, his conduct is upright. [9] It is better to live in a corner of a roof Than in a house shared with a contentious woman. [10] The soul of the wicked desires evil; His neighbor finds no favor in his eyes. [11] When the scoffer is punished, the naive becomes wise; But when the wise is instructed, he receives knowledge. [12] The righteous one considers the house of the wicked, Turning the wicked to ruin. [13] He who shuts his ear to the cry of the poor Will also cry himself and not be answered. [14] A gift in secret subdues anger, And a bribe in the bosom, strong wrath.	פַּלְגֵי־מַיִם לֶב־מֶלֶךְ בְּיַד־יְהוָה עַל־כָּל־אֲשֶׁר יַחְפֹּץ יַטֶּנּוּ: 2כָּל־דֶּרֶךְ־אִישׁ יָשָׁר בְּעֵינָיו וְתֹכֵן לִבּוֹת יְהוָה: 3עֲשֹׂה צְדָקָה וּמִשְׁפָּט נִבְחָר לַיהוָה מִזָּבַח: 4רוּם־עֵינַיִם וּרְחַב־לֵב נֵר רְשָׁעִים חַטָּאת: 5מַחְשְׁבוֹת חָרוּץ אַךְ־לְמוֹתָר וְכָל־אָץ אַךְ־לְמַחְסוֹר: 6פֹּעַל אוֹצָרוֹת בִּלְשׁוֹן שָׁקֶר הֶבֶל נִדָּף מְבַקְשֵׁי־מָוֶת: 7שֹׁד־רְשָׁעִים יְגוֹרֵם כִּי מֵאֲנוּ לַעֲשׂוֹת מִשְׁפָּט: 8הֲפַכְפַּךְ דֶּרֶךְ אִישׁ וָזָר וְזַךְ יָשָׁר פָּעֳלוֹ: 9טוֹב לָשֶׁבֶת עַל־פִּנַּת־גָּג מֵאֵשֶׁת מִדְיָנִים וּבֵית חָבֶר: 10נֶפֶשׁ רָשָׁע אִוְּתָה־רָע לֹא־יֻחַן בְּעֵינָיו רֵעֵהוּ: 11בַּעֲנָשׁ־לֵץ יֶחְכַּם־פֶּתִי וּבְהַשְׂכִּיל לְחָכָם יִקַּח־דָּעַת: 12מַשְׂכִּיל צַדִּיק לְבֵית רָשָׁע מְסַלֵּף רְשָׁעִים לָרָע: 13אֹטֵם אָזְנוֹ מִזַּעֲקַת־דָּל גַּם־הוּא יִקְרָא וְלֹא יֵעָנֶה: 14מַתָּן בַּסֵּתֶר יִכְפֶּה־אָף וְשֹׁחַד בַּחֵק חֵמָה עַזָּה: 15שִׂמְחָה לַצַּדִּיק עֲשׂוֹת מִשְׁפָּט וּמְחִתָּה לְפֹעֲלֵי אָוֶן: 16אָדָם תּוֹעֶה מִדֶּרֶךְ הַשְׂכֵּל בִּקְהַל רְפָאִים יָנוּחַ:

¹⁵ The exercise of justice is joy for the righteous, But is terror to the workers of iniquity.

¹⁶ A man who wanders from the way of understanding Will rest in the assembly of the dead.

¹⁷ He who loves pleasure *will become* a poor man; He who loves wine and oil will not become rich.

¹⁸ The wicked is a ransom for the righteous, And the treacherous is in the place of the upright.

¹⁹ It is better to live in a desert land Than with a contentious and vexing woman.

²⁰ There is precious treasure and oil in the dwelling of the wise, But a foolish man swallows it up.

²¹ He who pursues righteousness and loyalty Finds life, righteousness and honor.

²² A wise man scales the city of the mighty And brings down the stronghold in which they trust.

²³ He who guards his mouth and his tongue, Guards his soul from troubles.

²⁴ "Proud," "Haughty," "Scoffer," are his names, Who acts with insolent pride.

²⁵ The desire of the sluggard puts him to death, For his hands refuse to work;

²⁶ All day long he is craving, While the righteous gives and does not hold back.

²⁷ The sacrifice of the wicked is an abomination, How much more when he brings it with evil intent!

²⁸ A false witness will perish, But the man who listens *to the truth* will speak forever.

²⁹ A wicked man displays a bold face, But as for the upright, he makes his way sure.

17 אִישׁ מַחְסוֹר אֹהֵב שִׂמְחָה אֹהֵב יַיִן־וָשֶׁמֶן לֹא יַעֲשִׁיר:

18 כֹּפֶר לַצַּדִּיק רָשָׁע וְתַחַת יְשָׁרִים בּוֹגֵד:

19 טוֹב שֶׁבֶת בְּאֶרֶץ־מִדְבָּר מֵאֵשֶׁת (מִדוֹנִים) [מִדְיָנִים] וָכָעַס:

20 אוֹצָר נֶחְמָד וָשֶׁמֶן בִּנְוֵה חָכָם וּכְסִיל אָדָם יְבַלְּעֶנּוּ:

21 רֹדֵף צְדָקָה וָחָסֶד יִמְצָא חַיִּים צְדָקָה וְכָבוֹד:

22 עִיר גִּבֹּרִים עָלָה חָכָם וַיֹּרֶד עֹז מִבְטֶחָה:

23 שֹׁמֵר פִּיו וּלְשׁוֹנוֹ שֹׁמֵר מִצָּרוֹת נַפְשׁוֹ:

24 זֵד יָהִיר לֵץ שְׁמוֹ עוֹשֶׂה בְּעֶבְרַת זָדוֹן:

25 תַּאֲוַת עָצֵל תְּמִיתֶנּוּ כִּי־מֵאֲנוּ יָדָיו לַעֲשׂוֹת:

26 כָּל־הַיּוֹם הִתְאַוָּה תַאֲוָה וְצַדִּיק יִתֵּן וְלֹא יַחְשֹׂךְ:

27 זֶבַח רְשָׁעִים תּוֹעֵבָה אַף כִּי־בְזִמָּה יְבִיאֶנּוּ:

28 עֵד־כְּזָבִים יֹאבֵד וְאִישׁ שׁוֹמֵעַ לָנֶצַח יְדַבֵּר:

29 הֵעֵז אִישׁ רָשָׁע בְּפָנָיו וְיָשָׁר הוּא‪ ‬(יָכִין) [יָבִין] (דְּרָכָיו) [דַּרְכּוֹ]:

30 אֵין חָכְמָה וְאֵין תְּבוּנָה וְאֵין עֵצָה לְנֶגֶד יְהוָה: פ

31 סוּס מוּכָן לְיוֹם מִלְחָמָה וְלַיהוָה הַתְּשׁוּעָה:

³⁰ There is no wisdom and no understanding And no counsel against the LORD. ³¹ The horse is prepared for the day of battle, But victory belongs to the LORD.	

Process of Discovery

Linguistics Section

Linguistic Structure

The king's heart is *like* channels of water in the hand of the LORD; He turns it wherever He wishes.

² Every man's way is right in his own eyes, But the LORD weighs the hearts.

³ To do righteousness and justice Is desired by the LORD more than sacrifice.

⁴ Haughty eyes and a proud heart, The lamp of the wicked, is sin.

⁵ The plans of the diligent *lead* surely to advantage, But everyone who is hasty *comes* surely to poverty.

⁶ The acquisition of treasures by a lying tongue Is a fleeting vapor, the pursuit of death.

⁷ The violence of the wicked will drag them away, Because they refuse to act with justice.

⁸ The way of a guilty man is crooked, But as for the pure, his conduct is upright.

⁹ It is better to live in a corner of a roof Than in a house shared with a contentious woman.

¹⁰ The soul of the wicked desires evil; His neighbor finds no favor in his eyes.

¹¹ When the scoffer is punished, the naive becomes wise; But when the wise is instructed, he receives knowledge.

¹² The righteous one considers the house of the wicked, Turning the wicked to ruin.

¹³ He who shuts his ear to the cry of the poor Will also cry himself and not be answered.

¹⁴ A gift in secret subdues anger, And a bribe in the bosom, strong wrath.

¹⁵ The exercise of justice is joy for the righteous, But is terror to the workers of iniquity.

¹⁶ A man who wanders from the way of understanding Will rest in the assembly of the dead.

¹⁷ He who loves pleasure *will become* a poor man; He who loves wine and oil will not become rich.

¹⁸ The wicked is a ransom for the righteous, And the treacherous is in the place of the upright.

¹⁹ It is better to live in a desert land Than with a contentious and vexing woman.

²⁰ There is precious treasure and oil in the dwelling of the wise, But a foolish man swallows it up.

²¹ He who pursues righteousness and loyalty Finds life, righteousness and honor.

²² A wise man scales the city of the mighty And brings down the stronghold in which they trust.

²³ He who guards his mouth and his tongue, Guards his soul from troubles.

²⁴ "Proud," "Haughty," "Scoffer," are his names, Who acts with insolent pride.

²⁵ The desire of the sluggard puts him to death, For his hands refuse to work;

²⁶ All day long he is craving, While the righteous gives and does not hold back.

[27] The sacrifice of the wicked is an abomination, How much more when he brings it with evil intent!

[28] A false witness will perish, But the man who listens *to the truth* will speak forever.

[29] A wicked man displays a bold face, But as for the upright, he makes his way sure.

[30] There is no wisdom and no understanding And no counsel against the LORD.

[31] The horse is prepared for the day of battle, But victory belongs to the LORD

Discussion

This chapter continues to offer wisdom sayings of King Solomon.

Questioning the Passage

1. What does verse thirty-one mean?

This verse says that a person must not rely on a miracle from the LORD, especially when he/she can take care of the situation.[99]

Culture Section

Questioning the passage

1. What is the lesson in verse nine?

Housing was scarce in the Near East. Many times several families lived in the same house. If the parents were alive, the married and unmarried sons with their families lived in the same house. When a person could not find a place to sleep in the house, the rooftop was used. It was not unusual to see people eating in the streets or holding meetings on the rooftops. The verse means that it is better to remain single and sleep anywhere than to have a quarrelsome wife and live in a spacious home with luxuries.[100]

---

[99] Eliezer Ginsburg and Nosson Scherman, *Mishlei: Proverbs = Mishlei: a New Translation with a Commentary Anthologized from Talmudic, Midrashic and Rabbinic Sources* (Brooklyn, NY: Mesorah, 2003) Volume Two.

[100] Rocco A. Errico and George M. Lamsa, *Aramaic Light on Ezra through the Song of Solomon* (Smyma, GA: Noohra Foundation, 2010).

2. What does verse fourteen mean?

Offering a tribute to a higher authority was called a gift in the Scripture. The land of Judea and Samaria sent gifts to the Kings of Assyria, Babylon, and Egypt to gain favor from them. These larger nations offered protection in exchange for the tribute. However, when the tribute was stopped, they were invaded and taxed more than the original tribute.

3. What does verse twenty mean?

In biblical times treasures were an accumulation of gold, silver, and precious stones. Since banks did not exist, these treasures would be hidden inside the home, buried in a field, or placed in caves. Butter and oil have always been a significant part of the culture of the Near East. Olive oil and butter were used as currency. It is prudent not to spend all your money to have some for a "rainy day."[101]

Thoughts

This chapter contains additional sayings of King Solomon.

---

[101] IBID.

Chapter Twenty-Two

Language

New American Standard 1995	Hebrew
[1] A *good* name is to be more desired than great wealth, Favor is better than silver and gold.	נִבְחָר שֵׁם מֵעֹשֶׁר רָב מִכֶּסֶף וּמִזָּהָב חֵן טוֹב: [2]עָשִׁיר וָרָשׁ נִפְגָּשׁוּ עֹשֵׂה כֻלָּם יְהוָה:
[2] The rich and the poor have a common bond, The LORD is the maker of them all.	[3]עָרוּם רָאָה רָעָה (וְיִסָּתֵר) [וְנִסְתָּר] וּפְתָיִים עָבְרוּ וְנֶעֱנָשׁוּ:
[3] The prudent sees the evil and hides himself, But the naive go on, and are punished for it.	[4]עֵקֶב עֲנָוָה יִרְאַת יְהוָה עֹשֶׁר וְכָבוֹד וְחַיִּים:
[4] The reward of humility *and* the fear of the LORD Are riches, honor and life.	[5]צִנִּים פַּחִים בְּדֶרֶךְ עִקֵּשׁ שׁוֹמֵר נַפְשׁוֹ יִרְחַק מֵהֶם:
[5] Thorns *and* snares are in the way of the perverse; He who guards himself will be far from them.	[6]חֲנֹךְ לַנַּעַר עַל־פִּי דַרְכּוֹ גַּם כִּי־יַזְקִין לֹא־יָסוּר מִמֶּנָּה:
[6] Train up a child in the way he should go, Even when he is old he will not depart from it.	[7]עָשִׁיר בְּרָשִׁים יִמְשׁוֹל וְעֶבֶד לֹוֶה לְאִישׁ מַלְוֶה:
[7] The rich rules over the poor, And the borrower *becomes* the lender's slave.	[8]זוֹרֵעַ עַוְלָה (יִקְצוֹר־) [יִקְצָר־]אָוֶן וְשֵׁבֶט עֶבְרָתוֹ יִכְלֶה:
[8] He who sows iniquity will reap vanity, And the rod of his fury will perish.	[9]טוֹב־עַיִן הוּא יְבֹרָךְ כִּי־נָתַן מִלַּחְמוֹ לַדָּל:
[9] He who is generous will be blessed, For he gives some of his food to the poor.	[10]גָּרֵשׁ לֵץ וְיֵצֵא מָדוֹן וְיִשְׁבֹּת דִּין וְקָלוֹן:
[10] Drive out the scoffer, and contention will go out, Even strife and dishonor will cease.	[11]אֹהֵב (טְהוֹר־) [טְהָר־]לֵב חֵן שְׂפָתָיו רֵעֵהוּ מֶלֶךְ:
[11] He who loves purity of heart *And* whose speech is gracious, the king is his friend.	[12]עֵינֵי יְהוָה נָצְרוּ דָעַת וַיְסַלֵּף דִּבְרֵי בֹגֵד:
[12] The eyes of the LORD preserve knowledge, But He overthrows the words of the treacherous man.	[13]אָמַר עָצֵל אֲרִי בַחוּץ בְּתוֹךְ רְחֹבוֹת אֵרָצֵחַ:
[13] The sluggard says, "There is a lion outside; I will be killed in the streets!"	[14]שׁוּחָה עֲמֻקָּה פִּי זָרוֹת זְעוּם יְהוָה (יִפּוֹל־) [יִפָּל־]שָׁם:
	[15]אִוֶּלֶת קְשׁוּרָה בְלֶב־נָעַר שֵׁבֶט מוּסָר יַרְחִיקֶנָּה מִמֶּנּוּ:
	[16]עֹשֵׁק דָּל לְהַרְבּוֹת לוֹ נֹתֵן לְעָשִׁיר אַךְ־לְמַחְסוֹר:
	[17]הַט אָזְנְךָ וּשְׁמַע דִּבְרֵי חֲכָמִים וְלִבְּךָ תָּשִׁית לְדַעְתִּי:
	[18]כִּי־נָעִים כִּי־תִשְׁמְרֵם בְּבִטְנֶךָ יִכֹּנוּ יַחְדָּו עַל־שְׂפָתֶיךָ:
	[19]לִהְיוֹת בַּיהוָה מִבְטַחֶךָ הוֹדַעְתִּיךָ הַיּוֹם אַף־אָתָּה:
	[20]הֲלֹא כָתַבְתִּי לְךָ (שִׁלְשׁוֹם) [שָׁלִשִׁים] בְּמוֹעֵצֹת וָדָעַת:

¹⁴ The mouth of an adulteress is a deep pit; He who is cursed of the LORD will fall into it.

¹⁵ Foolishness is bound up in the heart of a child; The rod of discipline will remove it far from him.

¹⁶ He who oppresses the poor to make more for himself Or who gives to the rich, *will* only *come to* poverty.

¹⁷ Incline your ear and hear the words of the wise, And apply your mind to my knowledge;

¹⁸ For it will be pleasant if you keep them within you, That they may be ready on your lips.

¹⁹ So that your trust may be in the LORD, I have taught you today, even you.

²⁰ Have I not written to you excellent things Of counsels and knowledge,

²¹ To make you know the certainty of the words of truth That you may correctly answer him who sent you?

²² Do not rob the poor because he is poor, Or crush the afflicted at the gate;

²³ For the LORD will plead their case And take the life of those who rob them.

²⁴ Do not associate with a man *given* to anger; Or go with a hot-tempered man,

²⁵ Or you will learn his ways And find a snare for yourself.

²⁶ Do not be among those who give pledges, Among those who become guarantors for debts.

²⁷ If you have nothing with which to pay, Why should he take your bed from under you?

²⁸ Do not move the ancient boundary Which your fathers have set.

²¹ לְהוֹדִיעֲךָ קֹשְׁטְ אִמְרֵי אֱמֶת לְהָשִׁיב אֲמָרִים אֱמֶת לְשֹׁלְחֶיךָ׃ פ

²² אַל־תִּגְזָל־דָּל כִּי דַל־הוּא וְאַל־תְּדַכֵּא עָנִי בַשָּׁעַר׃

²³ כִּי־יְהוָה יָרִיב רִיבָם וְקָבַע אֶת־קֹבְעֵיהֶם נָפֶשׁ׃

²⁴ אַל־תִּתְרַע אֶת־בַּעַל אָף וְאֶת־אִישׁ חֵמוֹת לֹא תָבוֹא׃

²⁵ פֶּן־תֶּאֱלַף (אֹרְחָתוֹ) [אֹרְחֹתָיו] וְלָקַחְתָּ מוֹקֵשׁ לְנַפְשֶׁךָ׃

²⁶ אַל־תְּהִי בְתֹקְעֵי־כָף בַּעֹרְבִים מַשָּׁאוֹת׃

²⁷ אִם־אֵין־לְךָ לְשַׁלֵּם לָמָּה יִקַּח מִשְׁכָּבְךָ מִתַּחְתֶּיךָ׃

²⁸ אַל־תַּסֵּג גְּבוּל עוֹלָם אֲשֶׁר עָשׂוּ אֲבוֹתֶיךָ׃

²⁹ חָזִיתָ אִישׁ מָהִיר בִּמְלַאכְתּוֹ לִפְנֵי־מְלָכִים יִתְיַצָּב בַּל־יִתְיַצֵּב לִפְנֵי חֲשֻׁכִּים׃ פ

[29] Do you see a man skilled in his work? He will stand before kings; He will not stand before obscure men.	

Process of Discovery

Linguistics Section

Linguistic Structure

[1] A *good* name is to be more desired than great wealth, Favor is better than silver and gold.

[2] The rich and the poor have a common bond, The LORD is the maker of them all.

[3] The prudent sees the evil and hides himself, But the naive go on, and are punished for it.

[4] The reward of humility *and* the fear of the LORD Are riches, honor and life.

[5] Thorns *and* snares are in the way of the perverse; He who guards himself will be far from them.

[6] Train up a child in the way he should go, Even when he is old he will not depart from it.

[7] The rich rules over the poor, And the borrower *becomes* the lender's slave.

[8] He who sows iniquity will reap vanity, And the rod of his fury will perish.

[9] He who is generous will be blessed, For he gives some of his food to the poor.

[10] Drive out the scoffer, and contention will go out, Even strife and dishonor will cease.

[11] He who loves purity of heart *And* whose speech is gracious, the king is his friend.

[12] The eyes of the LORD preserve knowledge, But He overthrows the words of the treacherous man.

[13] The sluggard says, "There is a lion outside; I will be killed in the streets!"

[14] The mouth of an adulteress is a deep pit; He who is cursed of the LORD will fall into it.

[15] Foolishness is bound up in the heart of a child; The rod of discipline will remove it far from him.

[16] He who oppresses the poor to make more for himself Or who gives to the rich, *will* only *come to* poverty.

[17] Incline your ear and hear the words of the wise, And apply your mind to my knowledge; [18] For it will be pleasant if you keep them within you, That they may be ready on your lips.

[19] So that your trust may be in the LORD, I have taught you today, even you.

[20] Have I not written to you excellent things Of counsels and knowledge, [21] To make you know the certainty of the words of truth That you may correctly answer him who sent you?

[22] Do not rob the poor because he is poor, Or crush the afflicted at the gate;

[23] For the LORD will plead their case And take the life of those who rob them.

[24] Do not associate with a man *given* to anger; Or go with a hot-tempered man, [25] Or you will learn his ways And find a snare for yourself.

[26] Do not be among those who give pledges, Among those who become guarantors for debts.

[27] If you have nothing with which to pay, Why should he take your bed from under you?

[28] Do not move the ancient boundary Which your fathers have set.

[29] Do you see a man skilled in his work? He will stand before kings; He will not stand before obscure men.

Discussion

These are more sayings of King Solomon.

Questioning the Passage

1. What are the ways of thorns and snares? (v. 5)

    This verse says that a person who looks for a short cut to riches and honor will not find it. Instead, the person will find that the road they selected is filled with difficulties that would not have been experienced if they traveled on the known path to success.[102]

2. What is the "rod of his fury?" (v. 8)

    An equivalent saying today is "what goes around comes around." A person who cheats other persons will one day find themselves on the receiving end. If a person is rude and obnoxious during their life, the person will find in old age that no one wants to talk or deal with him/her.

---

[102] Eliezer Ginsburg and Nosson Scherman, *Mishlei: Proverbs = Mishlei: a New Translation with a Commentary Anthologized from Talmudic, Midrashic and Rabbinic Sources* (Brooklyn, NY: Mesorah, 2003) Volume Two.

3. What does verse thirteen mean?"

    This verse demonstrates that a lazy person will come up with ridiculous excuses so that he/she does not have to work.

4. What is the meaning of verses seventeen and eighteen?

    The Sage Alshich said that this verse answers a fundamental question about the Torah. Why did the oral Torah have to be transmitted orally originally? Would it not have been better to have had it written down immediately?[103] Eventually, it was written down. This writing is called the Mishnah.

    The Sage Rashi said that a person could guard his/her wisdom so that he/she will not forget it by speaking the words aloud.[104]

5. What does verse twenty-three mean?

    It was believed that the LORD decides who will be poor. Therefore, anyone who mocks or robs the poor is, in essence, insulting the LORD. The LORD can then reverse the fortunes of the robber, giving the fortune to a poor person.

Thoughts

This chapter contains more sayings of King Solomon.

---

[103] IBID.
[104] IBID.

Chapter Twenty-Three

Language

New American Standard 1995	Hebrew
[1] When you sit down to dine with a ruler, Consider carefully what is before you,

3ךְ אִם־בַּעַל נֶפֶשׁ אָתָּה: אַל־תִּתְאָו

לְמַטְעַמּוֹתָיו וְהוּא לֶחֶם כְּזָבִים:

4אַל־תִּיגַע לְהַעֲשִׁיר מִבִּינָתְךָ חֲדָל:

5(הֲתָעוּף) [הֲתָעִיף] עֵינֶיךָ בּוֹ וְאֵינֶנּוּ כִּי

עָשֹׂה יַעֲשֶׂה־לּוֹ כְנָפַיִם כְּנֶשֶׁר (וְעָיֵף) [יָעוּף]

הַשָּׁמָיִם פ

6אַל־תִּלְחַם אֶת־לֶחֶם רַע עָיִן וְאַל־(תִּתְאָו)

[תִּתְאָיו] לְמַטְעַמֹּתָיו:

7כִּי כְּמוֹ־שָׁעַר בְּנַפְשׁוֹ כֶּן־הוּא אֱכֹל וּשְׁתֵה

יֹאמַר לָךְ וְלִבּוֹ בַּל־עִמָּךְ:

8פִּתְּךָ־אָכַלְתָּ תְקִיאֶנָּה וְשִׁחַתָּ דְּבָרֶיךָ

הַנְּעִימִים:

9בְּאָזְנֵי כְסִיל אַל־תְּדַבֵּר כִּי־יָבוּז לְשֵׂכֶל

מִלֶּיךָ:

10אַל־תַּסֵּג גְּבוּל עוֹלָם וּבִשְׂדֵי יְתוֹמִים אַל־

תָּבֹא:

11כִּי־גֹאֲלָם חָזָק הוּא־יָרִיב אֶת־רִיבָם אִתָּךְ:

12הָבִיאָה לַמּוּסָר לִבֶּךָ וְאָזְנֶךָ לְאִמְרֵי־דָעַת:

13אַל־תִּמְנַע מִנַּעַר מוּסָר כִּי־תַכֶּנּוּ בַשֵּׁבֶט

לֹא יָמוּת:

14אַתָּה בַּשֵּׁבֶט תַּכֶּנּוּ וְנַפְשׁוֹ מִשְּׁאוֹל תַּצִּיל:

15בְּנִי אִם־חָכַם לִבֶּךָ יִשְׂמַח לִבִּי גַם־אָנִי:

16וְתַעְלֹזְנָה כִלְיוֹתָי בְּדַבֵּר שְׂפָתֶיךָ מֵישָׁרִים:

17אַל־יְקַנֵּא לִבְּךָ בַּחַטָּאִים כִּי אִם־בְּיִרְאַת־

יְהֹוָה כָּל־הַיּוֹם:

18כִּי אִם־יֵשׁ אַחֲרִית וְתִקְוָתְךָ לֹא תִכָּרֵת:

19שְׁמַע־אַתָּה בְּנִי וַחֲכָם וְאַשֵּׁר בַּדֶּרֶךְ לִבֶּךָ:

20אַל־תְּהִי בְסֹבְאֵי־יָיִן בְּזֹלֲלֵי בָשָׂר לָמוֹ:

21כִּי־סֹבֵא וְזוֹלֵל יִוָּרֵשׁ וּקְרָעִים תַּלְבִּישׁ

נוּמָה:

22שְׁמַע לְאָבִיךָ זֶה יְלָדֶךָ וְאַל־תָּבוּז כִּי־זָקְנָה

אִמֶּךָ:

23אֱמֶת קְנֵה וְאַל־תִּמְכֹּר חָכְמָה וּמוּסָר

וּבִינָה:

 |
[2] And put a knife to your throat If you are a man of *great* appetite.	
[3] Do not desire his delicacies, For it is deceptive food.	
[4] Do not weary yourself to gain wealth, Cease from your consideration *of it*.	
[5] When you set your eyes on it, it is gone. For *wealth* certainly makes itself wings Like an eagle that flies *toward* the heavens.	
[6] Do not eat the bread of a selfish man, Or desire his delicacies;	
[7] For as he thinks within himself, so he is. He says to you, "Eat and drink!" But his heart is not with you.	
[8] You will vomit up the morsel you have eaten, And waste your compliments.	
[9] Do not speak in the hearing of a fool, For he will despise the wisdom of your words.	
[10] Do not move the ancient boundary Or go into the fields of the fatherless,	
[11] For their Redeemer is strong; He will plead their case against you.	
[12] Apply your heart to discipline And your ears to words of knowledge.	
[13] Do not hold back discipline from the child, Although you strike him with the rod, he will not die.	
[14] You shall strike him with the rod And rescue his soul from Sheol.	
[15] My son, if your heart is wise, My own heart also will be glad;	
[16] And my inmost being will rejoice When your lips speak what is right.	

¹⁷ Do not let your heart envy sinners, But *live* in the fear of the LORD always.

¹⁸ Surely there is a future, And your hope will not be cut off.

¹⁹ Listen, my son, and be wise, And direct your heart in the way.

²⁰ Do not be with heavy drinkers of wine, *Or* with gluttonous eaters of meat;

²¹ For the heavy drinker and the glutton will come to poverty, And drowsiness will clothe *one* with rags.

²² Listen to your father who begot you, And do not despise your mother when she is old.

²³ Buy truth, and do not sell *it, Get* wisdom and instruction and understanding.

²⁴ The father of the righteous will greatly rejoice, And he who sires a wise son will be glad in him.

²⁵ Let your father and your mother be glad, And let her rejoice who gave birth to you.

²⁶ Give me your heart, my son, And let your eyes delight in my ways.

²⁷ For a harlot is a deep pit And an adulterous woman is a narrow well.

²⁸ Surely she lurks as a robber, And increases the faithless among men.

²⁹ Who has woe? Who has sorrow? Who has contentions? Who has complaining? Who has wounds without cause? Who has redness of eyes?

³⁰ Those who linger long over wine, Those who go to taste mixed wine.

³¹ Do not look on the wine when it is red, When it sparkles in the cup, When it goes down smoothly;

³² At the last it bites like a serpent And stings like a viper.

---

24 (גּוֹל) [גִּיל] (יָגוֹל) [יָגִיל] אֲבִי צַדֵּיק (יוֹלֵד) [וְיוֹלֵד] חָכָם (וְיִשְׂמַח־)[יִשְׂמַח־]בּֽוֹ:

25 יִשְׂמַח־אָבִיךָ וְאִמֶּךָ וְתָגֵל יֽוֹלַדְתֶּֽךָ:

26 תְּנָה־בְנִי לִבְּךָ לִי וְעֵינֶיךָ דְּרָכַי (תִּרְצֶנָה) [תִּצֹּֽרְנָה]:

27 כִּי־שׁוּחָה עֲמֻקָּה זוֹנָה וּבְאֵר צָרָה נָכְרִיָּֽה:

28 אַף־הִיא כְּחֶתֶף תֶּאֱרֹב וּבוֹגְדִים בְּאָדָם תּוֹסִֽף:

29 לְמִי אוֹי לְמִי אֲבוֹי לְמִי (מדונים) [מִדְיָנִים] לְמִי שִׂיחַ לְמִי פְּצָעִים חִנָּם לְמִי חַכְלִלוּת עֵינָֽיִם:

30 לַמְאַחֲרִים עַל־הַיָּיִן לַבָּאִים לַחְקֹר מִמְסָֽךְ:

31 אַל־תֵּרֶא יַיִן כִּי יִתְאַדָּם כִּי־יִתֵּן (בכיס) [בַּכּוֹס] עֵינוֹ יִתְהַלֵּךְ בְּמֵישָׁרִֽים:

32 אַחֲרִיתוֹ כְּנָחָשׁ יִשָּׁךְ וּֽכְצִפְעֹנִי יַפְרִֽשׁ:

33 עֵינֶיךָ יִרְאוּ זָרוֹת וְלִבְּךָ יְדַבֵּר תַּהְפֻּכֽוֹת:

34 וְהָיִיתָ כְּשֹׁכֵב בְּלֶב־יָם וּֽכְשֹׁכֵב בְּרֹאשׁ חִבֵּֽל:

35 הִכּוּנִי בַל־חָלִיתִי הֲלָמוּנִי בַּל־יָדָעְתִּי מָתַי אָקִיץ אוֹסִיף אֲבַקְשֶׁנּוּ עֽוֹד:

<table>
<tr><td>

³³ Your eyes will see strange things And your mind will utter perverse things.

³⁴ And you will be like one who lies down in the middle of the sea, Or like one who lies down on the top of a mast.

³⁵ "They struck me, *but* I did not become ill; They beat me, *but* I did not know *it*. When shall I awake? I will seek another drink."

</td><td></td></tr>
</table>

Process of Discovery

Linguistics Section

Linguistic Structure

[1] When you sit down to dine with a ruler, Consider carefully what is before you, [2] And put a knife to your throat If you are a man of *great* appetite. [3] Do not desire his delicacies, For it is deceptive food.

[4] Do not weary yourself to gain wealth, Cease from your consideration *of it*. [5] When you set your eyes on it, it is gone. For *wealth* certainly makes itself wings Like an eagle that flies *toward* the heavens.

[6] Do not eat the bread of a selfish man, Or desire his delicacies; [7] For as he thinks within himself, so he is. He says to you, "Eat and drink!" But his heart is not with you. [8] You will vomit up the morsel you have eaten, And waste your compliments.

[9] Do not speak in the hearing of a fool, For he will despise the wisdom of your words.

[10] Do not move the ancient boundary Or go into the fields of the fatherless, [11] For their Redeemer is strong; He will plead their case against you.

[12] Apply your heart to discipline And your ears to words of knowledge.

[13] Do not hold back discipline from the child, Although you strike him with the rod, he will not die. [14] You shall strike him with the rod And rescue his soul from Sheol.

[15] My son, if your heart is wise, My own heart also will be glad; [16] And my inmost being will rejoice When your lips speak what is right.

[17] Do not let your heart envy sinners, But *live* in the fear of the LORD always. [18] Surely there is a future, And your hope will not be cut off. [19] Listen, my son, and be wise, And direct your heart in the way.

[20] Do not be with heavy drinkers of wine, *Or* with gluttonous eaters of meat; [21] For the heavy drinker and the glutton will come to poverty, And drowsiness will clothe *one* with rags.

[22] Listen to your father who begot you, And do not despise your mother when she is old.

[23] Buy truth, and do not sell *it*, *Get* wisdom and instruction and understanding.

[24] The father of the righteous will greatly rejoice, And he who sires a wise son will be glad in him.

[25] Let your father and your mother be glad, And let her rejoice who gave birth to you.

[26] Give me your heart, my son, And let your eyes delight in my ways.

[27] For a harlot is a deep pit And an adulterous woman is a narrow well. [28] Surely she lurks as a robber, And increases the faithless among men.

[29] Who has woe? Who has sorrow? Who has contentions? Who has complaining? Who has wounds without cause? Who has redness of eyes? [30] Those who linger long over wine, Those who go to taste mixed wine.

[31] Do not look on the wine when it is red, When it sparkles in the cup, When it goes down smoothly; [32] At the last it bites like a serpent And stings like a viper.

[33] Your eyes will see strange things And your mind will utter perverse things.

[34] And you will be like one who lies down in the middle of the sea, Or like one who lies down on the top of a mast.

[35] "They struck me, *but* I did not become ill; They beat me, *but* I did not know *it*. When shall I awake? I will seek another drink."

Discussion

This chapter contains additional sayings from King Solomon.

Questioning the Passage

1. What does a redeemer do? (v. 11)

    A redeemer is a person who extricates a close relative from financial distress (Leviticus 25:25). An example is when Boaz helped Ruth.

    Lev. 25:25 'If a fellow countryman of yours becomes so poor he has to sell part of his property, then his nearest kinsman is to come and buy back what his relative has sold.

Phrase Study

1. רַע עָיִן (v. 6) - this phrase means "evil eye." In the New American Standard 1995 Bible it is translated as "selfish." In the Targum used the translation "evil eye."

   The concept of the evil eye is: "The superstition of the influence of the "evil eye," so widely spread over the earth, has had a mighty influence on life and language in Palestine, though direct references to it are not frequent in the Scriptures (Deuteronomy 15:9; Deuteronomy 28:54, 56 Proverbs 23:6; Proverbs 28:22 Matthew 20:15 (compare Matthew 6:23 Luke 11:34); Mark 7:22). In the Bible the expression is synonymous with envy, jealousy and some forms of covetousness. In comparing Romans 1:29 with Mark 7:22 we find that ophthalmos poneros corresponds to phthonos. See Trench, New Testament Synonyms, under the word The eye of the envious (as also the tongue of the invidious by an apparently appreciative word, which, however, only disguises the strong desire of possessing the object of comment or of destroying it for its rightful owner) was supposed to have a baneful influence upon the wellbeing of others, especially of children. Therefore mothers bestowed constant care against the frustration of such fancied designs by means of innumerable sorts of charms. They often allowed their darlings to appear as unlovely as possible, through uncleanliness or rags, so as to spare them the harmful rising of envy in the hearts of others."[105]

---

[105] Topical Bible: Evil Eye, accessed November 26, 2020, https://biblehub.com/topical/e/evil_eye.htm.

2. גָּאַל *(gō'ēl)* I, redeemer. (v. 11)

"The participial from of the Qal stem of the verb has practically become a noun in its own right though it may properly be considered as merely a form of the verb.

The primary meaning of this root is to do the part of a kinsman and thus to redeem his kin from difficulty or danger. It is used with its derivatives 118 times. One difference between this root and the very similar root פָּדָה "redeem," is that there is usually an emphasis in גָּאַל on the redemption being the privilege or duty of a near relative. The participial form of the Qal stem has indeed been translated by some as "kinsman-redeemer" or as in KJV merely "kinsman." The root is to be distinguished from גָּאַל II, "defile" (which see).

The root is used in four basic situations covering the things a good and true man would do for his kinsman. First, it is used in the Pentateuchal legislation to refer to the repurchase of a field which was sold in time of need (Lev 25:25 ff.), or the freeing of an Israelite slave who sold himself in time of poverty (25:48ff.). Such purchase and restitution was the duty of the next of kin. Secondly, but associated with this usage was the "redemption" of property or non-sacrificial animals dedicated to the Lord, or the redemption of the firstborn of unclean animals (27:11ff.). The idea was that a man could give an equivalent to the Lord in exchange, but the redemption price was to be a bit extra to avoid dishonest exchanges. In these cases, the redeemer was not a relative, but the owner of the property.

Thirdly, the root is used to refer to the next of kin who is the "avenger of blood" (RSV "revenger") for a murdered man. The full phrase "avenger of blood" is almost always used (cf. Num. 35:12ff.). Apparently the idea is that the next of kin must effect the payment of life for life. As a house is repurchased or a slave redeemed by payment, so the lost life of the relative must be paid for by the equivalent life of the murderer. The kinsman is the avenger of blood. This system of execution must be distinguished from blood feuds for the גֹּאֵל was a guiltless executioner and not to be murdered in turn.

Finally, there is the very common usage prominent in the Psalms and prophets that God is Israel's Redeemer who will stand up for his people and vindicate them. There may be a hint of the Father's near kinship or ownership in the use of this word. A redemption price is not usually cited, though the idea of judgment on Israel's oppressors as a ransom is included in Isa 43:1–3. God, as it were, redeems his sons from a bondage worse than slavery.

Perhaps the best known instance of redemption of the poor is in the book of Ruth which is the most extensive OT witness for the law of levirate marriage. According to Deut 25:5–10, a widow without issue should be taken by her husband's brother to perpetuate seed and thus insure the succession of the land which was bound to the male descendants. The near relative here is called a יָבָם. The root גָּאַל is not used. In the situation in Ruth two things are mentioned, the field and the levirate marriage. The near kin was willing to buy the field, but not to marry Ruth.

The point is that when Naomi in her poverty had to sell the field the next of kin was obligated to buy it back for her. This he was willing to do for his brother's widow without issue. The land would presumably revert to him anyway at last. When he learned that he must marry Ruth and raise children who would maintain their inheritance, he refused and Boaz stepped in. But the two things, kinsman redemption and levirate marriage, are to be distinguished. The word גֹּאֵל "redeemer," does not refer to the latter institution.

In the famous verse Job 19:25 the word גֹּאֵל is translated "redeemer" in the AV and some have taken it to refer to the coming of Christ in his work of atonement. This would be expressed more characteristically by the Hebrew word פָּדָה (which see). This word in 19:25 is now more accurately referred to the work of God who as friend and kinsman through faith will [Vol. 1, p. 145] ultimately redeem Job from the dust of death. The enigmatic "after my skin" of v. 26 could well be read with different vowels "after I awake" (see NIV footnote and 14:12–14 where Job's question about resurrection is climaxed by his hope that God will have regard for him at last and that Job like a tree will have a second growth- חֲלִיפָה, v. 14, which answers to the חָלַף of v. 7). In any case Job expects with his own eyes to see God his גֹּאֵל at last.

Bibliography: A. R. Johnson, "The Primary Meaning of the Root *g'l*," Supp VT 1: 67–77. AI, 11–12, 21–23. Leggett, Donald A., *The Levirate Goel*

Institutions in the OT, Presbyterian & Reformed Press. TDOT, II, pp. 350–55."[106]

Culture Section

Questioning the passage

1. What does the Proverb in verses 1 through 3 mean?

   The "knife" in this verse is used allegorically to mean "poison." When Near Eastern people eat something that tasted bad or was poisonous, they said, "It cuts me like a knife." Drinking poison injures the throat of the victim who consumes it. Enemies were often killed by using poison. An elaborate banquet was held, and the guest of honor was the person who was to be poisoned. People who could afford it hired taste testers to try all the presented food and wine. Before eating or drinking, the person would secretly examine the food and drink before ingesting it.

   Poisoning was an old Eastern custom to do away with one's enemies. Alexander the Great was poisoned at a banquet in Babylon. Muhammad was poisoned by a woman whose relatives were slain in battle against him.

   When Yeshua prayed to the LORD before His arrest, he asked for the cup to pass away from him (Matthew 26:39). The term "cup" became symbolical for treachery because of the custom of poisoning enemies. The Temple leadership's treachery was about to happen and led Yeshua to the cross and death. The corruption in the Temple leadership, along with the Roman

---

[106] R. Laird Harris, Gleason L. Archer, and Bruce K. Waltke, *Theological Wordbook of the Old Testament* (Chicago: Moody Press, 2004).

overlords, caused Yeshua's death. What happened to Yeshua was equivalent to His drinking a cup of wine with poison.[107]

2. What do verses six and seven mean?

Some wicked people planned evil acts at a table during meals. Many times the person they wanted to snare was the guest. They held lavish banquets and entertainment, and all the while, they were plotting. This proverb connects to verse two about poisoning an honored guest. The NASB uses the translation of "selfish." The Hebrew says, "evil eye." A person with the evil eye is usually plotting evil.

3. What does it mean to vomit up the morsel? (v. 8)

"Vomit up" is an Eastern Idiom that means that the person will pay for something by force or fraudulent means. To eat something that has the evil eye means to put the person in extreme danger.[108]

4. What does verse twenty-seven mean?

A pit was used in biblical times as a trap. A man would be lowered into a pit so that he could not escape. Joseph's brothers placed him in a pit until they decided to sell him as a slave. The adulterous woman, harlots, were any woman who was not the man's wife. Prostitutes are likened to a narrow pit because it is simple to get away from her because there was no emotional investment. The harlot is a deep pit because it is difficult to leave her. After all, the man usually falls in love with her.

---

[107] Rocco A. Errico and George M. Lamsa, *Aramaic Light on Ezra through the Song of Solomon* (Smyma, GA: Noohra Foundation, 2010).
[108] IBID.

5. What does "red eyes" symbolize? (v. 29)

   Red eyes symbolize drunkenness. It can also symbolize material prosperity. Drunkenness can bring about trouble because a drunk often loses control of their words and actions.

6. What is the significance of red wine? (v. 31)

   Red wine was rare in the Near East. Red grapes were scarce. White wine was abundant. Red wine was expensive and difficult to obtain. The desire to have red wine could make people do things that they normally would not do. It is a warning against allowing the flesh to control the soul.

7. What does it mean to lie down in the middle of the sea? (v. 34)

   This phrase is an Eastern idiom, that means the person is lost or does not know what he/she is doing. This usually occurs from drunkenness. The warning is against drinking too much.[109]

Thoughts

This chapter is another list of wisdom from King Solomon.

---

[109] IBID.

Chapter Twenty-Four

Language

New American Standard 1995	Hebrew
[1] Do not be envious of evil men, Nor desire to be with them; [2] For their minds devise violence, And their lips talk of trouble. [3] By wisdom a house is built, And by understanding it is established; [4] And by knowledge the rooms are filled With all precious and pleasant riches. [5] A wise man is strong, And a man of knowledge increases power. [6] For by wise guidance you will wage war, And in abundance of counselors there is victory. [7] Wisdom is *too* exalted for a fool, He does not open his mouth in the gate. [8] One who plans to do evil, Men will call a schemer. [9] The devising of folly is sin, And the scoffer is an abomination to men. [10] If you are slack in the day of distress, Your strength is limited. [11] Deliver those who are being taken away to death, And those who are staggering to slaughter, Oh hold *them* back. [12] If you say, "See, we did not know this," Does He not consider *it* who weighs the hearts? And does He not know *it* who keeps your soul? And will He not render to man according to his work? [13] My son, eat honey, for it is good, Yes, the honey from the comb is sweet to your taste;	אַל־תְּקַנֵּא בְּאַנְשֵׁי רָעָה וְאַל־(תִּתְאָו) [תִּתְאָיו] לִהְיוֹת אִתָּם: [2]כִּי־שֹׁד יֶהְגֶּה לִבָּם וְעָמָל שִׂפְתֵיהֶם תְּדַבֵּרְנָה: [3]בְּחָכְמָה יִבָּנֶה בָּיִת וּבִתְבוּנָה יִתְכּוֹנָן: [4]וּבְדַעַת חֲדָרִים יִמָּלְאוּ כָּל־הוֹן יָקָר וְנָעִים: [5]גֶּבֶר־חָכָם בַּעוֹז וְאִישׁ־דַּעַת מְאַמֶּץ־כֹּחַ: [6]כִּי בְתַחְבֻּלוֹת תַּעֲשֶׂה־לְּךָ מִלְחָמָה וּתְשׁוּעָה בְּרֹב יוֹעֵץ: [7]רָאמוֹת לֶאֱוִיל חָכְמוֹת בַּשַּׁעַר לֹא יִפְתַּח־פִּיהוּ: [8]מְחַשֵּׁב לְהָרֵעַ לוֹ בַּעַל־מְזִמּוֹת יִקְרָאוּ: [9]זִמַּת אִוֶּלֶת חַטָּאת וְתוֹעֲבַת לְאָדָם לֵץ: [10]הִתְרַפִּיתָ בְּיוֹם צָרָה צַר כֹּחֶכָה: [11]הַצֵּל לְקֻחִים לַמָּוֶת וּמָטִים לַהֶרֶג אִם־תַּחְשׂוֹךְ: [12]כִּי־תֹאמַר הֵן לֹא־יָדַעְנוּ זֶה הֲלֹא־תֹכֵן לִבּוֹת הוּא־יָבִין וְנֹצֵר נַפְשְׁךָ הוּא יֵדָע וְהֵשִׁיב לְאָדָם כְּפָעֳלוֹ: [13]אֱכָל־בְּנִי דְבַשׁ כִּי־טוֹב וְנֹפֶת מָתוֹק עַל־חִכֶּךָ: [14]כֵּן דְּעֶה חָכְמָה לְנַפְשֶׁךָ אִם־מָצָאתָ וְיֵשׁ אַחֲרִית וְתִקְוָתְךָ לֹא תִכָּרֵת: פ [15]אַל־תֶּאֱרֹב רָשָׁע לִנְוֵה צַדִּיק אַל־תְּשַׁדֵּד רִבְצוֹ:

¹⁴ Know *that* wisdom is thus for your soul; If you find *it*, then there will be a future, And your hope will not be cut off.

¹⁵ Do not lie in wait, O wicked man, against the dwelling of the righteous; Do not destroy his resting place;

¹⁶ For a righteous man falls seven times, and rises again, But the wicked stumble in *time of* calamity.

¹⁷ Do not rejoice when your enemy falls, And do not let your heart be glad when he stumbles;

¹⁸ Or the LORD will see *it* and be displeased, And turn His anger away from him.

¹⁹ Do not fret because of evildoers Or be envious of the wicked;

²⁰ For there will be no future for the evil man; The lamp of the wicked will be put out.

²¹ My son, fear the LORD and the king; Do not associate with those who are given to change,

²² For their calamity will rise suddenly, And who knows the ruin *that comes* from both of them?

²³ These also are sayings of the wise. To show partiality in judgment is not good.

²⁴ He who says to the wicked, "You are righteous," Peoples will curse him, nations will abhor him;

²⁵ But to those who rebuke the *wicked* will be delight, And a good blessing will come upon them.

²⁶ He kisses the lips Who gives a right answer.

²⁷ Prepare your work outside And make it ready for yourself in the field; Afterwards, then, build your house.

כִּי שֶׁבַע ׀ יִפּוֹל צַדִּיק וָקָם וּרְשָׁעִים יִכָּשְׁלוּ בְרָעָה: ¹⁶

בִּנְפֹל (אוֹיִבֶיךָ) [אֽוֹיִבְךָ] אַל־תִּשְׂמָח וּבִכָּשְׁלוֹ אַל־יָגֵל לִבֶּךָ: ¹⁷

פֶּן־יִרְאֶה יְהוָה וְרַע בְּעֵינָיו וְהֵשִׁיב מֵעָלָיו אַפּוֹ: ¹⁸

אַל־תִּתְחַר בַּמְּרֵעִים אַל־תְּקַנֵּא בָּרְשָׁעִים: ¹⁹

כִּי ׀ לֹא־תִהְיֶה אַחֲרִית לָרָע נֵר רְשָׁעִים יִדְעָךְ: ²⁰

יְרָא־אֶת־יְהוָה בְּנִי וָמֶלֶךְ עִם־שׁוֹנִים אַל־תִּתְעָרָב: ²¹

כִּי־פִתְאֹם יָקוּם אֵידָם וּפִיד שְׁנֵיהֶם מִי יוֹדֵעַ: ס ²²

גַּם־אֵלֶּה לַחֲכָמִים הַכֵּר־פָּנִים בְּמִשְׁפָּט בַּל־טוֹב: ²³

אֹמֵר ׀ לְרָשָׁע צַדִּיק אָתָּה יִקְּבֻהוּ עַמִּים יִזְעָמוּהוּ לְאֻמִּים: ²⁴

וְלַמּוֹכִיחִים יִנְעָם וַעֲלֵיהֶם תָּבוֹא בִרְכַּת־טוֹב: ²⁵

שְׂפָתַיִם יִשָּׁק מֵשִׁיב דְּבָרִים נְכֹחִים: ²⁶

הָכֵן בַּחוּץ ׀ מְלַאכְתֶּךָ וְעַתְּדָהּ בַּשָּׂדֶה לָךְ אַחַר וּבָנִיתָ בֵיתֶךָ: פ ²⁷

אַל־תְּהִי עֵד־חִנָּם בְּרֵעֶךָ וַהֲפִתִּיתָ בִּשְׂפָתֶיךָ: ²⁸

אַל־תֹּאמַר כַּאֲשֶׁר עָשָׂה־לִי כֵּן אֶעֱשֶׂה־לּוֹ אָשִׁיב לָאִישׁ כְּפָעֳלוֹ: ²⁹

עַל־שְׂדֵה אִישׁ־עָצֵל עָבַרְתִּי וְעַל־כֶּרֶם אָדָם חֲסַר־לֵב: ³⁰

וְהִנֵּה עָלָה כֻלּוֹ ׀ קִמְּשֹׂנִים כָּסּוּ פָנָיו חֲרֻלִּים וְגֶדֶר אֲבָנָיו נֶהֱרָסָה: ³¹

וָאֶחֱזֶה אָנֹכִי אָשִׁית לִבִּי רָאִיתִי לָקַחְתִּי מוּסָר: ³²

[28] Do not be a witness against your neighbor without cause, And do not deceive with your lips.

[29] Do not say, "Thus I shall do to him as he has done to me; I will render to the man according to his work."

[30] I passed by the field of the sluggard And by the vineyard of the man lacking sense,

[31] And behold, it was completely overgrown with thistles; Its surface was covered with nettles, And its stone wall was broken down.

[32] When I saw, I reflected upon it; I looked, *and* received instruction.

[33] "A little sleep, a little slumber, A little folding of the hands to rest,"

[34] Then your poverty will come *as* a robber And your want like an armed man.

מְעַט שֵׁנוֹת מְעַט תְּנוּמוֹת מְעַט| [33]
חִבֻּק יָדַיִם לִשְׁכָּב:
וּבָא־מִתְהַלֵּךְ רֵישֶׁךָ וּמַחְסֹרֶיךָ כְּאִישׁ [34]
מָגֵן: פ

Process of Discovery

Linguistics Section

Linguistic Structure

[1] Do not be envious of evil men, Nor desire to be with them;[2] For their minds devise violence, And their lips talk of trouble.

[3] By wisdom a house is built, And by understanding it is established; [4] And by knowledge the rooms are filled With all precious and pleasant riches.

[5] A wise man is strong, And a man of knowledge increases power.
[6] For by wise guidance you will wage war, And in abundance of counselors there is victory.
[7] Wisdom is *too* exalted for a fool, He does not open his mouth in the gate.
[8] One who plans to do evil, Men will call a schemer.
[9] The devising of folly is sin, And the scoffer is an abomination to men.
[10] If you are slack in the day of distress, Your strength is limited.
[11] Deliver those who are being taken away to death, And those who are staggering to slaughter, Oh hold *them* back.
[12] If you say, "See, we did not know this," Does He not consider *it* who weighs the hearts? And does He not know *it* who keeps your soul? And will He not render to man according to his work?

[13] My son, eat honey, for it is good, Yes, the honey from the comb is sweet to your taste; [14] Know *that* wisdom is thus for your soul; If you find *it*, then there will be a future, And your hope will not be cut off.

[15] Do not lie in wait, O wicked man, against the dwelling of the righteous; Do not destroy his resting place; [16] For a righteous man falls seven times, and rises again, But the wicked stumble in *time of* calamity.

[17] Do not rejoice when your enemy falls, And do not let your heart be glad when he stumbles; [18] Or the LORD will see *it* and be displeased, And turn His anger away from him.

[19] Do not fret because of evildoers Or be envious of the wicked; [20] For there will be no future for the evil man; The lamp of the wicked will be put out.

[21] My son, fear the LORD and the king; Do not associate with those who are given to change, [22] For their calamity will rise suddenly, And who knows the ruin *that comes* from both of them?

[23] These also are sayings of the wise. To show partiality in judgment is not good.

[24] He who says to the wicked, "You are righteous," Peoples will curse him, nations will abhor him; [25] But to those who rebuke the *wicked* will be delight, And a good blessing will come upon them.

[26] He kisses the lips Who gives a right answer.
[27] Prepare your work outside And make it ready for yourself in the field; Afterwards, then, build your house.
[28] Do not be a witness against your neighbor without cause, And do not deceive with your lips.
[29] Do not say, "Thus I shall do to him as he has done to me; I will render to the man according to his work."

[30] I passed by the field of the sluggard And by the vineyard of the man lacking sense, [31] And behold, it was completely overgrown with thistles; Its surface was covered with nettles, And its stone wall was broken down.

[32] When I saw, I reflected upon it; I looked, *and* received instruction.

[33] "A little sleep, a little slumber, A little folding of the hands to rest," [34] Then your poverty will come *as* a robber And your want like an armed man.

Discussion

This chapter contains more sayings of King Solomon

Questioning the Passage

1. What does verse sixteen mean?

    A righteous person may fall (fail at a task) but will always pick themselves up and try again. The number seven in this proverb is used to denote many. When a wicked person fails at a task, they generally do not try it again.[110]

Culture Section

Questioning the passage

1. What does it mean to open one's mouth at the gate? (v. 7)
    This phrase means that the person never offered any counsel when sitting with the elders at the gate of the city.[111] The city gate was the place that the administration of the city was conducted. Judges were also at the city gate. A fool never offers anything profound, especially when he/she is at the city gate.

2. What is Solomon advising his son to do in verse twenty-one?
    King Solomon was advising his son to show reverence to the LORD when he became King. He was to reign over the people as their monarch. However, as King, he answered to the LORD. A King was expected to give counsel to his people. King Solomon counseled his son about being King.

---

[110] R. Laird Harris, Gleason L. Archer, and Bruce K. Waltke, *Theological Wordbook of the Old Testament* (Chicago: Moody Press, 2004).

[111] Rocco A. Errico and George M. Lamsa, *Aramaic Light on Ezra through the Song of Solomon* (Smyma, GA: Noohra Foundation, 2010).

3. Is verse twenty-nine the Golden Rule?

    This proverb is the beginning of the Golden Rule. King Solomon discovered that rendering evil for evil did more harm than good. He admonished his people to leave vengeance to the LORD, who was the right judge of humankind. Many prophets said that vengeance was a long struggle for Israel in the Gentile world.[112]

Thoughts

This chapter contains more sayings of King Solomon.

---

[112] IBID.

Chapter Twenty-Five

Language

New American Standard 1995	Hebrew
[1] These also are proverbs of Solomon which the men of Hezekiah, king of Judah, transcribed.	גַּם־אֵלֶּה מִשְׁלֵי שְׁלֹמֹה אֲשֶׁר הֶעְתִּיקוּ אַנְשֵׁי חִזְקִיָּה מֶלֶךְ־יְהוּדָה: [2] כְּבֹד אֱלֹהִים הַסְתֵּר דָּבָר וּכְבֹד מְלָכִים חֲקֹר דָּבָר:
[2] It is the glory of God to conceal a matter, But the glory of kings is to search out a matter.	[3] שָׁמַיִם לָרוּם וָאָרֶץ לָעֹמֶק וְלֵב מְלָכִים אֵין חֵקֶר:
[3] *As* the heavens for height and the earth for depth, So the heart of kings is unsearchable.	[4] הָגוֹ סִיגִים מִכָּסֶף וַיֵּצֵא לַצֹּרֵף כֶּלִי:
[4] Take away the dross from the silver, And there comes out a vessel for the smith;	[5] הָגוֹ רָשָׁע לִפְנֵי־מֶלֶךְ וְיִכּוֹן בַּצֶּדֶק כִּסְאוֹ:
[5] Take away the wicked before the king, And his throne will be established in righteousness.	[6] אַל־תִּתְהַדַּר לִפְנֵי־מֶלֶךְ וּבִמְקוֹם גְּדֹלִים אַל־תַּעֲמֹד:
[6] Do not claim honor in the presence of the king, And do not stand in the place of great men;	[7] כִּי טוֹב אֲמָר־לְךָ עֲלֵה הֵנָּה מֵהַשְׁפִּילְךָ לִפְנֵי נָדִיב אֲשֶׁר רָאוּ עֵינֶיךָ:
[7] For it is better that it be said to you, "Come up here," Than for you to be placed lower in the presence of the prince, Whom your eyes have seen.	[8] אַל־תֵּצֵא לָרִב מַהֵר פֶּן מַה־תַּעֲשֶׂה בְּאַחֲרִיתָהּ בְּהַכְלִים אֹתְךָ רֵעֶךָ:
[8] Do not go out hastily to argue *your case*; Otherwise, what will you do in the end, When your neighbor humiliates you?	[9] רִיבְךָ רִיב אֶת־רֵעֶךָ וְסוֹד אַחֵר אַל־תְּגָל:
[9] Argue your case with your neighbor, And do not reveal the secret of another,	[10] פֶּן־יְחַסֶּדְךָ שֹׁמֵעַ וְדִבָּתְךָ לֹא תָשׁוּב:
[10] Or he who hears *it* will reproach you, And the evil report about you will not pass away.	[11] תַּפּוּחֵי זָהָב בְּמַשְׂכִּיּוֹת כָּסֶף דָּבָר דָּבֻר עַל־אָפְנָיו:
[11] *Like* apples of gold in settings of silver Is a word spoken in right circumstances.	[12] נֶזֶם זָהָב וַחֲלִי־כָתֶם מוֹכִיחַ חָכָם עַל־אֹזֶן שֹׁמָעַת:
[12] *Like* an earring of gold and an ornament of fine gold Is a wise reprover to a listening ear.	[13] כְּצִנַּת־שֶׁלֶג בְּיוֹם קָצִיר צִיר נֶאֱמָן לְשֹׁלְחָיו וְנֶפֶשׁ אֲדֹנָיו יָשִׁיב: פ
	[14] נְשִׂיאִים וְרוּחַ וְגֶשֶׁם אָיִן אִישׁ מִתְהַלֵּל בְּמַתַּת־שָׁקֶר:
	[15] בְּאֹרֶךְ אַפַּיִם יְפֻתֶּה קָצִין וְלָשׁוֹן רַכָּה תִּשְׁבָּר־גָּרֶם:
	[16] דְּבַשׁ מָצָאתָ אֱכֹל דַּיֶּךָ פֶּן־תִּשְׂבָּעֶנּוּ וַהֲקֵאתוֹ:
	[17] הֹקַר רַגְלְךָ מִבֵּית רֵעֶךָ פֶּן־יִשְׂבָּעֲךָ וּשְׂנֵאֶךָ:
	[18] מֵפִיץ וְחֶרֶב וְחֵץ שָׁנוּן אִישׁ עֹנֶה בְרֵעֵהוּ עֵד שָׁקֶר:
	[19] שֵׁן רֹעָה וְרֶגֶל מוּעָדֶת מִבְטָח בּוֹגֵד בְּיוֹם צָרָה:
	[20] מַעֲדֶה בֶּגֶד בְּיוֹם קָרָה חֹמֶץ עַל־נָתֶר וְשָׁר בַּשִּׁרִים עַל לֶב־רָע: פ

¹³ Like the cold of snow in the time of harvest Is a faithful messenger to those who send him, For he refreshes the soul of his masters.

¹⁴ *Like* clouds and wind without rain Is a man who boasts of his gifts falsely.

¹⁵ By forbearance a ruler may be persuaded, And a soft tongue breaks the bone.

¹⁶ Have you found honey? Eat *only* what you need, That you not have it in excess and vomit it.

¹⁷ Let your foot rarely be in your neighbor's house, Or he will become weary of you and hate you.

¹⁸ *Like* a club and a sword and a sharp arrow Is a man who bears false witness against his neighbor.

¹⁹ *Like* a bad tooth and an unsteady foot Is confidence in a faithless man in time of trouble.

²⁰ *Like* one who takes off a garment on a cold day, *or like* vinegar on soda, Is he who sings songs to a troubled heart.

²¹ If your enemy is hungry, give him food to eat; And if he is thirsty, give him water to drink;

²² For you will heap burning coals on his head, And the LORD will reward you.

²³ The north wind brings forth rain, And a backbiting tongue, an angry countenance.

²⁴ It is better to live in a corner of the roof Than in a house shared with a contentious woman.

²⁵ *Like* cold water to a weary soul, So is good news from a distant land.

²⁶ *Like* a trampled spring and a polluted well Is a righteous man who gives way before the wicked.

21 אִם־רָעֵב שֹׂנַאֲךָ הַאֲכִלֵהוּ לָחֶם וְאִם־צָמֵא הַשְׁקֵהוּ מָיִם׃

22 כִּי גֶחָלִים אַתָּה חֹתֶה עַל־רֹאשׁוֹ וַיהֹוָה יְשַׁלֶּם־לָךְ׃

23 רוּחַ צָפוֹן תְּחוֹלֵל גָּשֶׁם וּפָנִים נִזְעָמִים לְשׁוֹן סָתֶר׃

24 טוֹב שֶׁבֶת עַל־פִּנַּת־גָּג מֵאֵשֶׁת (מדונים) [מִדְיָנִים] וּבֵית חָבֶר׃

25 מַיִם קָרִים עַל־נֶפֶשׁ עֲיֵפָה וּשְׁמוּעָה טוֹבָה מֵאֶרֶץ מֶרְחָק׃

26 מַעְיָן נִרְפָּשׂ וּמָקוֹר מָשְׁחָת צַדִּיק מָט לִפְנֵי־רָשָׁע׃

27 אָכֹל דְּבַשׁ הַרְבּוֹת לֹא־טוֹב וְחֵקֶר כְּבֹדָם כָּבוֹד׃

28 עִיר פְּרוּצָה אֵין חוֹמָה אִישׁ אֲשֶׁר אֵין מַעְצָר לְרוּחוֹ׃

²⁷ It is not good to eat much honey, Nor is it glory to search out one's own glory. ²⁸ *Like* a city that is broken into *and* without walls Is a man who has no control over his spirit.	

Process of Discovery

Linguistics Section

Linguistic Structure

[1] These also are proverbs of Solomon which the men of Hezekiah, king of Judah, transcribed.

[2] It is the glory of God to conceal a matter, But the glory of kings is to search out a matter.

[3] *As* the heavens for height and the earth for depth, So the heart of kings is unsearchable.

[4] Take away the dross from the silver, And there comes out a vessel for the smith; [5] Take away the wicked before the king, And his throne will be established in righteousness.

[6] Do not claim honor in the presence of the king, And do not stand in the place of great men; [7] For it is better that it be said to you, "Come up here," Than for you to be placed lower in the presence of the prince, Whom your eyes have seen.

[8] Do not go out hastily to argue *your case*; Otherwise, what will you do in the end, When your neighbor humiliates you? [9] Argue your case with your neighbor, And do not reveal the secret of another, [10] Or he who hears *it* will reproach you, And the evil report about you will not pass away.

[11] *Like* apples of gold in settings of silver Is a word spoken in right circumstances.

[12] *Like* an earring of gold and an ornament of fine gold Is a wise reprover to a listening ear.

[13] Like the cold of snow in the time of harvest Is a faithful messenger to those who send him, For he refreshes the soul of his masters.

[14] *Like* clouds and wind without rain Is a man who boasts of his gifts falsely.

[15] By forbearance a ruler may be persuaded, And a soft tongue breaks the bone.

[16] Have you found honey? Eat *only* what you need, That you not have it in excess and vomit it.

[17] Let your foot rarely be in your neighbor's house, Or he will become weary of you and hate you. [18] *Like* a club and a sword and a sharp arrow Is a man who bears false witness against his neighbor. [19] *Like* a bad tooth and an unsteady foot Is confidence in a faithless man in time of trouble. [20] *Like* one who takes off a garment on a cold day, *or like* vinegar on soda, Is he who sings songs to a troubled heart.

[21] If your enemy is hungry, give him food to eat; And if he is thirsty, give him water to drink; [22] For you will heap burning coals on his head, And the LORD will reward you.

[23] The north wind brings forth rain, And a backbiting tongue, an angry countenance. [24] It is better to live in a corner of the roof Than in a house shared with a contentious woman. [25] *Like* cold water to a weary soul, So is good news from a distant land. [26] *Like* a trampled spring and a polluted well Is a righteous man who gives way before the wicked.

[27] It is not good to eat much honey, Nor is it glory to search out one's own glory. [28] *Like* a city that is broken into *and* without walls Is a man who has no control over his spirit.

Discussion

The book of Proverbs is divided into several sections. Chapters one to twenty-four are proverbs that King Solomon had written down for the general population to read. This next section is proverbs that King Solomon said but was not written down by Solomon. The scholars under King Hezekiah decided to reveal these proverbs to the people.[113]

Culture Section

Questioning the passage

1. What was Near Eastern etiquette about sitting and standing before the King and at banquets? (v. 6-7)

It was the custom of the day to have the wealthy people and noblemen stand or sit close to the King at a banquet. Sometimes men would try to get close to the King. It made a big difference where one was seated or standing when a King came to visit. This custom was also true at wedding feasts and banquets. Some men would arrive early to the event and sit in

---

[113] R. Laird Harris, Gleason L. Archer, and Bruce K. Waltke, *Theological Wordbook of the Old Testament* (Chicago: Moody Press, 2004).

the high places reserved for prominent guests because the food was more abundant. When the prominent guests arrived, the interloper would be told to move. This situation was an embarrassing moment for the men who had to move to a lower class seat.[114]

2. What does verse twenty mean?

    Robes and coats were used by the poor as pledges of surety when borrowing money from a stranger. Even on a cold day, a lender would take the robe from a borrower. According to the Mosaic law, the robe was supposed to be returned by evening. When it was used as collateral, it was not returned until the debt was paid.

    The broken heart causes sorrow, which is likened to a moth on a garment and a boring-worm on a tree. They caused suffering for the person by eating the insides.[115]

3. Why should one be good to enemies? (v. 21-22)

    The phrase "heap burning coals on his head" is a Near Eastern idiom that means to embarrass him or to cause him suffering." It is embarrassing for an enemy to accept bread and water from someone he has hated or wronged.[116] Showing kindness to one's enemy might change their heart and become a friend.

---

[114] Rocco A. Errico and George M. Lamsa, *Aramaic Light on Ezra through the Song of Solomon* (Smyma, GA: Noohra Foundation, 2010).
[115] IBID.
[116] IBID.

Thoughts

This chapter contains more proverbs of King Solomon, which were revealed to the people by the scholars of King Hezekiah. Several of the proverbs found at the beginning of the chapter are concerning the glory of the King. The King was considered the LORD's anointed and were to be shown the respect due. The King was supposed to be a counselor whose job was to take care of the people and lead them in the Torah of the LORD. Many of the Kings between Solomon and Hezekiah turned away from the LORD. These Kings did not deserve the respect of the people. Since there are several proverbs about the King, these proverbs might have been hidden because they did not fit for the idolatrous King.

Chapter Twenty-Six

Language

New American Standard 1995	Hebrew

כַּשֶּׁלֶג׀ בַּקַּיִץ וְכַמָּטָר בַּקָּצִיר כֵּן לֹא־נָאוֶה לִכְסִיל כָּבוֹד: 2 כַּצִּפּוֹר לָנוּד כַּדְּרוֹר לָעוּף כֵּן קִלְלַת חִנָּם (לא) [לוֹ] תָבֹא: 3 שׁוֹט לַסּוּס מֶתֶג לַחֲמוֹר וְשֵׁבֶט לְגֵו כְּסִילִים: 4 אַל־תַּעַן כְּסִיל כְּאִוַּלְתּוֹ פֶּן־תִּשְׁוֶה־לּוֹ גַם־ אָתָּה: 5 עֲנֵה כְסִיל כְּאִוַּלְתּוֹ פֶּן־יִהְיֶה חָכָם בְּעֵינָיו: 6 מְקַצֶּה רַגְלַיִם חָמָס שֹׁתֶה שֹׁלֵחַ דְּבָרִים בְּיַד־כְּסִיל: 7 דַּלְיוּ שֹׁקַיִם מִפִּסֵּחַ וּמָשָׁל בְּפִי כְסִילִים: 8 כִּצְרוֹר אֶבֶן בְּמַרְגֵּמָה כֵּן־נוֹתֵן לִכְסִיל כָּבוֹד: 9 חוֹחַ עָלָה בְיַד־שִׁכּוֹר וּמָשָׁל בְּפִי כְסִילִים: 10 רַב מְחוֹלֵל־כֹּל וְשֹׂכֵר כְּסִיל וְשֹׂכֵר עֹבְרִים: 11 כְּכֶלֶב שָׁב עַל־קֵאוֹ כְּסִיל שׁוֹנֶה בְאִוַּלְתּוֹ: 12 רָאִיתָ אִישׁ חָכָם בְּעֵינָיו תִּקְוָה לִכְסִיל מִמֶּנּוּ: 13 אָמַר עָצֵל שַׁחַל בַּדָּרֶךְ אֲרִי בֵּין הָרְחֹבוֹת: 14 הַדֶּלֶת תִּסּוֹב עַל־צִירָהּ וְעָצֵל עַל־מִטָּתוֹ: 15 טָמַן עָצֵל יָדוֹ בַּצַּלָּחַת נִלְאָה לַהֲשִׁיבָהּ אֶל־ פִּיו: 16 חָכָם עָצֵל בְּעֵינָיו מִשִּׁבְעָה מְשִׁיבֵי טָעַם: 17 מַחֲזִיק בְּאָזְנֵי־כָלֶב עֹבֵר מִתְעַבֵּר עַל־רִיב לֹא־לוֹ: 18 כְּמִתְלַהְלֵהַּ הַיֹּרֶה זִקִּים חִצִּים וָמָוֶת: 19 כֵּן־אִישׁ רִמָּה אֶת־רֵעֵהוּ וְאָמַר הֲלֹא־ מְשַׂחֵק אָנִי: 20 בְּאֶפֶס עֵצִים תִּכְבֶּה־אֵשׁ וּבְאֵין נִרְגָּן יִשְׁתֹּק מָדוֹן: 21 פֶּחָם לְגֶחָלִים וְעֵצִים לְאֵשׁ וְאִישׁ (מדונים) [מִדְיָנִים] לְחַרְחַר־רִיב: פ 22 דִּבְרֵי נִרְגָּן כְּמִתְלַהֲמִים וְהֵם יָרְדוּ חַדְרֵי־ בָטֶן:

1 Like snow in summer and like rain in harvest, So honor is not fitting for a fool.
2 Like a sparrow in *its* flitting, like a swallow in *its* flying, So a curse without cause does not alight.
3 A whip is for the horse, a bridle for the donkey, And a rod for the back of fools.
4 Do not answer a fool according to his folly, Or you will also be like him.
5 Answer a fool as his folly *deserves*, That he not be wise in his own eyes.
6 He cuts off *his own* feet *and* drinks violence Who sends a message by the hand of a fool.
7 *Like* the legs *which* are useless to the lame, So is a proverb in the mouth of fools.
8 Like one who binds a stone in a sling, So is he who gives honor to a fool.
9 *Like* a thorn *which* falls into the hand of a drunkard, So is a proverb in the mouth of fools.
10 *Like* an archer who wounds everyone, So is he who hires a fool or who hires those who pass by.
11 Like a dog that returns to its vomit Is a fool who repeats his folly.
12 Do you see a man wise in his own eyes? There is more hope for a fool than for him.
13 The sluggard says, "There is a lion in the road! A lion is in the open square!"
14 *As* the door turns on its hinges, So *does* the sluggard on his bed.

15 The sluggard buries his hand in the dish; He is weary of bringing it to his mouth again.

16 The sluggard is wiser in his own eyes Than seven men who can give a discreet answer.

17 *Like* one who takes a dog by the ears Is he who passes by *and* meddles with strife not belonging to him.

18 Like a madman who throws Firebrands, arrows and death,

19 So is the man who deceives his neighbor, And says, "Was I not joking?"

20 For lack of wood the fire goes out, And where there is no whisperer, contention quiets down.

21 *Like* charcoal to hot embers and wood to fire, So is a contentious man to kindle strife.

22 The words of a whisperer are like dainty morsels, And they go down into the innermost parts of the body.

23 *Like* an earthen vessel overlaid with silver dross Are burning lips and a wicked heart.

24 He who hates disguises *it* with his lips, But he lays up deceit in his heart.

25 When he speaks graciously, do not believe him, For there are seven abominations in his heart.

26 *Though his* hatred covers itself with guile, His wickedness will be revealed before the assembly.

27 He who digs a pit will fall into it, And he who rolls a stone, it will come back on him.

28 A lying tongue hates those it crushes, And a flattering mouth works ruin.

כֶּסֶף סִיגִים מְצֻפֶּה עַל־חָרֶשׂ שְׂפָתַיִם 23 דֹּלְקִים וְלֶב־רָע:

(בְּשִׂפְתוֹ) [בִּשְׂפָתָיו] יִנָּכֵר שׂוֹנֵא וּבְקִרְבּוֹ 24 יָשִׁית מִרְמָה:

כִּי־יְחַנֵּן קוֹלוֹ אַל־תַּאֲמֶן־בּוֹ כִּי שֶׁבַע 25 תּוֹעֵבוֹת בְּלִבּוֹ:

תִּכַּסֶּה שִׂנְאָה בְּמַשָּׁאוֹן תִּגָּלֶה רָעָתוֹ 26 בְקָהָל:

כֹּרֶה־שַּׁחַת בָּהּ יִפֹּל וְגֹלֵל אֶבֶן אֵלָיו תָּשׁוּב: 27

לְשׁוֹן־שֶׁקֶר יִשְׂנָא דַכָּיו וּפֶה חָלָק יַעֲשֶׂה 28 מִדְחֶה:

Process of Discovery

Linguistics Section

Linguistic Structure

[1] Like snow in summer and like rain in harvest, So honor is not fitting for a fool.

[2] Like a sparrow in *its* flitting, like a swallow in *its* flying, So a curse without cause does not alight.

[3] A whip is for the horse, a bridle for the donkey, And a rod for the back of fools.

[4] Do not answer a fool according to his folly, Or you will also be like him.

[5] Answer a fool as his folly *deserves*, That he not be wise in his own eyes.

[6] He cuts off *his own* feet *and* drinks violence Who sends a message by the hand of a fool.

[7] *Like* the legs *which* are useless to the lame, So is a proverb in the mouth of fools.

[8] Like one who binds a stone in a sling, So is he who gives honor to a fool.

[9] *Like* a thorn *which* falls into the hand of a drunkard, So is a proverb in the mouth of fools.

[10] *Like* an archer who wounds everyone, So is he who hires a fool or who hires those who pass by.

[11] Like a dog that returns to its vomit Is a fool who repeats his folly.

[12] Do you see a man wise in his own eyes? There is more hope for a fool than for him.

[13] The sluggard says, "There is a lion in the road! A lion is in the open square!"

[14] *As* the door turns on its hinges, So *does* the sluggard on his bed.

[15] The sluggard buries his hand in the dish; He is weary of bringing it to his mouth again.

[16] The sluggard is wiser in his own eyes Than seven men who can give a discreet answer.

[17] *Like* one who takes a dog by the ears Is he who passes by *and* meddles with strife not belonging to him.

[18] Like a madman who throws Firebrands, arrows and death, [19] So is the man who deceives his neighbor, And says, "Was I not joking?"

[20] For lack of wood the fire goes out, And where there is no whisperer, contention quiets down.

[21] *Like* charcoal to hot embers and wood to fire, So is a contentious man to kindle strife.

[22] The words of a whisperer are like dainty morsels, And they go down into the innermost parts of the body.

[23] *Like* an earthen vessel overlaid with silver dross Are burning lips and a wicked heart.
[24] He who hates disguises *it* with his lips, But he lays up deceit in his heart.
[25] When he speaks graciously, do not believe him, For there are seven abominations in his heart.
[26] *Though his* hatred covers itself with guile, His wickedness will be revealed before the assembly.
[27] He who digs a pit will fall into it, And he who rolls a stone, it will come back on him.
[28] A lying tongue hates those it crushes, And a flattering mouth works ruin.

Discussion

This chapter is a continuation of wisdom from King Solomon.

Questioning the Passage

1. Who are the seven men in verse sixteen?

   The Sages say that the seven men were the ones that King Solomon called together when he wanted to decide whether to declare a leap year.[117]

Culture Section

Questioning the passage

1. What does the simile of the thorn mean in verse nine?

   In biblical times the Near East had an abundance of thorns and briers. These thorns and briers were present all year round. Since the field workers did not have leather gloves, the thorns and briers would get stuck in their hands. When a person is drunk, they cannot feel the thorns that have pricked their hands. The proverb is about money. A person who drinks too much will end up in poverty. The poverty is slow-moving but increases as the person drinks

---

[117] R. Laird Harris, Gleason L. Archer, and Bruce K. Waltke, *Theological Wordbook of the Old Testament* (Chicago: Moody Press, 2004).

more to get drunk. A fool does not know how to relate a parable to his/her life because he/she does not understand it.[118]

2. What does verse eleven mean?

Dogs in biblical times were generally not fed. They would search the streets looking for food. If they found the remains of a dead animal they would eat as much as they could. If the dead animal was decayed enough it would upset them and they would vomit it out. But being hungry they would eat their vomit. A fool commits a folly or error. The connection is that the fool does not learn from the error and will commit it again in the same way that the dog will eat the rotten food he vomited up.[119]

Thoughts

The first past of this chapter is devoted to the work of a fool, while the second half is about a sluggard.

---

[118] Rocco A. Errico and George M. Lamsa, *Aramaic Light on Ezra through the Song of Solomon* (Smyma, GA: Noohra Foundation, 2010).
[119] IBID.

Chapter Twenty-Seven

Language

New American Standard 1995	Hebrew
[1] Do not boast about tomorrow, For you do not know what a day may bring forth. [2] Let another praise you, and not your own mouth; A stranger, and not your own lips. [3] A stone is heavy and the sand weighty, But the provocation of a fool is heavier than both of them. [4] Wrath is fierce and anger is a flood, But who can stand before jealousy? [5] Better is open rebuke Than love that is concealed. [6] Faithful are the wounds of a friend, But deceitful are the kisses of an enemy. [7] A sated man loathes honey, But to a famished man any bitter thing is sweet. [8] Like a bird that wanders from her nest, So is a man who wanders from his home. [9] Oil and perfume make the heart glad, So a man's counsel is sweet to his friend. [10] Do not forsake your own friend or your father's friend, And do not go to your brother's house in the day of your calamity; Better is a neighbor who is near than a brother far away. [11] Be wise, my son, and make my heart glad, That I may reply to him who reproaches me. [12] A prudent man sees evil *and* hides himself, The naive proceed *and* pay the penalty. [13] Take his garment when he becomes surety for a stranger; And for an adulterous woman hold him in pledge.	אַל־תִּתְהַלֵּל בְּיוֹם מָחָר כִּי לֹא־תֵדַע מַה־יֵּלֶד יוֹם: [2] יְהַלֶּלְךָ זָר וְלֹא־פִיךָ נָכְרִי וְאַל־שְׂפָתֶיךָ: [3] כֹּבֶד־אֶבֶן וְנֵטֶל הַחוֹל וְכַעַס אֱוִיל כָּבֵד מִשְּׁנֵיהֶם: [4] אַכְזְרִיּוּת חֵמָה וְשֶׁטֶף אָף וּמִי יַעֲמֹד לִפְנֵי קִנְאָה: [5] טוֹבָה תּוֹכַחַת מְגֻלָּה מֵאַהֲבָה מְסֻתָּרֶת: [6] נֶאֱמָנִים פִּצְעֵי אוֹהֵב וְנַעְתָּרוֹת נְשִׁיקוֹת שׂוֹנֵא: [7] נֶפֶשׁ שְׂבֵעָה תָּבוּס נֹפֶת וְנֶפֶשׁ רְעֵבָה כָּל־מַר מָתוֹק: [8] כְּצִפּוֹר נוֹדֶדֶת מִן־קִנָּהּ כֵּן־אִישׁ נוֹדֵד מִמְּקוֹמוֹ: [9] שֶׁמֶן וּקְטֹרֶת יְשַׂמַּח־לֵב וּמֶתֶק רֵעֵהוּ מֵעֲצַת־נָפֶשׁ: [10] רֵעֲךָ (וְרֵעֶה) [וְרֵעַ] אָבִיךָ אַל־תַּעֲזֹב וּבֵית אָחִיךָ אַל־תָּבוֹא בְּיוֹם אֵידֶךָ טוֹב שָׁכֵן קָרוֹב מֵאָח רָחוֹק: [11] חֲכַם בְּנִי וְשַׂמַּח לִבִּי וְאָשִׁיבָה חֹרְפִי דָבָר: [12] עָרוּם רָאָה רָעָה נִסְתָּר פְּתָאיִם עָבְרוּ נֶעֱנָשׁוּ: [13] קַח־בִּגְדוֹ כִּי־עָרַב זָר וּבְעַד נָכְרִיָּה חַבְלֵהוּ: [14] מְבָרֵךְ רֵעֵהוּ בְּקוֹל גָּדוֹל בַּבֹּקֶר הַשְׁכֵּים קְלָלָה תֵּחָשֶׁב לוֹ: [15] דֶּלֶף טוֹרֵד בְּיוֹם סַגְרִיר וְאֵשֶׁת (מִדוֹנִים) [מִדְיָנִים] נִשְׁתָּוָה: [16] צֹפְנֶיהָ צָפַן־רוּחַ וְשֶׁמֶן יְמִינוֹ יִקְרָא: [17] בַּרְזֶל בְּבַרְזֶל יָחַד וְאִישׁ יַחַד פְּנֵי־רֵעֵהוּ: [18] נֹצֵר תְּאֵנָה יֹאכַל פִּרְיָהּ וְשֹׁמֵר אֲדֹנָיו יְכֻבָּד: [19] כַּמַּיִם הַפָּנִים לַפָּנִים כֵּן לֵב־הָאָדָם לָאָדָם: [20] שְׁאוֹל (וַאֲבַדֹּה) [וַאֲבַדּוֹ] לֹא תִשְׂבַּעְנָה וְעֵינֵי הָאָדָם לֹא תִשְׂבַּעְנָה:

¹⁴ He who blesses his friend with a loud voice early in the morning, It will be reckoned a curse to him.

¹⁵ A constant dripping on a day of steady rain And a contentious woman are alike;

¹⁶ He who would restrain her restrains the wind, And grasps oil with his right hand.

¹⁷ Iron sharpens iron, So one man sharpens another.

¹⁸ He who tends the fig tree will eat its fruit, And he who cares for his master will be honored.

¹⁹ As in water face *reflects* face, So the heart of man *reflects* man.

²⁰ Sheol and Abaddon are never satisfied, Nor are the eyes of man ever satisfied.

²¹ The crucible is for silver and the furnace for gold, And each *is tested* by the praise accorded him.

²² Though you pound a fool in a mortar with a pestle along with crushed grain, *Yet* his foolishness will not depart from him.

²³ Know well the condition of your flocks, *And* pay attention to your herds;

²⁴ For riches are not forever, Nor does a crown *endure* to all generations.

²⁵ *When* the grass disappears, the new growth is seen, And the herbs of the mountains are gathered in,

²⁶ The lambs *will be* for your clothing, And the goats *will bring* the price of a field,

²⁷ And *there will be* goats' milk enough for your food, For the food of your household, And sustenance for your maidens.

מַצְרֵף לַכֶּסֶף וְכוּר לַזָּהָב וְאִישׁ לְפִי מַהֲלָלוֹ: ²¹

אִם תִּכְתּוֹשׁ־אֶת־הָאֱוִיל בַּמַּכְתֵּשׁ בְּתוֹךְ הָרִיפוֹת בַּעֱלִי לֹא־תָסוּר מֵעָלָיו אִוַּלְתּוֹ: פ ²²

יָדֹעַ תֵּדַע פְּנֵי צֹאנֶךָ שִׁית לִבְּךָ לַעֲדָרִים: ²³

כִּי לֹא לְעוֹלָם חֹסֶן וְאִם־נֵזֶר לְדוֹר (דוֹר) [וָדוֹר]: ²⁴

גָּלָה חָצִיר וְנִרְאָה־דֶשֶׁא וְנֶאֶסְפוּ עִשְּׂבוֹת הָרִים: ²⁵

כְּבָשִׂים לִלְבוּשֶׁךָ וּמְחִיר שָׂדֶה עַתּוּדִים: ²⁶

וְדֵי חֲלֵב עִזִּים לְלַחְמְךָ לְלֶחֶם בֵּיתֶךָ וְחַיִּים לְנַעֲרוֹתֶיךָ: ²⁷

Process of Discovery

Linguistics Section

Linguistic Structure

[1] Do not boast about tomorrow, For you do not know what a day may bring forth.

[2] Let another praise you, and not your own mouth; A stranger, and not your own lips.

[3] A stone is heavy and the sand weighty, But the provocation of a fool is heavier than both of them.

[4] Wrath is fierce and anger is a flood, But who can stand before jealousy?

[5] Better is open rebuke Than love that is concealed.

[6] Faithful are the wounds of a friend, But deceitful are the kisses of an enemy.

[7] A sated man loathes honey, But to a famished man any bitter thing is sweet.

[8] Like a bird that wanders from her nest, So is a man who wanders from his home.

[9] Oil and perfume make the heart glad, So a man's counsel is sweet to his friend.

[10] Do not forsake your own friend or your father's friend, And do not go to your brother's house in the day of your calamity; Better is a neighbor who is near than a brother far away.

[11] Be wise, my son, and make my heart glad, That I may reply to him who reproaches me.

[12] A prudent man sees evil *and* hides himself, The naive proceed *and* pay the penalty.

[13] Take his garment when he becomes surety for a stranger; And for an adulterous woman hold him in pledge.

[14] He who blesses his friend with a loud voice early in the morning, It will be reckoned a curse to him.

[15] A constant dripping on a day of steady rain And a contentious woman are alike; [16] He who would restrain her restrains the wind, And grasps oil with his right hand.

[17] Iron sharpens iron, So one man sharpens another.

[18] He who tends the fig tree will eat its fruit, And he who cares for his master will be honored.

[19] As in water face *reflects* face, So the heart of man *reflects* man.

[20] Sheol and Abaddon are never satisfied, Nor are the eyes of man ever satisfied.

[21] The crucible is for silver and the furnace for gold, And each *is tested* by the praise accorded him.

[22] Though you pound a fool in a mortar with a pestle along with crushed grain, *Yet* his foolishness will not depart from him.

23 Know well the condition of your flocks, *And* pay attention to your herds; 24 For riches are not forever, Nor does a crown *endure* to all generations.

25 *When* the grass disappears, the new growth is seen, And the herbs of the mountains are gathered in, 26 The lambs *will be* for your clothing, And the goats *will bring* the price of a field, 27 And *there will be* goats' milk enough for your food, For the food of your household, And sustenance for your maidens.

Discussion

This chapter consists of wisdom from King Solomon.

Culture Section

Questioning the passage

1. What does verse nine mean?

   In the Near East, people did not bathe. Water was scarce and was not used in this manner. Open skin sores would develop because of the lack of hygiene. Oils, perfumes, and balms were used on open skin wounds. The oil would allow the dirt to be cleaned off the wound and help it to heal. The person would then be glad to be rid of the skin sores, a delight to the heart. This is likened to a friend's counsel. A good counsel's advice sinks into the mind and heals it, just like the oil heals dry skin and sores.[120]

---

[120] Rocco A. Errico and George M. Lamsa, *Aramaic Light on Ezra through the Song of Solomon* (Smyma, GA: Noohra Foundation, 2010).

2. What does verse fourteen mean?

    The blessings are flattery. When flattering another person, the flatterer will raise their voice for all to hear.[121] When this is done on unworthy people, it is deceitful and sinful. It will become a curse on the flatterer.

3. What does verse fifteen mean?

    The dripping of the day refers to rainwater that would leak from the roof of the home. The roof was generally made of thatch and mud. Leaks were common. When a leak occurred, vessels would be placed under the leak to catch the rainwater. Beds would be moved if necessary. The leaks were annoying and could cause damage to valuables and clothing. This is likened to a quarrelsome wife who was dissatisfied with life and continuously annoyed her husband and the neighbors with her constant complaining.[122]

Thoughts

This chapter consists of more wisdom saying from King Solomon.

---

[121] IBID.
[122] IBID.

Chapter Twenty-Eight

Language

New American Standard 1995	Hebrew
[1] The wicked flee when no one is pursuing, But the righteous are bold as a lion.	נָסוּ וְאֵין־רֹדֵף רָשָׁע וְצַדִּיקִים כִּכְפִיר יִבְטָח: [2] בְּפֶשַׁע אֶרֶץ רַבִּים שָׂרֶיהָ וּבְאָדָם מֵבִין יֹדֵעַ כֵּן יַאֲרִיךְ: [3] גֶּבֶר רָשׁ וְעֹשֵׁק דַּלִּים מָטָר סֹחֵף וְאֵין לָחֶם: [4] עֹזְבֵי תוֹרָה יְהַלְלוּ רָשָׁע וְשֹׁמְרֵי תוֹרָה יִתְגָּרוּ בָם: פ [5] אַנְשֵׁי־רָע לֹא־יָבִינוּ מִשְׁפָּט וּמְבַקְשֵׁי יְהוָה יָבִינוּ כֹל: [6] טוֹב־רָשׁ הוֹלֵךְ בְּתֻמּוֹ מֵעִקֵּשׁ דְּרָכַיִם וְהוּא עָשִׁיר: [7] נוֹצֵר תּוֹרָה בֵּן מֵבִין וְרֹעֶה זוֹלְלִים יַכְלִים אָבִיו: [8] מַרְבֶּה הוֹנוֹ בְּנֶשֶׁךְ (וּבְתַרְבִּית) [וְתַרְבִּית] לְחוֹנֵן דַּלִּים יִקְבְּצֶנּוּ: [9] מֵסִיר אָזְנוֹ מִשְּׁמֹעַ תּוֹרָה גַּם־תְּפִלָּתוֹ תּוֹעֵבָה: [10] מַשְׁגֶּה יְשָׁרִים בְּדֶרֶךְ רָע בִּשְׁחוּתוֹ הוּא־יִפּוֹל וּתְמִימִים יִנְחֲלוּ־טוֹב: [11] חָכָם בְּעֵינָיו אִישׁ עָשִׁיר וְדַל מֵבִין יַחְקְרֶנּוּ: [12] בַּעֲלֹץ צַדִּיקִים רַבָּה תִפְאָרֶת וּבְקוּם רְשָׁעִים יְחֻפַּשׂ אָדָם: [13] מְכַסֶּה פְשָׁעָיו לֹא יַצְלִיחַ וּמוֹדֶה וְעֹזֵב יְרֻחָם: [14] אַשְׁרֵי אָדָם מְפַחֵד תָּמִיד וּמַקְשֶׁה לִבּוֹ יִפּוֹל בְּרָעָה:
[2] By the transgression of a land many are its princes, But by a man of understanding *and* knowledge, so it endures.	
[3] A poor man who oppresses the lowly Is *like* a driving rain which leaves no food.	
[4] Those who forsake the law praise the wicked, But those who keep the law strive with them.	
[5] Evil men do not understand justice, But those who seek the LORD understand all things.	
[6] Better is the poor who walks in his integrity Than he who is crooked though he be rich.	
[7] He who keeps the law is a discerning son, But he who is a companion of gluttons humiliates his father.	
[8] He who increases his wealth by interest and usury Gathers it for him who is gracious to the poor.	
[9] He who turns away his ear from listening to the law, Even his prayer is an abomination.	
[10] He who leads the upright astray in an evil way Will himself fall into his own pit, But the blameless will inherit good.	
[11] The rich man is wise in his own eyes, But the poor who has understanding sees through him.	

¹² When the righteous triumph, there is great glory, But when the wicked rise, men hide themselves.

¹³ He who conceals his transgressions will not prosper, But he who confesses and forsakes *them* will find compassion.

¹⁴ How blessed is the man who fears always, But he who hardens his heart will fall into calamity.

¹⁵ *Like* a roaring lion and a rushing bear Is a wicked ruler over a poor people.

¹⁶ A leader who is a great oppressor lacks understanding, *But* he who hates unjust gain will prolong *his* days.

¹⁷ A man who is laden with the guilt of human blood Will be a fugitive until death; let no one support him.

¹⁸ He who walks blamelessly will be delivered, But he who is crooked will fall all at once.

¹⁹ He who tills his land will have plenty of food, But he who follows empty *pursuits* will have poverty in plenty.

²⁰ A faithful man will abound with blessings, But he who makes haste to be rich will not go unpunished.

²¹ To show partiality is not good, Because for a piece of bread a man will transgress.

²² A man with an evil eye hastens after wealth And does not know that want will come upon him.

²³ He who rebukes a man will afterward find *more* favor Than he who flatters with the tongue.

²⁴ He who robs his father or his mother And says, "It is not a transgression," Is the companion of a man who destroys.

²⁵ An arrogant man stirs up strife, But he who trusts in the LORD will prosper.

אֲרִי־נֹהֵם וְדֹב שׁוֹקֵק מֹשֵׁל רָשָׁע עַל ¹⁵
עַם־דָּל:

נָגִיד חֲסַר תְּבוּנוֹת וְרַב מַעֲשַׁקּוֹת ¹⁶
(שֹׂנְאֵי) [שֹׂנֵא] בֶצַע יַאֲרִיךְ יָמִים: פ

אָדָם עָשֻׁק בְּדַם־נָפֶשׁ עַד־בּוֹר יָנוּס ¹⁷
אַל־יִתְמְכוּ־בוֹ:

הוֹלֵךְ תָּמִים יִוָּשֵׁעַ וְנֶעְקַשׁ דְּרָכַיִם ¹⁸
יִפּוֹל בְּאֶחָת:

עֹבֵד אַדְמָתוֹ יִשְׂבַּע־לָחֶם וּמְרַדֵּף ¹⁹
רֵקִים יִשְׂבַּע־רִישׁ:

אִישׁ אֱמוּנוֹת רַב־בְּרָכוֹת וְאָץ ²⁰
לְהַעֲשִׁיר לֹא יִנָּקֶה:

הַכֵּר־פָּנִים לֹא־טוֹב וְעַל־פַּת־לֶחֶם ²¹
יִפְשַׁע־גָּבֶר:

נִבֳהָל לַהוֹן אִישׁ רַע עָיִן וְלֹא־יֵדַע כִּי־ ²²
חֶסֶר יְבֹאֶנּוּ:

מוֹכִיחַ אָדָם אַחֲרַי חֵן יִמְצָא מִמַּחֲלִיק ²³
לָשׁוֹן:

גּוֹזֵל אָבִיו וְאִמּוֹ וְאֹמֵר אֵין־פָּשַׁע ²⁴
חָבֵר הוּא לְאִישׁ מַשְׁחִית:

רְחַב־נֶפֶשׁ יְגָרֶה מָדוֹן וּבוֹטֵחַ עַל־ ²⁵
יְהוָה יְדֻשָּׁן:

בּוֹטֵחַ בְּלִבּוֹ הוּא כְסִיל וְהוֹלֵךְ ²⁶
בְּחָכְמָה הוּא יִמָּלֵט:

נוֹתֵן לָרָשׁ אֵין מַחְסוֹר וּמַעְלִים עֵינָיו ²⁷
רַב־מְאֵרוֹת:

בְּקוּם רְשָׁעִים יִסָּתֵר אָדָם וּבְאָבְדָם ²⁸
יִרְבּוּ צַדִּיקִים:

<table>
<tr><td>

[26] He who trusts in his own heart is a fool, But he who walks wisely will be delivered.

[27] He who gives to the poor will never want, But he who shuts his eyes will have many curses.

[28] When the wicked rise, men hide themselves; But when they perish, the righteous increase.

</td><td></td></tr>
</table>

Process of Discovery

Linguistics Section

Linguistic Structure

[1] The wicked flee when no one is pursuing, But the righteous are bold as a lion.
[2] By the transgression of a land many are its princes, But by a man of understanding *and* knowledge, so it endures.
[3] A poor man who oppresses the lowly Is *like* a driving rain which leaves no food.
[4] Those who forsake the law praise the wicked, But those who keep the law strive with them.
[5] Evil men do not understand justice, But those who seek the LORD understand all things.
[6] Better is the poor who walks in his integrity Than he who is crooked though he be rich.
[7] He who keeps the law is a discerning son, But he who is a companion of gluttons humiliates his father.
[8] He who increases his wealth by interest and usury Gathers it for him who is gracious to the poor.
[9] He who turns away his ear from listening to the law, Even his prayer is an abomination.
[10] He who leads the upright astray in an evil way Will himself fall into his own pit, But the blameless will inherit good.
[11] The rich man is wise in his own eyes, But the poor who has understanding sees through him.
[12] When the righteous triumph, there is great glory, But when the wicked rise, men hide themselves.
[13] He who conceals his transgressions will not prosper, But he who confesses and forsakes *them* will find compassion.
[14] How blessed is the man who fears always, But he who hardens his heart will fall into calamity.
[15] *Like* a roaring lion and a rushing bear Is a wicked ruler over a poor people.
[16] A leader who is a great oppressor lacks understanding, *But* he who hates unjust gain will prolong *his* days.
[17] A man who is laden with the guilt of human blood Will be a fugitive until death; let no one support him.
[18] He who walks blamelessly will be delivered, But he who is crooked will fall all at once.
[19] He who tills his land will have plenty of food, But he who follows empty *pursuits* will have poverty in plenty.

²⁰ A faithful man will abound with blessings, But he who makes haste to be rich will not go unpunished.

²¹ To show partiality is not good, Because for a piece of bread a man will transgress.

²² A man with an evil eye hastens after wealth And does not know that want will come upon him.

²³ He who rebukes a man will afterward find *more* favor Than he who flatters with the tongue.

²⁴ He who robs his father or his mother And says, "It is not a transgression," Is the companion of a man who destroys.

²⁵ An arrogant man stirs up strife, But he who trusts in the LORD will prosper.

²⁶ He who trusts in his own heart is a fool, But he who walks wisely will be delivered.

²⁷ He who gives to the poor will never want, But he who shuts his eyes will have many curses.

²⁸ When the wicked rise, men hide themselves; But when they perish, the righteous increase.

Discussion

This chapter contains additional wisdom sayings of King Solomon.

Questioning the Passage

1. What does verse two mean?

The monarchy kept the nation together in Solomon's day. The King said that it is essential to keep the monarchy going. If the monarchy fell, then anarchy and chaos would spread over the land. It is better to have a government than anarchy.[123] There are times when the monarchy should have been overthrown, and a new government put in place. The evil of Israel's kings brought the LORD's punishment upon them. Judea then followed the same path of having evil kings who led the LORD to bring the

---

[123] R. Laird Harris, Gleason L. Archer, and Bruce K. Waltke, *Theological Wordbook of the Old Testament* (Chicago: Moody Press, 2004).

Exile. Blind trust in the monarchy is what Solomon said here. He must not have anticipated that his descendants would bring evil unto the land.

2. What does verse eight imply?

   Usury (the collecting of interest for a loan) is forbidden according to Leviticus. A person who gets rich by collecting interest from his own people will discover that the LORD will take the money away from him and give it to the poor.[124]

3. What does verse twenty-six mean?

   Persons have a tendency to trust their own thoughts and not listen to other people who may have more wisdom. One should seek the opinions of other people and then evaluate the situation.

Culture Section

Questioning the passage

1. What was the "formula" for the forgiveness of sin? (v. 13)

   To confess means to acknowledge and reveal what a person has done. In biblical times the confessions were made in a place of worship, or the Temple in Jerusalem. Confession of sin removes the burden of the guilt of the sin. Forgiveness for sin cannot be purchased with money. The Torah demanded that confession occur before one can receive forgiveness from the LORD.[125] Mercy will come from the LORD to all sinners who

---

[124] IBID.

[125] Rocco A. Errico and George M. Lamsa, *Aramaic Light on Ezra through the Song of Solomon* (Smyrna, GA: Noohra Foundation, 2010).

openly acknowledge their sin and pray for the LORD's mercy and forgiveness.

Thoughts

This chapter contains to offer the wisdom of King Solomon.

Chapter Twenty-nine

Language

New American Standard 1995	Hebrew
[1] A man who hardens *his* neck after much reproof Will suddenly be broken beyond remedy.	אִישׁ תּוֹכָחוֹת מַקְשֶׁה־עֹרֶף פֶּתַע יִשָּׁבֵר וְאֵין מַרְפֵּא: [2] בִּרְבוֹת צַדִּיקִים יִשְׂמַח הָעָם וּבִמְשֹׁל רָשָׁע יֵאָנַח עָם:
[2] When the righteous increase, the people rejoice, But when a wicked man rules, people groan.	[3] אִישׁ־אֹהֵב חָכְמָה יְשַׂמַּח אָבִיו וְרֹעֶה זוֹנוֹת יְאַבֶּד־הוֹן:
[3] A man who loves wisdom makes his father glad, But he who keeps company with harlots wastes *his* wealth.	[4] מֶלֶךְ בְּמִשְׁפָּט יַעֲמִיד אָרֶץ וְאִישׁ תְּרוּמוֹת יֶהֶרְסֶנָּה:
[4] The king gives stability to the land by justice, But a man who takes bribes overthrows it.	[5] גֶּבֶר מַחֲלִיק עַל־רֵעֵהוּ רֶשֶׁת פּוֹרֵשׂ עַל־פְּעָמָיו:
[5] A man who flatters his neighbor Is spreading a net for his steps.	[6] בְּפֶשַׁע אִישׁ רָע מוֹקֵשׁ וְצַדִּיק יָרוּן וְשָׂמֵחַ:
[6] By transgression an evil man is ensnared, But the righteous sings and rejoices.	[7] יֹדֵעַ צַדִּיק דִּין דַּלִּים רָשָׁע לֹא־יָבִין דָּעַת:
[7] The righteous is concerned for the rights of the poor, The wicked does not understand *such* concern.	[8] אַנְשֵׁי לָצוֹן יָפִיחוּ קִרְיָה וַחֲכָמִים יָשִׁיבוּ אָף:
[8] Scorners set a city aflame, But wise men turn away anger.	[9] אִישׁ־חָכָם נִשְׁפָּט אֶת־אִישׁ אֱוִיל וְרָגַז וְשָׂחַק וְאֵין נָחַת:
[9] When a wise man has a controversy with a foolish man, The foolish man either rages or laughs, and there is no rest.	[10] אַנְשֵׁי דָמִים יִשְׂנְאוּ־תָם וִישָׁרִים יְבַקְשׁוּ נַפְשׁוֹ:
[10] Men of bloodshed hate the blameless, But the upright are concerned for his life.	[11] כָּל־רוּחוֹ יוֹצִיא כְסִיל וְחָכָם בְּאָחוֹר יְשַׁבְּחֶנָּה:
[11] A fool always loses his temper, But a wise man holds it back.	[12] מֹשֵׁל מַקְשִׁיב עַל־דְּבַר־שָׁקֶר כָּל־מְשָׁרְתָיו רְשָׁעִים:
[12] If a ruler pays attention to falsehood, All his ministers *become* wicked.	[13] רָשׁ וְאִישׁ תְּכָכִים נִפְגָּשׁוּ מֵאִיר־עֵינֵי שְׁנֵיהֶם יְהוָה:
[13] The poor man and the oppressor have this in common: The LORD gives light to the eyes of both.	[14] מֶלֶךְ שׁוֹפֵט בֶּאֱמֶת דַּלִּים כִּסְאוֹ לָעַד יִכּוֹן: [15] שֵׁבֶט וְתוֹכַחַת יִתֵּן חָכְמָה וְנַעַר מְשֻׁלָּח מֵבִישׁ אִמּוֹ:

¹⁴ If a king judges the poor with truth, His throne will be established forever.

¹⁵ The rod and reproof give wisdom, But a child who gets his own way brings shame to his mother.

¹⁶ When the wicked increase, transgression increases; But the righteous will see their fall.

¹⁷ Correct your son, and he will give you comfort; He will also delight your soul.

¹⁸ Where there is no vision, the people are unrestrained, But happy is he who keeps the law.

¹⁹ A slave will not be instructed by words *alone*; For though he understands, there will be no response.

²⁰ Do you see a man who is hasty in his words? There is more hope for a fool than for him.

²¹ He who pampers his slave from childhood Will in the end find him to be a son.

²² An angry man stirs up strife, And a hot-tempered man abounds in transgression.

²³ A man's pride will bring him low, But a humble spirit will obtain honor.

²⁴ He who is a partner with a thief hates his own life; He hears the oath but tells nothing.

²⁵ The fear of man brings a snare, But he who trusts in the LORD will be exalted.

²⁶ Many seek the ruler's favor, But justice for man *comes* from the LORD.

²⁷ An unjust man is abominable to the righteous, And he who is upright in the way is abominable to the wicked.

בִּרְבוֹת רְשָׁעִים יִרְבֶּה־פָּשַׁע וְצַדִּיקִים בְּמַפַּלְתָּם יִרְאוּ׃ ¹⁶

יַסֵּר בִּנְךָ וִינִיחֶךָ וְיִתֵּן מַעֲדַנִּים לְנַפְשֶׁךָ׃ פ ¹⁷

בְּאֵין חָזוֹן יִפָּרַע עָם וְשֹׁמֵר תּוֹרָה אַשְׁרֵהוּ׃ ¹⁸

בִּדְבָרִים לֹא־יִוָּסֶר עָבֶד כִּי־יָבִין וְאֵין מַעֲנֶה׃ ¹⁹

חָזִיתָ אִישׁ אָץ בִּדְבָרָיו תִּקְוָה לִכְסִיל מִמֶּנּוּ׃ ²⁰

מְפַנֵּק מִנֹּעַר עַבְדּוֹ וְאַחֲרִיתוֹ יִהְיֶה מָנוֹן׃ ²¹

אִישׁ־אַף יְגָרֶה מָדוֹן וּבַעַל חֵמָה רַב־פָּשַׁע׃ ²²

גַּאֲוַת אָדָם תַּשְׁפִּילֶנּוּ וּשְׁפַל־רוּחַ יִתְמֹךְ כָּבוֹד׃ ²³

חוֹלֵק עִם־גַּנָּב שׂוֹנֵא נַפְשׁוֹ אָלָה יִשְׁמַע וְלֹא יַגִּיד׃ ²⁴

חֶרְדַּת אָדָם יִתֵּן מוֹקֵשׁ וּבוֹטֵחַ בַּיהוָה יְשֻׂגָּב׃ ²⁵

רַבִּים מְבַקְשִׁים פְּנֵי־מוֹשֵׁל וּמֵיְהוָֹה מִשְׁפַּט־אִישׁ׃ ²⁶

תּוֹעֲבַת צַדִּיקִים אִישׁ עָוֶל וְתוֹעֲבַת רָשָׁע יְשַׁר־דָּרֶךְ׃ פ ²⁷

Process of Discovery

Linguistics Section

Linguistic Structure

[1] A man who hardens *his* neck after much reproof Will suddenly be broken beyond remedy.

[2] When the righteous increase, the people rejoice, But when a wicked man rules, people groan.

[3] A man who loves wisdom makes his father glad, But he who keeps company with harlots wastes *his* wealth.

[4] The king gives stability to the land by justice, But a man who takes bribes overthrows it.

[5] A man who flatters his neighbor Is spreading a net for his steps.

[6] By transgression an evil man is ensnared, But the righteous sings and rejoices.

[7] The righteous is concerned for the rights of the poor, The wicked does not understand *such* concern.

[8] Scorners set a city aflame, But wise men turn away anger.

[9] When a wise man has a controversy with a foolish man, The foolish man either rages or laughs, and there is no rest.

[10] Men of bloodshed hate the blameless, But the upright are concerned for his life.

[11] A fool always loses his temper, But a wise man holds it back.

[12] If a ruler pays attention to falsehood, All his ministers *become* wicked.

[13] The poor man and the oppressor have this in common: The LORD gives light to the eyes of both.

[14] If a king judges the poor with truth, His throne will be established forever.

[15] The rod and reproof give wisdom, But a child who gets his own way brings shame to his mother.

[16] When the wicked increase, transgression increases; But the righteous will see their fall.

[17] Correct your son, and he will give you comfort; He will also delight your soul.

[18] Where there is no vision, the people are unrestrained, But happy is he who keeps the law.

[19] A slave will not be instructed by words *alone*; For though he understands, there will be no response.

[20] Do you see a man who is hasty in his words? There is more hope for a fool than for him.

[21] He who pampers his slave from childhood Will in the end find him to be a son.

[22] An angry man stirs up strife, And a hot-tempered man abounds in transgression.

[23] A man's pride will bring him low, But a humble spirit will obtain honor.

[24] He who is a partner with a thief hates his own life; He hears the oath but tells nothing.

[25] The fear of man brings a snare, But he who trusts in the LORD will be exalted.

[26] Many seek the ruler's favor, But justice for man *comes* from the LORD.

[27] An unjust man is abominable to the righteous, And he who is upright in the way is abominable to the wicked.

Discussion

This chapter contains the wisdom sayings of King Solomon.

Questioning the Passage

1. What does verse eight mean?

   The Sage Ralbag[xiii] said that rabble-rousers could inflame an entire city into aggressive dispute. A wise person can restore calm and bring the people back to their senses.[126]

2. What does verse sixteen say about evil?

   The Sage Malbim said that evil will eventually reach its peak and will collapse upon itself.[127] The righteous need to wait until the fall of evil occurs. The evil persons may not be alive to witness the fall, but the righteous will be alive.

Culture Section

Questioning the passage

1. Why should a ruler not pay attention to gossip? (v. 12)

   In the Near East, a ruler had several servants. The servants would gossip about each other because they were envious of each other. If the ruler

---

126 R. Laird Harris, Gleason L. Archer, and Bruce K. Waltke, *Theological Wordbook of the Old Testament* (Chicago: Moody Press, 2004).

127 IBID.

listened to and reacted to the constant complaining, he would come to a false conclusion that all his servants were wicked.[128]

2. Why is it that when people have no vision, the people are unrestrained? (v. 18)

The Targum reads, "When the evil are many the people are broken, but happy is he who keeps the Law." [129] The Hebrew version uses the word חָזוֹן, which means "vision." King Solomon said that when the people and government do not have a vision for the future, then wicked people will rise in the leadership ranks. When this happens, the evil inclination will spread across the nation, and the people will be torn away from the Torah. If this happens, sinfulness and evil will spread across the nation and will bring idolatry. This was a warning to the future Kings to have a vision of improving the nation and counseling the people. Throughout Israel's history, the rise of evil leaders and Kings were a direct result of the lack of vision.

Thoughts

This chapter contains several statements of wisdom by King Solomon.

---

[128] Rocco A. Errico and George M. Lamsa, *Aramaic Light on Ezra through the Song of Solomon* (Smyma, GA: Noohra Foundation, 2010).
[129] Mangan Céline. *The Targum of Job.: the Targum of Proverbs U.a.* Liturgical Press, 1987.

Chapter Thirty

Language

New American Standard 1995	Hebrew
1 The words of Agur the son of Jakeh, the oracle. The man declares to Ithiel, to Ithiel and Ucal: 2 Surely I am more stupid than any man, And I do not have the understanding of a man. 3 Neither have I learned wisdom, Nor do I have the knowledge of the Holy One. 4 Who has ascended into heaven and descended? Who has gathered the wind in His fists? Who has wrapped the waters in His garment? Who has established all the ends of the earth? What is His name or His son's name? Surely you know! 5 Every word of God is tested; He is a shield to those who take refuge in Him. 6 Do not add to His words Or He will reprove you, and you will be proved a liar. 7 Two things I asked of You, Do not refuse me before I die: 8 Keep deception and lies far from me, Give me neither poverty nor riches; Feed me with the food that is my portion, 9 That I not be full and deny *You* and say, "Who is the LORD?" Or that I not be in want and steal, And profane the name of my God. 10 Do not slander a slave to his master, Or he will curse you and you will be found guilty. 11 There is a kind of *man* who curses his father And does not bless his mother.	דִּבְרֵי ׀ אָגוּר בִּן־יָקֶה הַמַּשָּׂא נְאֻם הַגֶּבֶר לְאִיתִיאֵל לְאִיתִיאֵל וְאֻכָל׃ 2 כִּי בַעַר אָנֹכִי מֵאִישׁ וְלֹא־בִינַת אָדָם לִי׃ 3 וְלֹא־לָמַדְתִּי חָכְמָה וְדַעַת קְדֹשִׁים אֵדָע׃ 4 מִי עָלָה־שָׁמַיִם ׀ וַיֵּרַד מִי אָסַף־רוּחַ ׀ בְּחָפְנָיו מִי צָרַר־מַיִם ׀ בַּשִּׂמְלָה מִי הֵקִים כָּל־אַפְסֵי־אָרֶץ מַה־שְּׁמוֹ וּמַה־שֶּׁם־בְּנוֹ כִּי תֵדָע׃ 5 כָּל־אִמְרַת אֱלוֹהַּ צְרוּפָה מָגֵן הוּא לַחֹסִים בּוֹ׃ 6 אַל־תּוֹסְףְּ עַל־דְּבָרָיו פֶּן־יוֹכִיחַ בְּךָ וְנִכְזָבְתָּ׃ פ 7 שְׁתַּיִם שָׁאַלְתִּי מֵאִתָּךְ אַל־תִּמְנַע מִמֶּנִּי בְּטֶרֶם אָמוּת׃ 8 שָׁוְא ׀ וּדְבַר־כָּזָב הַרְחֵק מִמֶּנִּי רֵאשׁ וָעֹשֶׁר אַל־תִּתֶּן־לִי הַטְרִיפֵנִי לֶחֶם חֻקִּי׃ 9 פֶּן אֶשְׂבַּע ׀ וְכִחַשְׁתִּי וְאָמַרְתִּי מִי יְהוָה וּפֶן־אִוָּרֵשׁ וְגָנַבְתִּי וְתָפַשְׂתִּי שֵׁם אֱלֹהָי׃ פ 10 אַל־תַּלְשֵׁן עֶבֶד אֶל־(אֲדֹנוֹ) [אֲדֹנָיו] פֶּן־יְקַלֶּלְךָ וְאָשָׁמְתָּ׃ 11 דּוֹר אָבִיו יְקַלֵּל וְאֶת־אִמּוֹ לֹא יְבָרֵךְ׃ 12 דּוֹר טָהוֹר בְּעֵינָיו וּמִצֹּאָתוֹ לֹא רֻחָץ׃ 13 דּוֹר מָה־רָמוּ עֵינָיו וְעַפְעַפָּיו יִנָּשֵׂאוּ׃ 14 דּוֹר חֲרָבוֹת שִׁנָּיו וּמַאֲכָלוֹת מְתַלְּעֹתָיו לֶאֱכֹל עֲנִיִּים מֵאֶרֶץ וְאֶבְיוֹנִים מֵאָדָם׃ פ

¹² There is a kind who is pure in his own eyes, Yet is not washed from his filthiness.

¹³ There is a kind-- oh how lofty are his eyes! And his eyelids are raised *in arrogance*.

¹⁴ There is a kind of *man* whose teeth are *like* swords And his jaw teeth *like* knives, To devour the afflicted from the earth And the needy from among men.

¹⁵ The leech has two daughters, "Give," "Give." There are three things that will not be satisfied, Four that will not say, "Enough":

¹⁶ Sheol, and the barren womb, Earth that is never satisfied with water, And fire that never says, "Enough."

¹⁷ The eye that mocks a father And scorns a mother, The ravens of the valley will pick it out, And the young eagles will eat it.

¹⁸ There are three things which are too wonderful for me, Four which I do not understand:

¹⁹ The way of an eagle in the sky, The way of a serpent on a rock, The way of a ship in the middle of the sea, And the way of a man with a maid.

²⁰ This is the way of an adulterous woman: She eats and wipes her mouth, And says, "I have done no wrong."

²¹ Under three things the earth quakes, And under four, it cannot bear up:

²² Under a slave when he becomes king, And a fool when he is satisfied with food,

²³ Under an unloved woman when she gets a husband, And a maidservant when she supplants her mistress.

²⁴ Four things are small on the earth, But they are exceedingly wise:

---

15 לַעֲלוּקָה ׀ שְׁתֵּי בָנוֹת הַב ׀ הַב שָׁלוֹשׁ הֵנָּה לֹא תִשְׂבַּעְנָה אַרְבַּע לֹא־אָמְרוּ הוֹן׃

16 שְׁאוֹל וְעֹצֶר רָחַם אֶרֶץ לֹא־שָׂבְעָה מַּיִם וְאֵשׁ לֹא־אָמְרָה הוֹן׃

17 עַיִן ׀ תִּלְעַג לְאָב וְתָבוּז לִיקֲּהַת־אֵם יִקְּרוּהָ עֹרְבֵי־נַחַל וְיֹאכְלוּהָ בְנֵי־נָשֶׁר׃ פ

18 שְׁלֹשָׁה הֵמָּה נִפְלְאוּ מִמֶּנִּי (וְאַרְבַּע) [וְאַרְבָּעָה] לֹא יְדַעְתִּים׃

19 דֶּרֶךְ הַנֶּשֶׁר ׀ בַּשָּׁמַיִם דֶּרֶךְ נָחָשׁ עֲלֵי צוּר דֶּרֶךְ־אֳנִיָּה בְלֶב־יָם וְדֶרֶךְ גֶּבֶר בְּעַלְמָה׃

20 כֵּן ׀ דֶּרֶךְ אִשָּׁה מְנָאָפֶת אָכְלָה וּמָחֲתָה פִיהָ וְאָמְרָה לֹא־פָעַלְתִּי אָוֶן׃ פ

21 תַּחַת שָׁלוֹשׁ רָגְזָה אֶרֶץ וְתַחַת אַרְבַּע לֹא־תוּכַל שְׂאֵת׃

22 תַּחַת־עֶבֶד כִּי יִמְלוֹךְ וְנָבָל כִּי יִשְׂבַּע־לָחֶם׃

23 תַּחַת שְׂנוּאָה כִּי תִבָּעֵל וְשִׁפְחָה כִּי־תִירַשׁ גְּבִרְתָּהּ׃ פ

24 אַרְבָּעָה הֵם קְטַנֵּי־אָרֶץ וְהֵמָּה חֲכָמִים מְחֻכָּמִים׃

25 הַנְּמָלִים עַם לֹא־עָז וַיָּכִינוּ בַקַּיִץ לַחְמָם׃

26 שְׁפַנִּים עַם לֹא־עָצוּם וַיָּשִׂימוּ בַסֶּלַע בֵּיתָם׃

27 מֶלֶךְ אֵין לָאַרְבֶּה וַיֵּצֵא חֹצֵץ כֻּלּוֹ׃

28 שְׂמָמִית בְּיָדַיִם תְּתַפֵּשׂ וְהִיא בְּהֵיכְלֵי מֶלֶךְ׃ פ

29 שְׁלֹשָׁה הֵמָּה מֵיטִיבֵי צָעַד וְאַרְבָּעָה מֵיטִבֵי לָכֶת׃

30 לַיִשׁ גִּבּוֹר בַּבְּהֵמָה וְלֹא־יָשׁוּב מִפְּנֵי־כֹל׃

25 The ants are not a strong people, But they prepare their food in the summer;

26 The shephanim are not mighty people, Yet they make their houses in the rocks;

27 The locusts have no king, Yet all of them go out in ranks;

28 The lizard you may grasp with the hands, Yet it is in kings' palaces.

29 There are three things which are stately in *their* march, Even four which are stately when they walk:

30 The lion *which* is mighty among beasts And does not retreat before any,

31 The strutting rooster, the male goat also, And a king *when his* army is with him.

32 If you have been foolish in exalting yourself Or if you have plotted *evil, put your* hand on your mouth.

33 For the churning of milk produces butter, And pressing the nose brings forth blood; So the churning of anger produces strife.

זַרְזִיר מָתְנַיִם אוֹ־תָיִשׁ וּמֶלֶךְ אַלְקוּם עִמּוֹ׃ ³¹

אִם־נָבַלְתָּ בְהִתְנַשֵּׂא וְאִם־זַמּוֹתָ יָד לְפֶה׃ ³²

כִּי מִיץ חָלָב יוֹצִיא חֶמְאָה וּמִיץ־אַף יוֹצִיא דָם וּמִיץ אַפַּיִם יוֹצִיא רִיב׃ פ ³³

Process of Discovery

Linguistics Section

Linguistic Structure

A1[1] The words of Agur the son of Jakeh, the oracle. The man declares to Ithiel, to Ithiel and Ucal: [2] Surely I am more stupid than any man, And I do not have the understanding of a man. [3] Neither have I learned wisdom, Nor do I have the knowledge of the Holy One. [4] Who has ascended into heaven and descended? Who has gathered the wind in His fists? Who has wrapped the waters in His garment? Who has established all the ends of the earth? What is His name or His son's name? Surely you know! [5] Every word of God is tested; He is a shield to those who take refuge in Him. [6] Do not add to His words Or He will reprove you, and you will be proved a liar.

A2 [7] Two things I asked of You, Do not refuse me before I die: [8] Keep deception and lies far from me, Give me neither poverty nor riches; Feed me with the food that is my portion, [9] That I not be full and deny *You* and say, "Who is the LORD?" Or that I not be in want and steal, And profane the name of my God.

A3 [10] Do not slander a slave to his master, Or he will curse you and you will be found guilty. [11] There is a kind of *man* who curses his father And does not bless his mother. [12] There is a kind who is pure in his own eyes, Yet is not washed from his filthiness. [13] There is a kind-- oh how lofty are his eyes! And his eyelids are raised *in arrogance*. [14] There is a kind of *man* whose teeth are *like* swords And his jaw teeth *like* knives, To devour the afflicted from the earth And the needy from among men.

A4 [15] The leech has two daughters, "Give," "Give." There are three things that will not be satisfied, Four that will not say, "Enough": [16] Sheol, and the barren womb, Earth that is never satisfied with water, And fire that never says, "Enough." [17] The eye that mocks a father And scorns a mother, The ravens of the valley will pick it out, And the young eagles will eat it.

A5 [18] There are three things which are too wonderful for me, Four which I do not understand: [19] The way of an eagle in the sky, The way of a serpent on a rock, The way of a ship in the middle of the sea, And the way of a man with a maid. [20] This is the way of an adulterous woman: She eats and wipes her mouth, And says, "I have done no wrong."

A6 [21] Under three things the earth quakes, And under four, it cannot bear up: [22] Under a slave when he becomes king, And a fool when he is satisfied with food, [23] Under an unloved woman when she gets a husband, And a maidservant when she supplants her mistress.

A7 [24] Four things are small on the earth, But they are exceedingly wise: [25] The ants are not a strong people, But they prepare their food in the summer; [26] The shephanim are not mighty people, Yet they make their houses in the rocks; [27] The locusts have no king, Yet all of them go out in ranks; [28] The lizard you may grasp with the hands, Yet it is in kings' palaces.

A8 [29] There are three things which are stately in *their* march, Even four which are stately when they walk: [30] The lion *which* is mighty among beasts And does not retreat before any, [31] The strutting rooster, the male goat also, And a king *when his* army is with him.

A9 [32] If you have been foolish in exalting yourself Or if you have plotted *evil, put your* hand on your mouth. [33] For the churning of milk produces butter, And pressing the nose brings forth blood; So the churning of anger produces strife.

A1(30:1-6)   Five questions about the Holy One.
A2(30:7-9)   Two wishes
A3(30:10-14)   Four groups
A4(30:15-17)   Four never say, Enough
A5(30:18-20)   Four I cannot understand
A6(30:21-23)   Under four it cannot bear up
A7(30:24-28)   Four things are among the smallest on the earth
A8(30:29-31)   Four are stately in their carriage
A9(30:32-33)   Three objects are produced

A: Lists.[130]

Discussion

The sayings in this chapter are attributed to Agur Ben Jakeh.

---

[130] Hajime Murai, "Literary Structure (Chiasm, Chiasmus) of Book of Proverbs," Literary structure (chiasm, chiasmus) of each pericopes of Book of Proverbs, accessed June 25, 2020, http://www.bible.literarystructure.info/bible/20_Proverbs_pericope_e.html.

Questioning the Passage

1. What does verse six mean?

    This is a warning that the inspired Word of the LORD cannot be changed, deleted, or added unto.

Biblical Personalities

1. Agur[131]

By: J. Frederic McCurdy, Louis Ginzberg

—Biblical Data:

The compiler of a collection of proverbs found in Prov. xxx. The text (ver. 1) seems to say that he was a "Massaite," the gentilic termination not being indicated in the traditional writing "Ha-Massa" (compare Gen. xxv. 14). This place has been identified by some Assyriologists with the land of Mash, a district between Palestine and Babylonia, and the traces of nomadic or seminomadic life and thought found in Gen. xxxi. and xxxii. give some support to the hypothesis. Graetz, followed by Bickell and Cheyne, conjectures that the original reading is "Ha-Moshel," "the collector of proverbs." The true explanation is still uncertain.

—In Rabbinical Literature:

"Agur," and the enigmatical names and words which follow in Prov. xxx. 1, are interpreted by the Haggadah as epithets of Solomon, playing upon the words as follows: "Agur" denotes "the compiler; the one who first gathered maxims together." "The son of Jakeh" denotes "the one who spat out," that is, "despised" (from קיא, "to spit"), le-Ithiel, "the words of God" (ot,

---

[131] "JewishEncyclopedia.com," AGUR BEN JAKEH - JewishEncyclopedia.com, accessed November 29, 2020, http://jewishencyclopedia.com/articles/927-agur-ben-jakeh.

"word"; *El*, "God"), exclaiming, "I can [*ukal*] transgress the law against marrying many wives without fear of being misled by them." Another exposition is that "Agur" means "the one who is brave in the pursuit of wisdom"; "the son of Jakeh" signifies "he who is free from sin" (from *naKi*, "pure"); *ha-massa* ("the burden"), "he who bore the yoke of God"; *le-Ithiel*, "he who understood the signs" (*ot*, "sign") and deeds of God, or he who understood the alphabet of God, that is the creative "letters" (*ot*, "letter") (see Ber. 55*a*); *we-Ukal*, "the master" (Tan., Waera, ed. Buber, 2, p. 18; Midr. Prov. xxx. 1; YalK. on the passage, § 962).

Culture Section

Questioning the passage

1. What does it mean that a person's teeth are like knives? (v. 14)

   Table knives were not known in biblical times. People used their front teeth to cut meat. The metaphor is that there were men who exploited the poor. It was said that their teeth were like swords. Today we call these people "sharks."[132]

2. What does it mean "the way of a man with a maid?" (v. 14)

   In the Near East, until recently, young men never kept company with women. Marriages were prearranged by the parents of the bride and the bridegroom. Young men found it difficult to make decisions or what to do with themselves in the years between boyhood and marriage. Often when older people spoke about young men, they would say, "They are in

---

[132] Rocco A. Errico and George M. Lamsa, *Aramaic Light on Ezra through the Song of Solomon* (Smyma, GA: Noohra Foundation, 2010).

the air" which meant they did not know what they were doing. Men were not allowed to speak in a council meeting until they were thirty years old.[133] It could be said that the young man did not know what his future was before he was married. He would have learned his Torah and his occupation but knew nothing about what his family would become.

Thoughts

These are sayings from Agur Ben Jakeh.

---

[133] IBID.

Chapter Thirty-One

Language

New American Standard 1995	Hebrew
[1] The words of King Lemuel, the oracle which his mother taught him:	דִּבְרֵי לְמוּאֵל מֶלֶךְ מַשָּׂא אֲשֶׁר־יִסְּרַתּוּ אִמּֽוֹ׃ [2]
[2] What, O my son? And what, O son of my womb? And what, O son of my vows?	מַה־בְּרִי וּמַה־בַּר־בִּטְנִי וּמֶה בַּר־נְדָרָֽי׃
[3] Do not give your strength to women, Or your ways to that which destroys kings.	אַל־תִּתֵּן לַנָּשִׁים חֵילֶךָ וּדְרָכֶיךָ לַמְחוֹת מְלָכִֽין׃ [3]
[4] It is not for kings, O Lemuel, It is not for kings to drink wine, Or for rulers to desire strong drink,	אַל לַמְלָכִים לְמוֹאֵל אַל לַמְלָכִים שְׁתוֹ־יָיִן וּלְרוֹזְנִים (אֵו) [אֵי] שֵׁכָֽר׃ [4]
[5] For they will drink and forget what is decreed, And pervert the rights of all the afflicted.	פֶּן־יִשְׁתֶּה וְיִשְׁכַּח מְחֻקָּק וִישַׁנֶּה דִּין כָּל־בְּנֵי־עֹֽנִי׃ [5]
[6] Give strong drink to him who is perishing, And wine to him whose life is bitter.	תְּנוּ־שֵׁכָר לְאוֹבֵד וְיַיִן לְמָרֵי נָֽפֶשׁ׃ [6]
[7] Let him drink and forget his poverty And remember his trouble no more.	יִשְׁתֶּה וְיִשְׁכַּח רִישׁוֹ וַעֲמָלוֹ לֹא יִזְכָּר־עֽוֹד׃ [7]
[8] Open your mouth for the mute, For the rights of all the unfortunate.	פְּתַח־פִּיךָ לְאִלֵּם אֶל־דִּין כָּל־בְּנֵי חֲלֽוֹף׃ [8]
[9] Open your mouth, judge righteously, And defend the rights of the afflicted and needy.	פְּתַח־פִּיךָ שְׁפָט־צֶדֶק וְדִין עָנִי וְאֶבְיֽוֹן׃ פ [9]
[10] An excellent wife, who can find? For her worth is far above jewels.	אֵֽשֶׁת־חַיִל מִי יִמְצָא וְרָחֹק מִפְּנִינִים מִכְרָֽהּ׃ [10]
[11] The heart of her husband trusts in her, And he will have no lack of gain.	בָּטַח בָּהּ לֵב בַּעְלָהּ וְשָׁלָל לֹא יֶחְסָֽר׃ [11]
[12] She does him good and not evil All the days of her life.	גְּמָלַתְהוּ טוֹב וְלֹא־רָע כֹּל יְמֵי חַיֶּֽיהָ׃ [12]
[13] She looks for wool and flax And works with her hands in delight.	דָּרְשָׁה צֶמֶר וּפִשְׁתִּים וַתַּעַשׂ בְּחֵפֶץ כַּפֶּֽיהָ׃ [13]
[14] She is like merchant ships; She brings her food from afar.	הָיְתָה כָּאֳנִיּוֹת סוֹחֵר מִמֶּרְחָק תָּבִיא לַחְמָֽהּ׃ [14]
[15] She rises also while it is still night And gives food to her household And portions to her maidens.	וַתָּקָם בְּעוֹד לַיְלָה וַתִּתֵּן טֶרֶף לְבֵיתָהּ וְחֹק לְנַעֲרֹתֶֽיהָ׃ [15]
	זָמְמָה שָׂדֶה וַתִּקָּחֵהוּ מִפְּרִי כַפֶּיהָ (נָטַע) [נָטְעָה] כָּֽרֶם׃ [16]
	חָגְרָה בְעוֹז מָתְנֶיהָ וַתְּאַמֵּץ זְרוֹעֹתֶֽיהָ׃ [17]
	טָעֲמָה כִּי־טוֹב סַחְרָהּ לֹא־יִכְבֶּה (בַלַּיִל) [בַלַּיְלָה] נֵרָֽהּ׃ [18]
	יָדֶיהָ שִׁלְּחָה בַכִּישׁוֹר וְכַפֶּיהָ תָּמְכוּ פָֽלֶךְ׃ [19]
	כַּפָּהּ פָּרְשָׂה לֶעָנִי וְיָדֶיהָ שִׁלְּחָה לָאֶבְיֽוֹן׃ [20]
	לֹא־תִירָא לְבֵיתָהּ מִשָּׁלֶג כִּי כָל־בֵּיתָהּ לָבֻשׁ שָׁנִֽים׃ [21]
	מַרְבַדִּים עָשְׂתָה־לָּהּ שֵׁשׁ וְאַרְגָּמָן לְבוּשָֽׁהּ׃ [22]
	נוֹדָע בַּשְּׁעָרִים בַּעְלָהּ בְּשִׁבְתּוֹ עִם־זִקְנֵי־אָֽרֶץ׃ [23]
	סָדִין עָשְׂתָה וַתִּמְכֹּר וַחֲגוֹר נָתְנָה לַֽכְּנַעֲנִֽי׃ [24]
	עֹז־וְהָדָר לְבוּשָׁהּ וַתִּשְׂחַק לְיוֹם אַחֲרֽוֹן׃ [25]

16 She considers a field and buys it; From her earnings she plants a vineyard.

17 She girds herself with strength And makes her arms strong.

18 She senses that her gain is good; Her lamp does not go out at night.

19 She stretches out her hands to the distaff, And her hands grasp the spindle.

20 She extends her hand to the poor, And she stretches out her hands to the needy.

21 She is not afraid of the snow for her household, For all her household are clothed with scarlet.

22 She makes coverings for herself; Her clothing is fine linen and purple.

23 Her husband is known in the gates, When he sits among the elders of the land.

24 She makes linen garments and sells *them*, And supplies belts to the tradesmen.

25 Strength and dignity are her clothing, And she smiles at the future.

26 She opens her mouth in wisdom, And the teaching of kindness is on her tongue.

27 She looks well to the ways of her household, And does not eat the bread of idleness.

28 Her children rise up and bless her; Her husband *also*, and he praises her, *saying*:

29 "Many daughters have done nobly, But you excel them all."

30 Charm is deceitful and beauty is vain, *But* a woman who fears the LORD, she shall be praised.

31 Give her the product of her hands, And let her works praise her in the gates.

פִּיהָ פָּתְחָה בְחָכְמָה וְתוֹרַת־חֶסֶד עַל־ 26
לְשׁוֹנָהּ:

צוֹפִיָּה הֲלִיכוֹת בֵּיתָהּ וְלֶחֶם עַצְלוּת לֹא 27
תֹאכֵל:

קָמוּ בָנֶיהָ וַיְאַשְּׁרוּהָ בַּעְלָהּ וַיְהַלְלָהּ: 28

רַבּוֹת בָּנוֹת עָשׂוּ חָיִל וְאַתְּ עָלִית עַל־ 29
כֻּלָּנָה:

שֶׁקֶר הַחֵן וְהֶבֶל הַיֹּפִי אִשָּׁה יִרְאַת־יְהֹוָה 30
הִיא תִתְהַלָּל:

תְּנוּ־לָהּ מִפְּרִי יָדֶיהָ וִיהַלְלוּהָ בַשְּׁעָרִים 31
מַעֲשֶׂיהָ

Process of Discovery

Linguistics Section

Linguistic Structure

[1] The words of King Lemuel, the oracle which his mother taught him: [2] What, O my son? And what, O son of my womb? And what, O son of my vows?

[3] Do not give your strength to women, Or your ways to that which destroys kings.
[4] It is not for kings, O Lemuel, It is not for kings to drink wine, Or for rulers to desire strong drink, [5] For they will drink and forget what is decreed, And pervert the rights of all the afflicted.

[6] Give strong drink to him who is perishing, And wine to him whose life is bitter.
[7] Let him drink and forget his poverty And remember his trouble no more.
[8] Open your mouth for the mute, For the rights of all the unfortunate.
[9] Open your mouth, judge righteously, And defend the rights of the afflicted and needy.
[10] An excellent wife, who can find? For her worth is far above jewels.
[11] The heart of her husband trusts in her, And he will have no lack of gain.
[12] She does him good and not evil All the days of her life.
[13] She looks for wool and flax And works with her hands in delight.
[14] She is like merchant ships; She brings her food from afar.
[15] She rises also while it is still night And gives food to her household And portions to her maidens.
[16] She considers a field and buys it; From her earnings she plants a vineyard.
[17] She girds herself with strength And makes her arms strong.
[18] She senses that her gain is good; Her lamp does not go out at night.
[19] She stretches out her hands to the distaff, And her hands grasp the spindle.
[20] She extends her hand to the poor, And she stretches out her hands to the needy.
[21] She is not afraid of the snow for her household, For all her household are clothed with scarlet.
[22] She makes coverings for herself; Her clothing is fine linen and purple.
[23] Her husband is known in the gates, When he sits among the elders of the land.
[24] She makes linen garments and sells *them*, And supplies belts to the tradesmen.
[25] Strength and dignity are her clothing, And she smiles at the future.
[26] She opens her mouth in wisdom, And the teaching of kindness is on her tongue.
[27] She looks well to the ways of her household, And does not eat the bread of idleness.
[28] Her children rise up and bless her; Her husband *also*, and he praises her, *saying*:
[29] "Many daughters have done nobly, But you excel them all."
[30] Charm is deceitful and beauty is vain, *But* a woman who fears the LORD, she shall be praised.

[31] Give her the product of her hands, And let her works praise her in the gates.

Discussion

This chapter is the sayings of King Lemuel.

Biblical Personalities

1. King Lemuel – "Proverbs 31:2-9 is introduced as the words of King Lemuel from prophecy that had been taught to him by his mother. Proverbs 31:1 states, "The words of king Lemuel, the prophecy that his mother taught him." Lemuel is mentioned only in this passage in the Bible (Proverbs 31:1, 4). This has left the door open to all kinds of speculation as to his true identity. He has been thought by interpreters to be imaginary, to be Solomon himself, to be Hezekiah, to be a Lemuel who was king of Massa (a play on the Hebrew words), or just some petty Arabian prince. In other words, no one really knows."[134]

Culture Section

Questioning the passage

1. What does verse six mean?

The Targum says, "Give liquor to those who mourn…"[135] In the Near East, a person mourns for a lost family member for a long time. The wine is supposed to help the person forget about their loss.

---

[134] "Learn The Bible," King Lemuel | Learn The Bible, accessed November 29, 2020, http://www.learnthebible.org/king-lemuel.html.
[135] Mangan Céline. *The Targum of Job.: the Targum of Proverbs U.a.* Liturgical Press, 1987.

2. What does verse eighteen say about a woman?

"Her lamp does not go out all night" is a Near Eastern expression that means that she works all night clear into the early morning hours. A virtuous woman who discovered that her merchandise was in great demand worked during the night. Most people went to sleep shortly after sunset. Olive oil that was used for lamps was expensive. Industrious women, on the other hand, worked through the night weaving and spinning clothing and rugs.[136]

3. What does it mean to sit at the gate? (v. 23)

This verse relates back to verses sixteen to twenty-two. The husband of a virtuous woman would wear nice clothing and would appear prosperous. The administration of the city was done at the gates. He would have been welcomed at the gate and could participate in the trials that might be occurring.[137]

Thoughts

The book of Proverbs concludes with the sayings and instructions of King Lemuel. This chapter is the only place in the Hebrew Bible where this name appears. It is not known who this person was nor what country he was King. The author of Proverbs decided that his sayings were important enough to be placed into this book.

---

[136] Rocco A. Errico and George M. Lamsa, *Aramaic Light on Ezra through the Song of Solomon* (Smyma, GA: Noohra Foundation, 2010).
[137] IBID.

BIBLIOGRAPHY

1986. *Back to School*. Directed by Paper Clip Productions.

Davis, Anne Kimball. 2012. *The Synoptic Gospels*. Albuquerque, NM.

Danker, Frederick W., Walter Bauer, and William F. Arndt. *A Greek-English Lexicon of the New Testament and Other Early Christian Literature*. Chicago: University of Chicago Press, 2000.

Errico, Rocco A., and George M. Lamsa. *Aramaic Light on Ezra through the Song of Solomon*. Smyma, GA: Noohra Foundation, 2010.

Ginsburg, Eliezer. *Mishlei = Proverbs: a New Translation with a Commentary Anthologized from Talmudic, Midrashic and Rabbinic Sources*. New York: Mesorah Publications Ltd, 1998.

Google Search. Google. Accessed June 1, 2020. https://www.google.com/search?sxsrf=ALeKk00INN_6n4EuhzGigiZP9onMg16p3Q%3A1591025699153&source=hp&ei=IyDVXpi8BsyHytMP3Ymp8Ac&q=satire%2Bdefinit&oq=satire%2Bdefinit&gs_lcp=CgZwc3ktYWIQAzIHCAAQRhD5ATICCAAyAggAMgIIADICCAAyAggAMgIIADICCAAyAggAMgIIADoHCCMQ6gIQJzoECCMQJzoFCAAQkQI6BQgAEIMBOgQIABAKOgkIABAKEEYQ-QFQzQ9YkypghERoAnAAeAKAAfUOiAGzLpIBDjExLjUuMS4wLjEuOC0ymAEAoAEBqgEHZ3dzLXdperABCg&sclient=psy-ab&ved=0ahUKEwjY2f7M-ODpAhXMg3IEHd1ECn4Q4dUDCAk&uact=5.

Harris, R. Laird, Gleason L. Archer, and Bruce K. Waltke. *Theological Wordbook of the Old Testament*. Chicago: Moody Press, 2004.

"JewishEncyclopedia.com." AGUR BEN JAKEH - JewishEncyclopedia.com. Accessed November 29, 2020. http://jewishencyclopedia.com/articles/927-agur-ben-jakeh.

"Learn The Bible." King Lemuel | Learn The Bible. Accessed November 29, 2020. http://www.learnthebible.org/king-lemuel.html.

Mangan Céline, and Martin McNamara. *The Aramaic Bible: the Targums*. Edinburgh: Clark, 1991.

Murai, Hajime. "Literary Structure (Chiasm, Chiasmus) of Book of Proverbs." Literary structure (chiasm, chiasmus) of each pericopes of Book of Proverbs. Accessed June 25, 2020. http://www.bible.literarystructure.info/bible/20_Proverbs_pericope_e.html.

Murai, Hajime. "Literary Structure (Chiasm, Chiasmus) of Book of Proverbs." Literary structure (chiasm, chiasmus) of each pericopes of Book of Proverbs. Accessed May 30, 2020. http://www.bible.literarystructure.info/bible/20_Proverbs_pericope_e.html.

Murai, Hajime. "Literary Structure (Chiasm, Chiasmus) of Book of Proverbs." Literary structure (chiasm, chiasmus) of each pericopes of Book of Proverbs. Accessed November 29, 2020. http://www.bible.literarystructure.info/bible/20_Proverbs_pericope_e.html.

END NOTES

---

[i] "Meïr Leibush ben Yehiel Michel Weisser (Malbim) was a rabbi, Hebrew grammarian, halachic scholar, and author of one of the most insightful and comprehensive Torah commentaries since medieval times. Known as the "ilui (prodigy) of Volhynia," he served in seven different rabbinic posts over the course of his lifetime. His staunch adherence to halacha and defense of tradition put him in direct confrontation with "enlightened" intellectuals who wished to introduce Reformist innovations in worship and other communal institutions. While serving as chief rabbi of Bucharest, he was falsely charged by his opponents and he only escaped imprisonment on the condition that he leave Romania. Persecution by reformers followed him to other rabbinic posts, including Lunchitz, where he was additionally attacked by a Chassidic faction that accused him of introducing enlightenment thought in his Torah commentary. On his way to accept a post in Krementchug, he fell sick in Kiev and died on the first day of Rosh HaShanah." Source: https://www.sefaria.org/person/Malbim

[ii] The name of Vilna Gaon Elijah ben Solomon Zalman, the greatest sage of the 18th century, the world-famous commentator of Torah and Talmud, made Vilnius famous as Lithuanian Jerusalem. His powerful intellect and erudition caused Vilnius to become a spiritual center of Jews that was, known all over the world. As Jacob S. Reizin wrote in the beginning of the 20th century, "After completing the Talmud, almost no expert of Jewish literature was better than or at least equal to Elijah of Vilnius." Source: http://www.jmuseum.lt/en/vilna-gaon-elijah-ben-solomon-zalman-2/i/156//

[iii] "With Jose bar Zevida, his early schoolmate and lifelong colleague and business partner, he studied under Ze'era I and Rav Ela.[1] When, as young men, they called

on <u>Abbahu</u> to express their sympathy with him in his bereavement, he treated them as prominent scholars.[2] But Jonah's special master was <u>Rav Jeremiah</u>.[3] From these masters and others, the youths acquired a thorough familiarity with the traditions, and gradually rose from pupils to fellows. Thus, it is said, "Haggai opened the discourse, and Jonah and Jose closed it".[4]

Finally they succeeded to the rectorate of the academy at <u>Tiberias</u>. In his office Jonah was distinguished by his paternal care for his pupils, to whom he gave both advice and material support.[5] According to the halakhic requirement he gave away the tithe of his income, but to those who studied <u>halachah</u>, not to <u>priests</u> or <u>Levites</u>, deriving his authority from II <u>Chronicles</u> 31:4.[6] When he discovered a worthy man who was poor, he would aid him in such a way as not to hurt his self-respect. "I understand," he would say to him, "that you have fallen heir to an estate" or "that your debtors will soon pay you; borrow some money of me, which you may repay when you come into possession of your fortune." As soon as the loan had been accepted, he would relieve the borrower from his promise by telling him, "This money is yours as a gift." This procedure he regarded as suggested by <u>Psalms</u>: "Blessed is he that considers [Hebr. משכיל = "is thoughtful towards"] the poor".[7]

Jonah also enjoyed a certain respect among the <u>Romans</u>.[8] He was included among those styled ("the mighty ones of the land of Israel"), because, the Rabbis explained, of the efficacy of his prayers in times of drought. The following miracle is related of him: Once, on <u>Shabbat</u>, fire broke out on his premises. A <u>Nabatean</u> whose property adjoined Jonah's attempted to extinguish it, but Jonah would not permit him thus to profane the Sabbath. "Do you rely on your good luck?" mockingly asked the Nabatean, to which Jonah replied, "Yes"; whereupon the fire was quenched.[9]

As rectors of the academy at Tiberias, Jonah and Jose had many disciples, some of whom became leaders in the next generation, and spread and perpetuated their master's doctrines. Jonah left a worthy son and successor in the person of <u>Mani II</u>."" Souce: https://en.wikipedia.org/wiki/Rabbi_Jonah

[iv] "The word "gaon" means genius and on no person could this title be more appropriately bestowed than on Rabbi Eliyahu of Vilna. Rabbi Eliyahu was probably the most influential Jewish leader in modern history.

Rabbi Eliyahu's great abilities began to show at a very early age. At the age of seven he gave his first public discourse and displayed a fully developed intellect. By the time he was ten he had advanced to the point where he no longer needed a teacher. When he was still a young man, Rabbi Eliyahu accepted upon himself "galus," self-imposed exile (a not unheard of practice at that time), in which he wandered from community to community as a beggar. This lasted for a period of some years whereupon he returned to the city of Vilna. Despite efforts on his part to hide his great righteousness and phenomenal knowledge, he was soon famed as a great tzadik (righteous man) and Torah scholar. At the age of 35 he was approached by one of the leading sages of that time, Rabbi Yonason Eybschutz, to act as an intermediary in the conflict between him and another great sage, Rabbi Yakov Emden. Source: https://www.jewishvirtuallibrary.org/rabbi-eliyahu-of-vilna-the-vilna-gaon

[v] "Rashi was the outstanding Biblical commentator of the Middle Ages. He was born in Troyes, France, and lived from 1040 to 1105, surviving the massacres of the First Crusade through Europe. His father Yitzchak was a great scholar, but very poor, making his living from the sale of wine. As a young man Rashi traveled to Worms, Germany, and other towns that were known for their scholars. In Mainz, he studied with Rabbenu Gershom and became his most brilliant student.At twenty-five, he founded his own academy in Troyes and was later elected Rabbi of the town. Rashi decided to write a

commentary in simple language, using the fewest words possible, to make it easy to understand the Torah." Source: https://www.jewishvirtuallibrary.org/rabbi-shlomo-yitzchaki-rashi

[vi] Metzudos was an Sage who wrote several commentaries about different biblical texts.

[vii] Bahya ben Joseph ibn Paquda (also: Pakuda, Bakuda, Hebrew: בחיי אבן פקודה, Arabic: بهية بن باكودا), c. 1050–1120,[1] was a Jewish philosopher and rabbi who lived at Zaragoza, Al-Andalus (now Spain). He was one of two people now known as Rabbeinu Behaye, the other being Bible commentator Bahya ben Asher. Source: https://en.wikipedia.org/wiki/Bahya_ibn_Paquda

---

[viii] Rabbi Moshe Alshich – "Renowned as one of the great *darshanim* (sermonizers) of the Jewish world, Rabbi Moshe Alshich was born in Adrianople, Turkey in 5268 (1508 CE) but lived most of his long and productive life in Safed. In his youth, he studied in the yeshivas headed by Rabbi Yosef Caro in Adrianople and Rabbi Yosef Taitatzak in Salonica. Rabbi Moshe revered Rabbi Yosef Caro and referred to him on occasion as "my father." At a relatively young age, he left for Israel together with Rabbi Caro and settled in Safed. There he was ordained by Rabbi Yosef Caro, eventually serving as one of the judges in Rabbi Yosef Caro's rabbinical court. The story is told that one day it was revealed to Rabbi Caro that his student had merited one of the seventy facets of Torah exegesis. Accordingly, Rabbi Caro compelled Rabbi Moshe to deliver the sermon on that Sabbath. The sermon was received with great acclaim, and from then on, Rabbi Moshe was given the unsought for honor of delivering a sermon every week. From these sermons, his famous *"Torat Moshe"* on the Pentateuch was compiled." Source: https://www.chabad.org/kabbalah/article_cdo/aid/380688/jewish/Rabbi-Moshe-Alshich.htm

[ix] "Rabbi David Altschuler of Prague (1687-1769), also known as Baal haMetzudot, was a Jewish Bible commentator, author of a classic commentary to Nevi'im and Ketuvim in the Hebrew Bible." Source: https://en.wikipedia.org/wiki/David_Altschuler

[x] "The title of the work *Chafetz Chaim* by Rabbi Yisrael Meir Kagan is taken from Psalms :

Come, children, hearken to me; I will teach you the fear of the Lord. Who is the man who desires life, who loves days to see goodness? Guard your tongue from evil and your lips from speaking deceitfully. Shun evil and do good, seek peace and pursue it.

— *Psalm 34:12–15*

The subject of the book is *hilchos shmiras halashon* (laws of clean speech). Rabbi Kagan provides copious sources from the Torah, Talmud and *Rishonim* (early commentators) about the severity of Jewish law on tale-mongering and gossip. Lashon hara, meaning *evil speech* (or loosely gossip and slander and prohibitions of defamation), is sometimes translated as *prohibitions of slander*, but in essence is concerning the *prohibitions of saying evil/bad/unpleasant things about a person, whether or not they are true.*

The book is divided into three parts:

- *Mekor Chayim* ("Source of Life"), the legal text.
- *Be'er mayim chayim* ("Well of living water"), the footnotes and legal argument.
- It is commonly printed together with the text *Shemirath ha-Lashon* ("Guarding of the tongue"), an ethical treatise on the proper use of the faculty of speech.

Souce: https://en.wikipedia.org/wiki/Chofetz_Chaim

[xi] "All histories of Jewish philosophy include an entry on Abraham Ibn Ezra, and, judging from his impact on the field, he certainly deserves the recognition that he has received. Just how he earned it, however, poses a difficult historical problem. Ibn Ezra contributed virtually nothing to any of the branches of philosophy; he authored little in the way of strictly philosophical tracts and, indeed, there is no reason for us to suppose that he enjoyed any rigorous training in philosophy. Yet he certainly left his mark on Jewish thought, and his pronouncements are recorded and treated with respect by those who came after him.

Ibn Ezra's philosophical legacy consists in the main of the following, rather short list of doctrines. The deity governs the terrestrial world by means of the heavenly bodies. Humans toil under astral destiny; though the stars are subservient, formally at least, to God, their domination over the material universe is for all practical purposes complete. Neither the precise structure of the human soul, nor the mode of its bonding with the body, may be known with certainty. However, one component or aspect of the human soul is of the same fiber as the supernal realm that is above the stars; nothing in existence is more similar to God. Nurturing this spiritual component offers the one hope of refuge from this world. Ibn Ezra's poetry in particular gives very powerful expression to the themes of the soul's alienation and longing to return to its heavenly abode. To be sure, weighty questions are involved in all of these teachings, but Ibn Ezra does not take any of them up in depth.

In sum, it appears that Ibn Ezra, much like Sa'adiah—the Jewish thinker who probably influenced him most strongly—adopted a mix of kalam and philosophical doctrines. There simply is no evidence that he trained in philosophy or studied anything more than a small sampling of the literature available in his day, which was considerable. His acknowledged sources are nearly all brief, gaonic, writings, which display the first grapplings of medieval Jewry with theological issues." Source: https://plato.stanford.edu/entries/ibn-ezra/

[xii] "Why is it hard to be good? It is a question Jewish thinkers have been asking for more than 1,000 years. While the commandments in the Torah and other Jewish texts are laid out pretty clearly, people often have a hard time following them.

Mussar (also spelled Musar), a Jewish spiritual practice that gives concrete instructions on how to live a meaningful and ethical life, arose as a response to this concern. Mussar is virtue-based ethics — based on the idea that by cultivating inner virtues, we improve ourselves. This is in contrast to most Jewish ethical teachings, which are rule-based. Today, a number of people who do not follow traditional Jewish rules and rituals are attracted to Mussar because it offers opportunities for personal transformation through a Jewish lens.

Mussar masters recognized that simply learning about kindness does not make us more kind. Moreover, they understood that our inner drives, wounds and appetites often manifest as the <u>Yetzer Hara</u> (the Evil Inclination), actively preventing us from behaving as we know we should. One Mussar teacher, Rabbi Elya Lopian (1876-1970), described Mussar as "teaching the heart what the mind already understands."" Source: https://www.myjewishlearning.com/article/the-musar-movement/

[xiii] Ralbag רלב"ג
(1288 - 1370 CE) (1288 - 1370 לספירה)

"Levi ben Gershon (Ralbag) was a Provencal philosopher, physician, mathematician, astronomer, Talmudic commentator and Torah commentator. He seems to never have accepted a rabbinic post, and little is known about his life – even the place and date of his death is unclear. Ralbag was a strict Aristotelian, and in his great philosophical work, Milchamot Hashem, he critiques Rambam on some points where he deviates from Aristotelian teaching. He was also a fervent believer in astrology, and astrological determinism pervades his philosophical work, though he did maintain the notion of human free-will. His philosophical views lead to opposition to his works in some circles. His mathematical works were sophisticated, influential and ground-breaking; he is noted for his work in combinatorics and early use of the principle of mathematical induction. Some of these works were even translated into Latin at the request of Christian scholars. The Ralbag was credited for inventing the 'Jacob's staff,' an astronomical device. Finally, he is perhaps best known today for his commentary on the Tanach, which displays his wide learning and interweaves halachic matters and rulings. He wrote several Talmudic works, most of which have since been lost." Source: https://www.sefaria.org/person/Ralbag